SCORPIONS IN A BOTTLE

CONFLICTING CULTURES IN

NORTHERN IRELAND

Minority Rights Group International (MRG) is a non-governmental organisation working to secure rights for ethnic, linguistic and religious minorities worldwide, and to promote cooperation and understanding between communities.

We publish readable, concise and accurate Reports on the issues facing oppressed groups around the world. We also produce books, education and training materials, and MRG's 800-page *World Directory of Minorities*.

We work with the United Nations, among other international bodies, to increase awareness of minority rights, often in conjunction with our partner organisations. We also coordinate training on minority rights internationally and work with different communities to counter racism and prejudice.

If you would like to know more about the work of MRG please contact the Communications Department, MRG, 379 Brixton Road, London SW9 7DE, United Kingdom.
Tel: +44 (0)171 978 9498. Fax: +44 (0)171 738 6265.
E mail: minority.rights@mrg.sprint.com
Web site: www.minorityrights.org (October 1997)

m

Minority Rights Publications is a series of books from Minority Rights Group. The series draws on the expertise and authority built up by MRG over 25 years of publishing. Titles include:

Armenia and Karabagh: The Struggle for Unity
edited by Christopher J. Walker (1991)

The Balkans: Minorities and States in Conflict
by Hugh Poulton (1993, 2nd edn)

Polar Peoples – Self-Determination and Development
edited by Minority Rights Group (1994)

Cutting the Rose – Female Genital Mutilation: The Practice and its Prevention
by Efua Dorkenoo (1994)

The Palestinians – The Road to Nationhood
by David McDowall (1994)

No Longer Invisible: Afro-Latin Americans Today
edited by Minority Rights Group (1995)

Roger M Schlosser
2001

SCORPIONS IN A BOTTLE

CONFLICTING CULTURES IN NORTHERN IRELAND

by

John Darby

Minority Rights Publications

© Minority Rights Group 1997

First published in the United Kingdom in 1997 by
Minority Rights Publications
379 Brixton Road
London SW9 7DE

British Library Cataloguing in Publication Data
A CIP catalogue record of this book is available from the British Library.

ISBN 1 873194 11 0 hardback
ISBN 1 873194 16 1 paperback

Library of Congress Cataloguing in Publication Data
CIP Data available from the Library of Congress

Cover design and typesetting in Stone Serif by Texture
Printed on chlorine-free paper in the UK by Redwood Books

Cover photo of Drumcree Parade 1995 along the Garvaghy Road
Stephen Davison/Pacemaker Press

This book has been commissioned and is published by Minority Rights
Publications as a contribution to public understanding of the issue
which forms its subject. The text and the views expressed do not
necessarily represent, in every detail and in all its aspects, the collective
view of Minority Rights Group.

CONTENTS

LIST OF FIGURES

LIST OF FIGURES

The cure at Troy

Human beings suffer,
They torture one another,
They get hurt and get hard.
No poem or play or song
Can fully right a wrong
Inflicted and endured.

The innocent in gaols
Beat on their bars together.
A hunger-striker's father
Stands in the graveyard dumb.
The police widow in veils
Faints at the funeral home.

History says, *Don't hope*
On this side of the grave.
But then, once in a lifetime
The longed-for tidal wave
Of justice can rise up,
And hope and history rhyme.

So hope for a great sea-change
On the far side of revenge.
Believe that a further shore
Is reachable from here.
Believe in miracles
And cures and healing wells.

Call miracle self-healing:
The utter, self-revealing
Double-take of feeling.
If there's fire on the mountain
Or lightning and storm
And a god speaks from the sky

That means someone is hearing
The outcry and the birth-cry
Of new life at its term.
It means, once in a lifetime
That justice can rise up,
And hope and history rhyme.

Seamus Heaney

Ceasefire

I
Put in mind of his own father and moved to tears
Achilles took him by the hand and pushed the old king
Gently away, but Priam curled up at his feet and
Wept with him until their sadness filled the building.

II
Taking Hector's corpse into his own hands Achilles
Made sure it was washed and, for the old king's sake,
Dressed in uniform, ready for Priam to carry
Wrapped like a present home to Troy at daybreak.

III
When they had eaten together, it pleased them both
To stare at each other's beauty as lovers might,
Achilles built like a god, Priam goodlooking still
And full of conversation, who earlier had sighed:

IV
'I get down on my knees and do what must be done
And kiss Achilles' hand, the killer of my son.'

Michael Longley

To my wife Marie

PREFACE AND ACKNOWLEDGEMENTS

Any divided community is like a bottle containing two scorpions. If the scorpions cannot be persuaded to mate, or at least to co-habit in a civilised manner within the same space, it may be better to recognise the fact, and to look around for another bottle.

The IRA ceasefire in 1994 and its ending in 1996 provide an opportunity to stand back and assess the extent to which relationships have altered and grievances have been addressed within Northern Ireland's bottle. A conflict cannot remain unaffected by 25 years of violence. The tension between majority and minority, between the state and the minority community, and between Britain and Ireland, have all changed significantly, and continue to change.

This book will focus on these changes, particularly within Northern Ireland, the theatre for the conflict. The 'Northern Ireland Problem' is not exclusively rooted in political or constitutional differences, or inequalities, or the use of violence or relationships between Catholics and Protestants. It is not even exclusively about the legitimacy of the state, for conflict is inevitable in any jurisdictional arrangement. The problem is an interlocking weave of these and other elements. This book aims to provide a case-study of that conflict and to put it within the broader context of conflict analysis. There will be an emphasis throughout on policy options for pluralist societies. It is laid out in three parts:

The first three chapters provide background information necessary to put the Northern Ireland material into context. They include a review of recent international trends in ethnic violence; an historical background on Ireland and Northern Ireland; and a short description of the current population of Northern Ireland.

The next four chapters are a case-study of a society in conflict. They examine respectively the nature of the problem and conflicting views about it, the years preceding and following the 1994 ceasefires of violence, and an assessment or audit of the state of minority rights. Chapter 8 considers any broader insights the Northern Ireland conflict might provide for other divided societies. Chapter 9 is a guide for those wishing to find out more information about the conflict. Appendix I shows the chronology of events since 1914; and Appendix II presents extracts from key political and constitutional documents.

The Northern Ireland conflict is described in the book as an ethnic conflict. The term 'ethnic' is used in its broad sense to include allegiances which are based on race, religion, language or other cultural manifestations, and which distinguish the group from those with different allegiances. These allegiances often include a political desire to live among 'one's own people'. The definition of one's own people often reflects what Benedict Anderson called 'imagined communities' rather than historical reality. Northern Ireland nationalists, for example, often look back to an independent Ireland which has never existed, and unionists variously express their allegiances to Britain and Ulster, a balance often determined by political circumstances. It is recognised, of course, that there are other definitions of ethnicity, but the broader definition allows a more comprehensive analysis of the issue. In relation to Northern Ireland, the broader 'ethnic' definition stands up to challenge better than other definitions which view it exclusively as a constitutional or religious conflict, or one based on economic, social or cultural inequalities. All of these, it is argued, are part of the problem, but none can claim exclusive rights to define it.

The term 'conflict' is also subject to dispute. It is recognised that conflict is often regarded as dysfunctional, a breakdown in normal relationships which needs to be remedied. That is not the definition of conflict adopted in this book. Instead, a distinction is made between conflict and violence. Violence is taken as evidence that acceptable forms of social intercourse have failed. Conflict is regarded as a normal consequence of any relationship – personal, group or national – where there are competing interests, interests which are normally handled by the operation of politics. It does not carry the negative implications of violence.

Conflict by this definition is a feature of every plural society. Since very few societies can claim to be homogeneous, virtually every society experiences ethnic conflict, or may experience it in the future. The question is why and how it is more successfully handled in some than in others.

Sectarian conflict is an emotional business, and no amount of academic analysis can get under the skin of objective grievances to the fears and aggression beneath. The best insights into the nature of sectarianism often come from creative writers, and I am grateful to Seamus Heaney and Michael Longley for permission to reproduce their poems. Thanks also to Martyn Turner, one of the most perceptive and sympathetic observers of events in Northern Ireland, for allowing me to select from his cartoons on the ceasefires, which appeared in the *Irish Times* and *The NOble Art of Politics* (1996). All the cartoons in the book are his, and reproduced with his kind permission.

This book is the product of work over a number of years, and its main support and victim has been my wife, Marie. I also wish to thank the Woodrow Wilson International Center for Scholars in Washington, DC, for inviting me to participate in its work on ethnicity during and after my studentship in 1992. The time spent at the Rockefeller Foundation's Center in Bellagio also allowed me to develop some of the ideas for this book, especially those relating to the factors which control ethnic conflict. The research commissioned by the United Nations Research Institute for Social Development (UNRISD) focused my mind on policy approaches to pluralism, and particular appreciation is recorded to Dharam Ghai. Many other colleagues and friends advised on specific aspects of the book, and I am grateful to them all: Rebecca Barkis, Paul Brennan, Seamus Dunn, Tony Gallagher, Tony

Hepburn, Dennis McCoy, Roger McGinty, Martin Melaugh, Dominic Murray, Niall O'Dochertaigh, Gillian Robinson; Edgar Jardine and his colleagues from the Northern Ireland Statistics and Research Agency for guidance through the jungle of official publications; those who compiled the tables reproduced from the Labour Force Survey and the various Social Attitudes surveys, including John Brewer, R. Cormack, Seamus Dunn, Tony Gallagher, Valerie Morgan, R. Osborne and Karen Trew; and Yvonne Murphy and Ciaran Crossey from the Linen Hall Library. The shortcomings in the book would have been much greater without their advice.

John Darby
1997

ABBREVATIONS

APNI	Alliance Party of Northern Ireland
CAIN	Conflict Archive on the Internet
CAJ	Committee on the Administration of Justice
CCRU	Central Community Relations Unit
DUP	Democratic Unionist Party
ESRC	Economic and Social Research Council
EU	European Union
FET	Fair Employment Tribunal
INCORE	Initiative on Conflict Resolution and Ethnicity
INLA	Irish National Liberation Army
IRA	Irish Republican Army
IRSP	Irish Republican Socialist Party
NICRA	Northern Ireland Civil Rights Association
NIHE	Northern Ireland Housing Executive
NILP	Northern Ireland Labour Party
NISRA	Northern Ireland Statistics and Research Agency
PD	People's Democracy
PUP	Progressive Unionist Party
RIR	Royal Irish Regiment
RUC	Royal Ulster Constabulary
RUCR	Royal Ulster Constabulary Reserve
SDLP	Social Democratic and Labour Party
UDA	Ulster Defence Association
UDP	Ulster Democratic Party
UDR	Ulster Defence Regiment
UFF	Ulster Freedom Fighters
UK	United Kingdom
UN	United Nations
UNRISD	United Nations Research Institute for Social Development
USA	United States of America
UUP	Ulster Unionist Party
UVF	Ulster Volunteer Force
UWC	Ulster Workers' Council
VUPP	Vanguard Unionist Progressive Party

1
ETHNIC CONFLICT: PLUS ÇA CHANGE...?

I s the world becoming more violent? Certainly, no conflict during the second half of the twentieth century has produced the number of deaths inflicted during the two world wars. However, if violence is measured by the number of conflicts rather than by casualties, the pattern changes. In recent years there has been a sharp increase in the number of localised conflicts, especially since the ending of the Cold War. The University of Uppsala has been monitoring the levels of violence throughout the world, classifying them by the number of casualties as minor armed conflicts (fewer than 25 deaths, and involving at least one state), intermediate armed conflicts (more than 25 deaths in one year, and more than 1,000 during the conflict) and wars (more than 1,000 deaths in one year). In the three years between 1989 and 1992 alone, the amalgamated total came to 82. Thirty-five of them were wars.[1]

Much of this violence emerged from ethnic conflicts. In 1992 the *New York Times* identified 48 ethnic conflicts throughout the world. These were geographically widely spread – 9 in Europe, 7 in the Middle East and North Africa, 15 in Africa south of the Sahara, 13 in Asia and 4 in Latin America.[2] The total is a substantial underestimate, for two main reasons. First, a number of situations omitted from the list would have qualified for admission under a broader definition of ethnic conflict: racist tensions in Europe; native American discontent in the United States of America (USA); disputes about aboriginal rights in Australia and

New Zealand. Second, the newspaper's decision to classify conflicts by the nation state in which they were located disguised
the complexities trapped within the enormous territories of
India, China and Russia, each of which contains a myriad of ethnic tensions.

A new phenomenon?

The number of states in the United Nations (UN) rose from 72 to
186 between its formation in 1945 and 1997. Most of the new
members had attained their independence as a result of the
decline of colonialism and the fall of empires. By 1984 there
remained fewer than 10 occupied or colonial territories across
the globe.[3] Many of these independence struggles were inspired
both by the desire to get rid of the colonial power and by an
aspiration for greater ethnic homogeneity, so that people could
live with those who shared the same ethnic background, culture
and aspirations. It did not seem unreasonable to expect that the
achievement of independence would reduce ethnic tensions.
Almost a half century after the start of decolonisation, the successor countries of the British, French, Dutch, Portuguese and,
more recently, Russian empires are among those which are suf-
fering most from ethnic violence.

So why has the dream of ethnic harmony become a nightmare?
The first reason is that ethnic homogeneity, on past evidence, is
almost always unattainable, and the search for it is usually vain.
In 1996 the Secretary-General of the Commonwealth, Emeka
Anyaoku, estimated that only four of the Commonwealth's 53
member states might be described as ethnically homogeneous.[4]
History, through a range of factors including political compromise, intermarriage, migration and the whim of cartographers,
has a habit of slackening the boundaries which groups use to
mark their distinctiveness. Apart from such rarities as the 'velvet
divorce' in the former Czechoslovakia, it is not easy to find examples where two ethnic or national groups were agreeably partitioned into two discrete states. Within the successor countries of
the former Soviet Union and Yugoslavia new minorities soon
emrgered, each demanding its own right to self-determination,

even in those countries which believed they had achieved a high level of ethnic uniformity. Their case is rarely received with sympathy. Nor, if they were to accomplish their objectives, is there any guarantee that they in turn would not be presented with similar demands from even smaller groups. Jonathan Swift put it neatly more than three centuries ago:

'So, naturalists observe, a flea
Hath smaller fleas that on him prey;
And these have smaller fleas to bite 'em,
And so proceed ad infinitum.'[5]

The danger is that a successful demand for self-determination by a minority often merely replicates the earlier problem in miniature, the only difference being that the previous minority has assumed control in a newly created state. Indeed, it is not impossible that such a development may lead to more, not less, violence. It may create a new minority too small or too dispersed to protect itself. In such circumstances it may be more sensible to seek reforms within the state, and the closer involvement of neighbouring states, than to demand secession from it. The question is, how can a distinction be made between different levels of minority discontent? Under what circumstances would accommodation within existing state boundaries offer the best opportunity for a more peaceful and fair future? Under what circumstances would self-determination and secession create stability?

Events in eastern Europe since 1989 are reminders that countries which appeared to be insulated against ethnic conflict were not. Ethnic identity, like the seeds discovered in Egyptian tombs, can lie dormant for centuries and, given the right conditions, spring into life. Ethnicity is an elastic and dynamic concept. It usually reflects a common perception of common origins, kinship ties, group loyalty and, usually, a common destiny. These may suggest that ethnicity is a primordial and impermeable force. In reality, however, ethnic identity is far from immutable. Every individual has a multiplicity of available identities, and ethnicity only becomes relevant when one of them becomes invested with social meaning and significance. Ethnicity is often

3

situationally determined and may wax or wane according to circumstances. The move towards a stronger European Union (EU),
for example, has been paralleled in a number of European countries by the growth of regional loyalties. In some cases these have
arisen from a divergence between regional and national economic
interests, but in others regional pride has taken on an ethnic
flavour. The growth of religious fundamentalism has added an
emotive force to ethnic conflicts in the Middle East, the former
Yugoslavia, Iraq, Sudan, India, Pakistan and other parts of south
Asia. The power of race as a recruiting sergeant for other discontent is evident on every continent. Ethnicity may be acquired or
divested according to the extent to which it aligns with, or
becomes dissociated from, other grievances.

The other principal reason for the recent growth of ethnic violence relates to changes in global politics. The ending of the Cold
War and the collapse of the Soviet Union may have reduced the
threat of a world war, but has also removed the stability and control produced by the deadlock between the superpowers. The con-
sequent relaxation of the controls over the expression of ethnic
identity has allowed it to emerge as an alternative source of
loyalty, a fixed constant in a changing world. Some commentators believe that subsequent developments have simply followed
a 'natural' course for ethnic conflict. The suppression of ethnic
expression for decades has also suppressed the mechanisms and
relationships which have served to manage differences in other
divided societies.[6] Hence, when the suppression is removed, ethnic rivalries are more likely to become violent and to spiral out of
control. What 'each side does is a response to the actual or anticipated moves of its opponents'.[7] Coleman described this process as
a chain reaction during which 'the harmful and dangerous elements drive out those which keep the conflict within bounds'.[8]
This process has been demonstrated in many contemporary conflicts: Croatia, Serbia, Nagorno-Karabakh, the Kurd homelands,
the Horn of Africa, Lebanon, Sri Lanka and other flashpoints in
the Indian sub-continent.[9]

Not all ethnic conflicts follow this pattern. If pluralist societies
were charted on a graph, according to how effectively they function, the pattern might be presented as an ascending line. At the

bottom of the line are peacefully regulated multi-cultural societies currently experiencing little or no violence, such as Switzerland, Canada and Australia; all of these have experienced ethnic tensions, and sometimes violence, in the past and may experience them again in the future, because permanent stability is unattainable. Moving along the ascending line, a large number of communities suffer relatively low levels of ethnic violence, including in the present or recent past the Basque region and, Northern Ireland. In all these places violence has been conducted by paramilitary organisations against the state or ethnic rivals, but has been controlled by the presence of an army or by indigenous social and economic mechanisms. At the top of the graph are societies in which violence has spiralled out of control, such as recently experienced in Bosnia, Rwanda and Burundi. These are often characterised by open warfare by organised armies.

Individual societies may move along the line of the graph in either direction. Some have completed the full course more than once, while others oscillate around one point over prolonged periods. It is sometimes possible, especially during the earlier phases of ethnic violence, to address grievances, and to initiate or strengthen progress towards a more peaceful accommodation, by the introduction of appropriate policies. It is also possible for low-violence ethnic conflicts to be suppressed temporarily rather than returning to the controlled but unresolved state from which they sprang. But if ethnic grievances are not addressed rapidly they tend to accelerate along the line of grievance and to become increasingly violent. When this happens, it becomes difficult to return to the fundamental causes of conflict, and the priority may shift to reducing the casualties and planning for a post-war settlement. The dynamic of each ethnic conflict does not follow a straight line along the graph paper. The risk is that the violence may follow a succession of curves along the graph, as ethnic violence rises, is suppressed or insufficiently addressed, and resumes at some future date. The most that one can plan for is to reach the plains at the bottom of the curve, and to maintain that position by fair policies and practices and, most of all, by constant vigilance for new signs of discontent. Permanent peace is not an attainable aspiration.

More than an internal problem

It is not merely the increased frequency of ethnic conflict which has raised international interest and concern. There is nothing new about ethnic conflict. What has changed is the context in which it is waged. Contrast the cases which come to mind when ethnic conflict was mentioned before the 1980s with those since. Before the 1980s the academic literature on ethnicity was dominated by long-established conflicts: the Basque region, Malaysia, Nigeria, Canada, Northern Ireland, Sri Lanka and the Lebanon. Ethnic conflict was presented primarily as internal and contained – an inconvenience to national governments certainly, but not a serious threat to world order. Those conflicts in the 1980s which had the potential to escalate into regional or international disputes – the Middle East, Yugoslavia, South Africa – were tacitly regarded as the proper province of one of the superpowers and treated accordingly. Such a position became untenable in the 1990s. Ethnic violence in the former Soviet Union, Yugoslavia and the Middle East affected power balances and had the potential to escalate into regional wars. Ethnic conflict had suddenly caught the world's attention because it had demonstrated its ability to disturb world peace.

The elevation of ethnic conflict from a local to a regional, and sometimes international, phenomenon partly arises from the social demography of ethnicity. Most ethnic minorities are not confined within a single nation state and many disputes arise from a mismatch between the claims of particular ethnic groups and those of recognised states. Ted Gurr's international study of minorities at risk found that 'of the 179 minorities identified in the survey, more than two thirds (122) have ethnic kindred in one or more adjacent countries'.[10] The cases of Serbs in Croatia and Bosnia, Russians within many of the successor states of the Soviet Union, the Kurds and the Chinese in many Asian countries illustrate that ethnic identity often ignores the borders of nation states. A 1991 study by the Institute of Geographers in Moscow, for example, concluded that only three of the 23 borders between the former republics of the Soviet Union were not disputed.[11] It is not uncommon for minority groups to look to neighbouring countries for protection, or for neighbouring countries to make irredentist claims, thus propelling local disputes on to the world stage. De Silva and May have described this process as the 'second law of ethnic conflict, that once such a conflict breaks out, sooner or later, indeed sooner rather than later in this era of instant communications, it will be internationalised.'[12] It is no longer realistic to regard ethnic violence, in contrast to international disputes, as a second-level threat to world order.

The new international concern with ethnic conflict was initially more reactive than positive. Relief at the ending of the Cold War was soon replaced by concern about the Pandora's box revealed behind the rubble of the Berlin Wall. Where had all these forgotten ethnic loyalties come from? It would have been difficult to anticipate the strong resurgence of Serbian nationalism or the full horror of the genocide in Rwanda and Burundi five years before they took place. Scholars of ethnicity, neglected for years, were catapulted to the fore in the search for explanations of the new phenomenon. They were often able to provide the historical antecedents of each local eruption. Occasionally they could outline the political and social forces which had led to violence, although it was hard to find basic up-to-date information on Burundi, Zaire or some of the republics of the former Soviet Union. In other words, the international community's initial concern about the spread of ethnic violence was to understand better its origins and causes. Only recently has the emphasis shifted from one end of the cycle of violence to the other, from focusing on the causes of conflict to seeking ways of ameliorating or resolving it.

Can conflict be resolved?

In 1965 Simpson and Yinger[13] clinically listed six possible policy approaches by which a stronger ethnic group may deal with its opponents:
- Assimilation, either forced or permitted;
- Pluralism;
- Legal protection for minorities;

- Population transfer, either negotiated or forced;
- Continued subjugation; and
- Extermination.

Historically, the most common approach to handling inconve-
nient minorities has hovered between the most violent of these
alternatives: subjugation and extermination. Recent events in
Bosnia, Rwanda and Burundi confirm that they are far from merely
historical. Part of the reason is the lack of an international organisation to apply effective sanction against such behaviour. Primary
responsibility for the resolution of internal disputes has traditionally resided with the nation state. If the conflict was between
groups within the state, any suggestion of external arbitration
was rigorously resisted, and the right of states to deal with their
own internal affairs is a key component of the UN Charter. If the
disputes were between states rather than within them, they were
treated through diplomatic negotiations, and sometimes, if they
failed, by war. These conventions were modified after the Second
World War by the division of power between the USA and the
Soviet Union, each of which exercised a form of protectorate
among the nations within its sphere of influence. In all of this
there was little opportunity for others – international, regional or
non-governmental organisations – to play an effective role in
international relations. Despite this, many of the most important
changes in international relationships since the 1950s have
emerged from developments outside the conventional diplomatic
field – what has been described as Track Two diplomacy.[14] Japan's
influence as a world power does not depend on its role in the UN,
but on its economic strength. The emergence of the European
Economic Community too had its roots in mundane agreements
about post-war trading in coal and steel. The USA's shift from the
Atlantic to the Pacific rim is another example of diplomatic interest following in the footprints of economic reality.

Ethnic conflicts were slower to respond to Track Two diplomacy.
During the 1970s and 1980s there was a growing tendency for
non-state actors to seek ways around some of the more intransigent ethnic conflicts, but none of these interventions produced
obvious results. In South Africa, for example, religious and business

leaders, anxious about governmental inaction and international pressure, attempted to act as mediators between the African National Congress (ANC) and individuals in government. Similar initiatives were tried in the Middle East, Northern Ireland and Cyprus.

These interventions both reflected and stimulated professional interest in conflict and conflict resolution. In Scandinavia, the Netherlands and, to some degree, Germany, conflict institutes, which had previously been dominated by issues of nuclear disarmament and human rights, adapted to include the analysis and resolution of ethnic conflict. The University of Uppsala, for example, and PIOOM (International Research Programme on Root Causes of Human Rights Violations) in the Netherlands, began to monitor incidents of violence across the world. The expansion of conflict resolution courses in the USA, many of which adopted similar approaches to the resolution of interstate, ethnic, industrial and domestic disputes, grew at a time when other academic departments were contracting. The emergence of similar centres within areas affected by ethnic violence – in Coleraine in Northern Ireland, in Onati in the Basque region, in Candy and Colombo in Sri Lanka, in Cape Town and Pretoria in South Africa – offered opportunities for collaboration and comparison. In the USA the private sector was not slow to follow the path beaten towards conflict resolution initiatives. The establishment by the UN University in 1993 of the Initiative on Conflict Resolution and Ethnicity (INCORE) in Northern Ireland marked a recognition that the systematic and comparative study of the causes, process and resolution of ethnic conflict is becoming a priority for the UN.

This burgeoning activity was complicated as well as stimulated by developments since the early 1990s. It has been accompanied by competing and often competitive approaches to mediation, political negotiation and conflict management and resolution. The emergence of new states, especially in eastern and central Europe, provided new areas to develop theory and practice. A serious demand also developed within the new states themselves for guidance in handling internal divisions. Much energy was spent in the early 1990s searching for a model for the successful management of pluralism. Planes to Moscow and other eastern European capitals, filled with western experts on constitutions, human rights and reconstruction, were passing planes flying in the opposite direction, filled with new members of new parliaments, administrators and members of minority interests. Academics were well represented in both directions. The destinations were sometimes curious ones. Northern Ireland may not seem an obvious model for the successful management of pluralism, but visitors from Russia, Bosnia, Azerbaijan, Armenia, Latvia and Lithuania beat a path there, perhaps seeking a lesson which would enable them to avoid their worst nightmares. The tempo established in those years has scarcely diminished. In 1996 the Fiji Constitution Reform Commission also based its inquiries on searching for successful and unsuccessful models for pluralism.

No such models exist. It is never possible to apply a template from one country to another. But it is often fruitful to borrow and adapt specific policies and procedures – the reversal of discriminatory procedures, constitutional arrangements, the protection of minorities, policing, educational provision, criminal procedures, policies for encouraging mutual understanding – from a variety of settings. The policies which the emerging nations sought to borrow or adapt were mainly political and constitutional. There was particular interest in federal structures, and how they might operate in regions where ethnic groups do not live in demographically exclusive districts, as they do in the Basque region of Spain, Sri Lanka and many other ethnically divided societies. In many of the new countries the conflicting groups are represented to some degree in almost every town, village and locality, creating a mosaic of intermingled relationships with greatly varying levels of social, economic and residential segregation and integration. How are such complexities to be handled?

The range of approaches suggested to deal with these problems cover a wide spectrum. Horowitz advocated the construction of constitutions and political systems which force ethnic rivals to make agreements before elections rather than form coalitions after them.[15] Montville and McDonald emphasised, in situations where political contacts between ethnic opponents are particularly difficult, the need to encourage and work through common non-political economic and cultural contacts.[16] The real growth in activity, however, has been among those who advocate bringing together small groups representing the conflicting parties for a variety of reasons: in order to identify and distinguish between needs and interests; to rehearse the problems which may emerge during real negotiations; to provide political experience; to establish social relationships between parties who cannot or do not meet within their country. The role of external negotiators has played an increasingly important part in getting rivals to the negotiating table. Certainly the experience and authority of Cyrus Vance and David Owen were unable to produce a permanent settlement in Bosnia. Nevertheless it was the intervention of the USA, especially during the Clinton presidency, which brokered the 1995 Dayton Accord between Serbia, Bosnia and Croatia, following mediation by a range of senior officials and politicians in the former Yugoslavia. Other external enterprises, such as the role of former USA president Jimmy Carter in Haiti, are more difficult to evaluate. The relative importance of external and internal actors in bringing together the South African government, the ANC and Inkatha is also still unclear, but a range of mediators can lay claim to contributing towards it. The intervention of USA Senator George Mitchell, with colleagues from Finland and Canada, helped to provide the basis for breaking the logjam over arms decommissioning in Northern Ireland in 1996, and his role continued through to the inter-party talks which followed. Perhaps the most important recent mediation was that which led to the Oslo Agreement in the Middle East, which involved academics, diplomats, officials and politicians at different stages. There is sceptical view that mediators are only useful in resolving ethnic conflicts when the parties have already reached the conclusion that a settlement is needed. These recent interventions suggest that the process varies greatly from place to place, and that more energy should be devoted to determining what form of mediation, internal or external, is appropriate to different phases of conflict.

The shift towards interest in conflict resolution coincided with, and may partly be explained by, apparently positive moves in a number of traditionally intransigent conflicts. Certainly the revival of violent ethnic conflict since the ending of the Cold War – in the former Soviet Union, Sri Lanka, Bosnia, Rwanda and Burundi – may mark out the 1990s as the decade when ethnic violence crept out from the cellar with a new energy. But shadowing this spectre is another phenomenon, less frequently observed. In the last few years a number of durable and traditional ethnic conflicts seem to be lurching along the continuum from violence towards settlement, or at least compromise.

- Perhaps the most dramatic was the rapid move in South Africa towards free elections and majority rule in April 1994. The constitutional settlement significantly shifted the emphasis to the need for fundamental social restructuring and more equitable distribution of resources.
- In the Middle East talks between Israel and the Palestine Liberation Organisation (PLO) provided sufficient momentum for the transfer of a level of autonomy. The violence after March 1996 seriously challenged the Oslo Agreement, but internal and international pressure may indicate that it is premature to write off the peace process there.
- After years of violence, concessions by the Spanish government gave the Basques greater, if not complete, control over their own affairs. The violent campaign by Euskad Ta Azkatasurra (ETA) did not end, but it has lost the support of many moderate Basques.
- The declaration of the Irish Republican Army (IRA) ceasefire in August 1994 ushered in the start of a cautious peace process in Northern Ireland. The ending of the IRA ceasefire in February 1996 reinforced the importance of distinguishing between ceasefires and peace processes.
- Perhaps even more surprisingly, given the short duration of the ceasefire declared by the Tamil Tigers in 1995, and the increased military activity since it ended, the impetus towards talks in Sri Lanka did not completely collapse.
- Cases can be made that there are at least elements of progress in other durable conflicts: in Mozambique, Chechnya, El Salvador, even in Corsica where a ceasefire was declared in January 1996.

The ending of violence brings its own problems, not least of which is the threat that it may return, as it did in Sri Lanka, the Middle East, Corsica and Northern Ireland. In addition, literally overnight, policy-makers whose concerns were dominated by security issues are faced with an entirely new set of questions. Are prisoners to be kept in prison, or will the new circumstances require symbolic acts of forgiveness? How are negotiations to be constructed between parties who have recently been engaged in violent conflict? How can the process handle the threat of well-armed fighters waiting outside the conference hall? Is it necessary to insist on the handing over of weapons, with its connotation of military defeat? How is a divided society to be policed, given the likelihood that violence has greatly inflated the number of police necessary to maintain law and order, and that those police are probably disproportionately recruited from the dominant community?

The literature on ethnicity, ethnic conflict and conflict resolution is substantial and growing rapidly, but there is very little empirical, and virtually no comparative, research on the management of peace processes. The coincidence of these developments across the world provides an opportunity for comparative research and for gaining a better understanding of processes towards peace. All of the circumstances cited above are vastly different. They include struggles for regional devolution, demands for secession and internal revolutions. The forms of violence used included wars between organised armies, irregular guerrilla campaigns and the calculated use of terror. Nevertheless, coming so close together, these changes suggested that ethnic conflict might be amenable to particular approaches rather than the inevitable victims of chance developments.

Together they provide a recent and varied set of experiences for examining the processes, difficulties and techniques involved in moving violent conflicts from violence to peace. All of them demonstrate how fragile is the process, and how easily it can be derailed. They underline the need to broaden the focus of concern from the historical analysis of violence to include a better understanding of its dynamic. Most of all, it must include the search for better ways of getting out of it.

The international community

The celebration of the UN's 50th anniversary in 1995 was dampened by an uncomfortable awareness that accelerating demands for its peace-keeping services were coinciding with a decline in the resources available to address them. The UN had established more peace-keeping missions in the last 5 years than during the first 45, and the rate showed no signs of diminishing. In 1995 the refusal by major contributors to pay their dues had forced the UN to finance peace-keeping missions by falling back on its core budget. At a time when ethnic disputes were escalating into international wars, international agencies were facing financial bankruptcy. They were also facing an intellectual crisis in redefining their role in the post-World War years. In 1992, Dr. Boutros Boutros-Ghali remarked, in *An Agenda for Peace*, that 'we have entered a time of global transition marked by uniquely contradictory trends'. On the one hand were encouraging signs of greater regional cooperation; on the other, new threats to state cohesion by 'brutal ethnic, religious, social, cultural or linguistic strife'.[17]

An Agenda for Peace has had many detractors, but the breadth and intensity of the debate that followed its publication was perhaps its greatest achievement. The four phases identified in the report set out a systematic analysis of the cycle of violence, and appropriate responses for each phase. Preventative diplomacy is intended to catch emerging trouble before it develops from disputes into conflicts, and hence towards violence. Peace-making seeks to bring hostile parties to agreement before they become violent. Peace-keeping – the phase with which the UN was most associated – comes into play when violence has broken out and it has become necessary to involve UN military, police personnel, and usually civilians too, in creating and maintaining the conditions necessary for peace. The final stage of peace-building follows the ending of violence and sets out to support structures for strengthening peace and returning the cycle to the first phase. This framework provided the intellectual basis for a continuing debate, which has since moved on to address more openly the circumstances when strong force might be used, as in the Bosnian air strikes in 1996. This extended debate introduced the need for a distinction between peace-keeping, with its emphasis on the UN as a force introduced to maintain peace after belligerents had reached agreement, and 'peace enforcement', an oxymoron which envisaged a new proactive war-waging role for the UN.

This debate reflects a pressing demand to raise the level of debate about the role of the UN itself, its future involvement in conflict resolution, and the extent to which it can share its responsibilities with other international, regional and non-governmental organisations. The former Secretary General sought to bring regional groups – such as the Organisation of African Unity, the Organisation of American States, the Conference on Security and Co-operation in Europe and the Commonwealth of Independent States – more directly into peacekeeping work. 'What is clear', he wrote in *An Agenda for Peace*, 'is that regional arrangements or agencies in many cases possess a potential that should be utilised in ... preventative diplomacy, peace-keeping, peace-making and post-conflict peace-building.'[18]

All these levels of intervention, whether by the UN or its regional associates, point to the difficulty in drawing a clear distinction between international wars and internal ethnic disputes. This, in turn, emphasises a fundamental tension between the right of states to manage their own internal affairs and the requirement on the UN to defend human rights without distinction as to 'race, colour, sex, language, religion, political or other opinion, national or social origin, property, birth or other status'.[19] Boutros-Ghali pointed out the dangers:

'The sovereignty, territorial integrity and independence of states within the established international system, and the principle of self-determination for peoples, both of great value and importance, must not be permitted to work against each other in the period ahead.'[20]

These problems – the move to involve regional partners in peace-keeping, and the tension between sovereignty and human rights – comprise part of the new debate about the future world order. The need to reform the UN budget is likely to provide the kick start for other systematic reforms, but the problems themselves are more fundamental. It was widely assumed that the ending of the Cold War would lead to a renaissance of the UN system. Instead the world of the 1990s became in some ways a more dangerous and unpredictable place, and the post-Cold War problems were no less threatening than those they replaced.

A postscript for pluralism

Also threatened are the positive benefits of ethnic pluralism: in particular, its contribution of cultural pluralism to music, literature, fine art and overall variety of life. When ethnic diversity is allowed to flourish, it enriches the human condition. In retrospect the optimism during the 1950s that racial and ethnic tensions were diminishing may today seem naive or utopian. Now the sour after-taste of ethnic violence runs the risk of tipping the balance too far in the opposite direction, where ethnic values are regarded as essentially dangerous.

The current increased interest in the management of ethnic diversity, if only because all the alternatives seem intolerable, has laid a good foundation for a more balanced approach to both the threats and the benefits associated with ethnicity. India, for example, despite its internal ethnic tensions, has taken great pride in its pluralist approach to an ethnic variety based on language, religion, tribes, castes and sects. So, in different ways and with different qualifications, have the USA, Malaysia, France and Switzerland. Civilisation would be diminished if ethnic variety comes to be regarded solely as a divisive and negative force.

Conflicts

13. Ethiopia (Afar)
14. Ethiopia (Harar)
15. Libya (Islamists)
16. Mozambique (RENAMO)
17. Uganda-Zaire
18. Senegal (Casamanche)
19. Somalia (Interclan)
20. Somalia (Somaliland)
21. Uganda (LRA)
22. Uganda (WNLF)
23. Uganda (DMA)
24. South Africa (Kwazulu-Natal)

North Africa and Middle East
25. Egypt (Copts, Islamists)
26. Iran (Kurds)
27. Iran (Mujahedeen)

28. Iraq (Kurds)
29. Iraq (Shi'ites)
30. Israel (Gaza & Westbank)
31. Lebanon (South)

Central and East Asia
32. Bangladesh (Chittagong)
33. India (Punjab)
34. India (Manipur)
35. India (Nagaland)
36. India (Tripura)
37. Burma (Karen)
38. Burma (Shan)
39. Burma (Arakan)
40. China (Xianjiang)
41. Pakistan (Punjab)
42. Pakistan (NWFP)

Chechnya
Tajikistan
Afghanistan
Pakistan
Kasjmir
Assam
Sri Lanka
Cambodia

Explanation of Symbols and Definitions

UN United Nations Peacekeeping Operation
(PK = Peacekeeping Mission, OB = Observer Mission)

Violent Political Conflict (conflict level 3: armed conflict that caused less than 100 deaths in the past year)

Low-intensity Conflict (conflict level 4: armed conflict that caused 100 to 1,000 deaths in the past year)

High-intensity Conflict (conflict level 5: large-scale armed conflict that caused more than 1,000 deaths in the past year)

Source: PIOOM Databank, Leiden University, Wassenaarseweg 52, 2333 AK Leiden, The Netherlands
tel.: 31-71-5273861, fax: 31-71-5273788, E-mail: pioom@rulfsw.leidenuniv.nl
©1997 - Infographic: Harry Kasemir Publicity & Design, Groningen

51. Israel-Syria (Golan Heights)
52. Kuwait-Iraq
53. Morocco (Western Sahara)
54. Saudi Arabia (Islamists)
55. Saudi Arabia-Yemen (Al-Kharakhir)

Central and East Asia
56. Bhutan (Banditism)
57. Uzbekistan (Fergana Valley)
58. China (Inner Mongolia)
59. China (Tibet)
60. China (Yunnan)
61. Phillipines (Moros)
62. Phillipines (Communists)
63. India/Pakistan (Siachen glacier)
64. India (Andra Pradesh)
65. India (West Bengal)
66. India (Bihar)
67. India (Uttar Pradesh)
68. India (Maharashtra)
69. Indonesia (East Timor)
70. Indonesia (Irian Jaya)
71. Indonesia (Aceh)
72. North/South Korea
73. Nepal (Maoists)
74. Papua New Guinea (Bougainville)

Low-intensity C

Central and South America
1. Guatemala (URNG)
2. Mexico (Guerrero)
3. Peru (Shining Path, MRTA)

West, Central and East Europe
4. Bosnia-Herzegovina
5. Azerbijan/Armenia (Nagorno K
6. Daghestan
7. Croatia

Africa
8. Angola (Cabinda)
9. Central. Afric. Rep. (Yakoma)
10. Ethiopia (Amhara)
11. Ethiopia (Oromo)
12. Ethiopia (Ogaden)

Other Peacekeeping Operations

Liberia (ECOMOG)	since 1990
Georgia (South Ossetia Joint Force)	since 1992
Moldova (Moldova Joint Force)	since 1992
Iraq (Operation Provide Comfort)	since 1992
Tajikistan (CIS Buffer Force)	since 1993
Georgia (CIS Peacekeeping Force)	since 1994
Bosnia-Herzegovina (SFOR)	since 1996

Algeria
Chad
Sudan
Sierra Leone
Liberia
Zaire
Rwanda
Burundi
Angola
Turkey

🔫 High-intensity conflicts

Estimated number of deaths in 1996

Burundi	10,000 - 50,000
Chechnya	>20,000
Rwanda	>10,000
Afghanistan	>10,000
Algeria	>10,000
Zaire (East)	>10,000
Turkey	>4,000
Liberia	>3,000
Sierra Leone	>3,000
Sri Lanka	>2,000
Angola	>1,000
Cambodia	>1,000
Colombia	>1,000
India (Assam)	>1,000
India (Kashmir)	>1,000
Pakistan (Sindh)	>1,000
Sudan (South)	>1,000
Tajikistan	>1,000
Chad (South)	>1,000

🔥 Violent Political Conflicts

Central and South America
1. Bolivia (Chaparé)
2. Brazil (Para)
3. El Salvador
4. Haiti
5. Mexico (Chiapas)
6. Mexico (Tabasco)
7. Mexico (Veracruz)
8. Mexico (Oaxaca)
9. Nicaragua (Contras, Re-contras)
10. Venezuela (Indians)

West, Central and East Europe
11. Armenia (Opposition)
12. Bosnia-H. (Herceg Bosna)
13. Bosnia-H. (Srpska Rep.)
14. Bulgarije (Opposition)
15. Cyprus
16. France (Corsica)
17. France (Algerian Islamists)
18. Greece-Turkey
   (Aegean Sea Islands)
19. Georgia (Abkhazia)
20. Georgia (Mkhedroni)
21. Croatia/Serbia (East Slavonia)
22. Moldova (Transdnistr)
23. United Kingdom (N. Ireland)
24. Serbia (Kosovo)
25. Serbia (Oppositie)

26. Spain (Basques)
27. Turkey (Alewites)
28. Ukraine (Krim)
29. Ukraine (Tatars)
30. Russia (Ingoeshe

Africa
31. Djibouti (Afar)
32. Eritrea (Border w
33. Ghana (North)
34. Guinea (Army)
35. Ivory Coast (Bet
36. Cameroon/Niger
37. Kenya (Rift Valle
38. Kenya (Turkana
39. Mali (Tuareg)
40. Mauritania-Sene
41. Niger (Tuareg)
42. Nigeria (Opposit
43. Nigeria (Ogoni)
44. Nigeria (Ijaw, Its
45. Nigeria (Kano, S
46. Tanzania (Zanzi
47. Togo (Oppositio
48. Zambia (Black M

North Africa and M
49. Algeria (Kabylia
50. Bahrein (Islamis

🔫 High-intensity conflicts

Estimated cumulative number of deaths

Cambodia (1975-)	>2,000,000
Afghanistan (1978-)	1-2,000,000
Sudan (South) (1983-)	>1,500,000
Angola (1975-)	500-900,000
Rwanda (1994-)	>800,000
Chad (South) (1966-)	100-300,000
Burundi (1993-)	>150,000
Liberia (1989-)	>150,000
Colombia (1964)	45-100,000
Tajikistan (1992-)	30-100,000
Chechnya (1994-1996)	40-80,000
Algeria (1992-)	>60,000
Sri Lanka (1983-)	50-60,000
India (Kashmir) (1989-)	30-50,000
Zaire (East) (1993-)	20-60,000
Sierra Leone (1991-)	20-30,000
Turkey (1983-)	20-25,000
Pakistan (Sindh) (1986-)	>14,000
India (Assam) (1979-)	>5,000

🇺🇳 Active United Nations Peacekeeping Operations

Egypt/Israel (UNTSO)	since 1948
Pakistan (UNMOGIP)	since 1949
Cyprus (UNFICYP)	since 1964
Syria (UNDOF)	since 1974
Lebanon (UNIFIL)	since 1978
Angola (UNAVEM III)	since 1991
Kuwait/Iraq (UNIKOM)	since 1991
West Sahara (MINURSO)	since 1991
El Salvador (ONUSAL)	since 1991
Mozambique (UNOMOZ)	since 1992
Georgia (UNOMIG)	since 1993
Liberia (UNOMIL)	since 1993
Haiti (UNMIH)	since 1993
Rwanda (UNAMIR)	since 1993
Tajikistan (UNMOT)	since 1994
Bosnia-Herz. (UNMIBH)	since 1995
Croatia (UNCRO)	since 1995
Macedonia (UNPREDEP)	since 1995
East Slavonia (UNTAES)	since 1996

2
HISTORICAL INHERITANCES

Sellar and Yeatman in their comic history of Britain, *1066 and All That*, decided to include only two dates in the book, because all others were 'not memorable'. They would have had much greater difficulty writing an equivalent volume on Irish history. 1170, 1641, 1690, 1798, 1912, 1916, 1921, 1969 – all these dates are fixed like beacons in the folklore and mythology of the Irish. They trip off the tongue during conversation like the latest football scores in other environments, and are recorded for posterity on gable walls all over Northern Ireland.

To some extent this chapter is a history of the above, and other, dates. It is not intended as a pocket history of Northern Ireland, and anyone who wishes a more comprehensive account of the history of Ulster or Ireland will have no difficulty in finding suitable books.[1] The intention here is to construct a short introduction for readers unfamiliar with Irish history and to provide a context for the outbreak of serious violence in 1969.

To say that Partition was created, and is maintained, by England for ulterior motives, is ... untrue. On the contrary all the English parties without exception have sought at one time or another to find a solution, even to the extent of betraying their Northern adherents. It was only through the determined clash of rival Irish wills that Partition became inevitable.

J. Horgan, 1955

19

Ulster[2] has a history of separateness which is not explainable in purely regional terms. Although the English monarchy had claimed Ireland since Henry II's invasion in the twelfth century, effective English control had been confined to a relatively small area, mainly around Dublin, until the fifteenth century. Before the Plantation of the early seventeenth century, Ulster was, apart from a few precarious coastal fortresses, the most Gaelic part of the country. It had successfully resisted English colonial ambitions. Its contacts with the rest of Ireland were largely confined to skirmishes across interminable battlefields. Western Scotland and eastern Ulster, however, had been exchanging migrants since long before the Middle Ages.

It would be a mistake to regard pre-Plantation Ulster as a cohesive unit. Like the rest of Ireland it was dominated by a number of territorially jealous chiefs. Internal wars and vendettas were common. But the dominance of the O'Donnells in Donegal, the MacDonalds in Antrim and particularly the O'Neills in the centre of the province did produce some islands of stability; it also produced military cohesion against Elizabeth I's armies and, for a time, success. It took nine years and a blockade of the province to bring the Ulster chiefs to their knees.

It was this very intransigence that accounted for the comprehensive nature of the Plantation of Ulster in 1609. There had been earlier attempts to colonise parts of Ireland during the sixteenth century, but they had consisted of little more than the confiscation of land and the grafting on of a new aristocracy. This also happened in Ulster. The leaders of the Ulster families were forced to flee to Europe, and their lands were confiscated and distributed to planters from Britain. By 1703, less than a century later, only 14 per cent of the land in Ireland remained in the hands of the Catholic Irish, and in Ulster the figure was 5 per cent. These figures are not the full measure of the changes introduced within the Plantation of Ulster. What made it unique among Irish plantations was the comprehensive attempt to attract colonists of all classes, and the fact that the colonists were Protestant and, to a large extent, culturally distinct from the indigenous population. The Catholic Irish remained, of course, but in conditions which emphasised their suppression. They were relegated to a state below servility, because the planters were not allowed to employ the native Irish as servants in the new towns which they built. The towns themselves were fortresses against the armed resentment of the Irish. Outside the towns they were banished from the land they had owned and worked, and were confined to the boggy mountainous regions. The reality differed from the intention, however. There were simply not enough settlers to achieve comprehensive control, and the Irish were quietly admitted to the towns.

The sum of the Plantation was the introduction to Ulster of a community of strangers who spoke a different language, worshipped apart and followed an alien culture and way of life. It had close commercial, cultural and political ties with Britain. The deep resentment of the Irish towards the planters, and the distrust of the planters towards the Irish, are the roots of the Ulster problem. Within 50 years of the Plantation the broad outlines of the current conflict in Northern Ireland had been sketched out: the same territory was occupied by two hostile groups, one believing the land had been usurped and the other fearing that its tenure was constantly under threat of rebellion; the two communities identified their differences in religious and cultural as well as territorial terms; sometimes they lived in separate quarters and, even when they did not, mutual suspicion reinforced their distinctiveness. The Plantation's heritage was one of hostility enlivened by periods of violence between the two communities. Colm Lennon's 1995 book on sixteenth-century Ireland was well named *The Incomplete Conquest*.[3]

The next two centuries supplied a lot of the dates and other trappings essential to the conflict. The Rising of 1641 against the planters provided a Protestant massacre, and the Cromwellian conquest in the 1650s a Catholic one. Most important of all was the Battle of the Boyne in 1690, sanctified on a hundred gable walls and Orange banners as the victory of the Protestant William III over the Catholic James II. The aftermath of William of Orange's victory at the Boyne was much more important than the campaign itself. It was a mark of the sustained hostility between planter and Gael that the penal laws, which feature strongly in the catalogue of England's evils in Ireland, were

21

enacted by Irishmen through the Irish parliament in Dublin. The laws were of vital importance in broadening the differences between the Irish establishment and its opponents. Having established an exclusively Protestant legislature in 1692, a comprehensive series of coercive acts against Catholics were implemented during the 1690s and after: they were excluded from the armed forces, the judiciary and the legal profession as well as from parliament; they were forbidden to carry arms or to own a horse worth more than £5; all their bishops and regular clergy were banished in 1697, although secular clergy could remain under licence; Catholics were forbidden to hold long leases on land or to buy land from a Protestant, and were forced to divide their property equally among their children in their wills, unless the eldest conformed to the Anglican faith; they were prohibited from conducting schools, or from sending their children to be educated abroad. Some of these laws, and notably those affecting property, were rigidly enforced, while others were unenforceable. Their main effects were to entrench the divide between Catholics and Protestants, to strengthen Irish Catholicism by adding a political component to it, and to drive underground some aspects of the Catholic Gaelic culture, notably education and public worship.

Most of the penal laws had been cautiously disregarded or repealed by the 1790s. Some of them had also applied to Presbyterians, and their repeal reflected an atmosphere of greater tolerance. A convention of the Irish Volunteers – an exclusively Protestant body aimed at creating greater independence from Britain – met at Dungannon in 1782 and passed a resolution 'that as men and as Irishmen, as Christians and as Protestants, we rejoice in the relaxation of the penal laws against our Roman Catholic fellow-subjects'.[4] The Volunteers, Protestant to a man, formed a guard of honour for Father Hugh O'Donnell as the first Catholic church in Belfast, St Mary's in Chapel Lane, was opened, and Protestants contributed £84 towards the cost of its building. The early success of the Society of United Irishmen in attracting both Presbyterians and Catholics into a revolutionary republican movement during the 1790s appeared to indicate a new Irish cohesion which disregarded religious denominationalism and was determined to establish an independent republic of Ireland. The abortive 1798 rebellion, best known for the Catholic rising in Wexford, also included risings in Antrim and Down; in the resulting judicial investigations 30 Presbyterian clergymen were accused of participation: three of them were hanged, seven imprisoned, four exiled or transported and at least five fled the country.[5]

This apparent cross-denominational solidarity could not disguise the emergence of strong community divisions. Secret organisations like the Defenders, the Peep O'Day Boys and the Steelboys, strongly sectarian and determined to ensure that tenancies were prevented from passing into the hands of the other religion, waged persistent and occasionally bloody skirmishes with each other in the country areas. Indeed it was one of these skirmishes in Armagh which led to the formation of the Orange Order, an organisation which stressed the common interests of all Protestants and effectively challenged the Presbyterian-Catholic alliance in the United Irishmen. Inside Belfast the level of tolerance towards Catholics was determined primarily by their numbers in the city. In 1707 George McCartney, the Sovereign of Belfast, reported to his superiors that 'thank God we are not under any great fears here, for ... we have not among us above seven papists'.[6] The industrial expansion of the city towards the beginning of the nineteenth century attracted Catholic immigration. Between 1800 and 1830 the proportion of Catholics in Belfast rose from 10 per cent to 30 per cent and the first signs of serious urban conflict occurred as a result of competition for jobs and houses. The same period saw considerable changes in attitudes among Presbyterians. The liberals within the Church came under increasing challenge from hardline opinion represented by Henry Cooke and those closely linked to the Orange Order. The dispute was along both theological and political lines, and resulted in a comprehensive victory for Cooke and his supporters. The liberals under Henry Montgomery broke away and formed the Non-subscribing Presbyterian Church. The community divisions in Ulster began to assume a form similar to that well-known today.

The first serious communal riot in Belfast took place on 12 July 1835, and a woman was killed. An English witness to the riot,

John Barrow, contrasted Belfast with the industrial cities in Britain where such disturbances were frequent. 'In Belfast, where everyone is too much engaged in his own business, and where neither religion nor politics have interfered to disturb the harmony of society, it could not fail to create a great and uneasy sensation.'[7] It was a sensation which Belfast citizens have experienced ever since. Andrew Boyd mentioned eight other years 'of the most serious rioting' during the rest of the nineteenth century, and indeed few years passed without some disturbances.[8] The main effect of these riots was to ensure that the expanding population of the city was separated into sectarian areas, and to fortify the communal differences between Catholics and Protestants.

The Act of Union in 1801, a direct consequence of the 1798 rebellion, abolished the Irish parliament and bound Ireland and Britain together as parts of the United Kingdom. The nineteenth century also witnessed a growing separation between Ulster and the rest of Ireland. The effects of the industrial revolution in Ireland were confined almost entirely to the northern part of the country, strapping even closer its industrial and commercial dependency on Britain. The greater prosperity of the north, its economic structure, even its physical appearance, increased its alienation from the rest of Ireland. The potato famine of the 1840s, undoubtedly the most far-reaching event in nineteenth-century Ireland, had much more severe consequences in the south and west than in the north, and had profound effects on political, economic and social developments there which were less dramatic in Ulster. Economic differences found a political voice when the campaign for the repeal of the Act of Union with Britain caused a petition to be organised as early as 1834 against repeal or, if a Dublin parliament was restored, in favour of a separate legislature in Ulster. In 1841 Daniel O'Connell, the champion of repeal, visited Belfast. His coach had to avoid an ambush, the meeting hall was stoned and his entourage was protected by a strong police force on its way southwards.

The most worthless Protestant, even if he had nothing else to boast of, at least found it pleasing to think that he was a member of the dominant race.

W. Lecky, 1892

It was the Home Rule campaign in the 1880s which was to give Protestant Ulster its organised basis and its tradition of separateness. As late as the general election of 1885, 17 out of 33 Ulster seats were carried by the Home Rule party. The next two decades transformed this picture and stiffened Ulster's resistance to Home Rule. The resistance was strengthened by the growing political alliance between Ulster unionism and the Conservative Party in Britain. The basis of the new Conservative policy was an identification with Protestant fears, and particularly with the province of Ulster. If the motive was frank political opportunism from the Conservatives, the Ulster unionists were glad of such powerful support. Nevertheless, although this support was important, it was events inside Ulster which gave the anti-Home Rule campaign its real power. Amidst the outbursts against Home Rule by churchmen, unionists, members of parliament and Conservative politicians, it was the Orange Order which emerged to provide the leadership and organisation. The Order's fortunes during the eighteenth century had been chequered. Outlawed and abused on many occasions, it had nevertheless survived. The anti-Home Rule campaign served to transform the Order from a disreputable to a respectable body. For its part the Order supplied the ready-made framework of an effective organisation for growing Protestant dissatisfaction, especially in Ulster. By 1905 it had played a major role in uniting disparate unionist voices within the Ulster Unionist Council – the coalition from which the Unionist Party was to emerge.

The Irish Parliamentary Party, which attempted to achieve Home Rule by legislative action, was at times complemented and at times rivalled by revolutionaries of both the physical force and the cultural variety. The Irish revolutionary tradition, represented by the Fenians from the 1850s, and later by the Irish

Republican Brotherhood, the IRA and others, loomed over the parliamentary campaign. It was strategically useful to Charles Stewart Parnell, the Irish nationalist leader, as a warning of what would happen if Home Rule were rejected – but it became a serious and, in the end, a more powerful rival to the Parliamentary Party as impatience grew with the slow progress towards independence. The formation of the Gaelic Athletic Association to encourage Irish sports, and the Gaelic League to encourage interest in the Irish language and literature, reflected an emerging nationalism which was more closely tuned to the revolutionary than the parliamentary tradition. These developments were adopted with enthusiasm by nationalists in the north of Ireland, just as the organisation of the anti-Home Rule campaign included branches all over the country. But as the crisis came to a head between 1906 and 1914, the quarrel was regarded in increasingly general geographical terms as one between the northern and southern parts of the country. Lip-service was paid to the existence of minorities within the enemy camps, but their causes did not receive really serious attention until the 1920s when their minority conditions had been confirmed within separate states.

The decade between 1912 and 1922 was a momentous one for Ireland. Civil conflict between north and south, where private armies were openly drilling, was averted by the outbreak of the First World War; the 1916 Easter rising in Dublin and the subsequent guerrilla campaign shifted the spotlight southward; the signing in 1921 of a treaty between the British government and Sinn Féin, the political wing of the IRA, led to the establishment of the Irish Free State from which Northern Ireland opted out. These events and the first years of both new states were accompanied by civil disorder. Belfast and other towns in the north suffered from a guerrilla campaign and sectarian conflicts. The new state of Northern Ireland was created in the midst of the troubles and divisions which were to characterise its later history.

The Government of Ireland Act 1920 proposed two states in Ireland, one for the six north-eastern counties and the other for the remainder of Ireland. Each was to have its own parliament to deal with domestic matters; each was to send representatives to

Westminster; and a Council of Ireland was to deal with matters of common interest. In fact the terms only came into operation in Northern Ireland, and the Council of Ireland never met. The new arrangements in Northern Ireland established a bi-cameral legislature, and a subordinate government in Belfast with authority over a number of devolved powers, including policing, education, local government and social services. London retained ultimate authority, with the power to suspend Northern Ireland's executive and legislative powers. Having fought against Home Rule for almost a century, unionists were, in the words of J.B. Armour, 'compelled to take a form of Home Rule that the devil himself could never have imagined'.[9]

The size of the new state was a case in point. The borders between Ireland's counties had never been intended as anything more than local administrative boundaries, and fairly arbitrary ones at that. Now some of them became international frontiers. As to why six counties had been selected rather than four or nine or any other number, the reasons were unashamedly straightforward. They formed essentially the largest area which could be comfortably held with a majority in favour of the union with Britain. The traditional nine counties of Ulster held 900,000 Protestants, most of whom supported the British connection, and 700,000 Catholics, most of whom wanted to end it. However, in the six counties which were later to become Northern Ireland, the religious breakdown was 820,000 Protestants and 430,000 Catholics. In 1920 C.C. Craig, brother of James Craig, the first Prime Minister of Northern Ireland, expressed the case frankly in the House of Commons: 'If we had a nine-county parliament, with 64 members, the unionist majority would be about three or four: but in a six-county parliament, with 52 members, the unionist majority would be about ten.'[10] It was this more than any other consideration which persuaded unionists to accept the six-county area.

Northern Ireland 1921–69: internal affairs

The new state was born amid bloodshed and communal disorder. In 1922, a total of 232 people were killed in the violence in

Northern Ireland, and almost 1,000 wounded, figures unsurpassed until 1972. The nationalist minority refused to recognise the new state; the 12 anti-partitionist members of parliament (MPs) refused to attend parliament; Catholic teachers shunned the educational system, submitting pupils for examinations in Dublin and even, for a time, refusing salaries. At the very time when the institutions of the new state were being established, a considerable minority of its citizens were refusing to participate on committees or to perform any action which might lend support to its authority.

As time passed, and the state remained, most nationalists decided on a reluctant acceptance of the need to come to some accommodation, at least in the short term. In some cases they found that the institutions which had been established and those which were still being set up were so arranged as to effectively exclude them from positions of power. Partly as a result of Catholic unwillingness to participate in a state whose existence they opposed, and partly as a result of discrimination by the establishment against a section of the community which it considered as traitorous, many of the institutions were heavily biased in favour of unionists. The local government franchise, for example, which remained unreformed until 1969, reflected property rather than population, excluding non-ratepayers and awarding many people with more than one property extra votes. Housing allocation and the gerrymandering of constituency boundaries were actively used in some cases, notably the city of Derry*, to maintain unionist majorities. In the membership of the police force and the Ulster Special Constabulary, formed to help combat the IRA threat in 1921, a combination of nationalist unwillingness and unionist distrust created forces which were to become largely Protestant. As late as the 1960s only 12 per cent of the Royal Ulster Constabulary (RUC) were Catholic, and the auxiliary 'B' Specials were exclusively Protestant. Education too was an area where Catholics felt bitterly that the system established by the Education Act (Northern Ireland) 1930 was one

---

* There is no acceptable compromise when referring to the city of Derry/Londonderry. The first term is favoured by nationalists, the latter by many unionists. Derry is the term commonly used by both communities in the city itself, and will be used in the rest of the book without political implication.

which had been tailored by Protestant pressure, producing a state education system which was in fact Protestant, and forcing Catholic schools to find 50 per cent of the cost of education. In the administration of justice Catholics have long believed that the Special Powers Act, which placed considerable emergency powers in the hands of the Minister of Home Affairs, was aimed exclusively against the nationalist minority. Further charges have been made, and vindicated by the Cameron Report in 1969 and by a strong body of academic research, about discrimination against Catholics in public employment.[11] The most serious general allegation in this field was that the government operated a policy of deliberate discrimination against part of the province – counties Londonderry and Fermanagh in particular – creating conditions which encouraged emigration to counter the higher Catholic birth rate in these areas. Disputes about the extent of institutional discrimination, and about the reasons for it, have always been particularly bitter, but one point is clear. Far from resolving intercommunal suspicion and fear, the establishment of the state actually helped to make them more precise.

The establishment of these institutions was a challenge to what some Irish republicans saw as unfinished business. The years immediately following the establishment of the state were among the most violent in Ulster's history. The republican objective of securing a united independent Ireland, by force if necessary, continued, and there were IRA campaigns in the 1920s, '40s and '50s. Sectarianism revived during the depression of the 1930s. Widespread riots in 1931, some of which involved the IRA, resulted in between 60 and 70 people being injured. The year 1932 saw riots in Belfast, Larne, Portadown and Ballymena. Twelve people were killed and 600 wounded in 1935. Incidents like the 1932 Shankill riots in support of the Falls hunger marchers, who had been baton charged by the police, disturbed the pattern but did not alter it. The frequency of sectarian violence gradually faded as the employment situation improved, but few believed that it had retreated far below the surface.

For many unionists these disturbances confirmed that the union itself could only be maintained with constant vigilance. Emergency legislation was introduced on a permanent basis; a police force and police reserve were established which were almost exclusively Protestant; local government electoral boundaries were openly gerrymandered; and a system of economic discrimination was introduced against the Catholic minority in Northern Ireland. Catholics formed about one-third of the population for most of the twentieth century.

Greater economic prosperity during the Second World War and post-war years saw a particular improvement in the prospects and conditions of the minority. The new industries introduced in the 1950s and '60s, many of which were branches of international combines, offered hopes to Catholics, especially from the middle and lower managerial classes who had formerly found promotion prospects restricted, although research suggests that the newcomers often came to adopt local practices.[12] Improvements were also evident in other spheres. The post-war legislation which greatly broadened the social benefits of the welfare state particularly benefited the poorer classes in society, and in Northern Ireland this included a disproportionate number of Catholics. The Education Act 1947 opened doors of educational opportunity by introducing free secondary education, and the subsequent rise in the number of Catholics attending university was one measure of its effectiveness. Although the extent of these changes is often debated, there is no doubt that the 1950s saw a growing tendency for Catholics to see their future in terms of a Northern Ireland context rather than in an all-Ireland state. One pointer to this change was the failure of the IRA offensive of 1956–62. Its defeat owed more to apathy than to the efficiency of law enforcement machinery, and this was recognised by the IRA in its statement formally ending the campaign: 'Foremost among the factors motivating this course of action has been the attitude of the general public whose minds have deliberately been distracted from the supreme issue facing the Irish people – the unity and freedom of Ireland.'[13]

The decision taken by the IRA shortly afterwards to abandon military methods and concentrate on socialist objectives by political means seemed to promise that the 1960s would be free of republican violence. In 1959 there were further signs of a possible erosion of traditional attitudes. The republican party, Sinn

Féin, lost its two seats at Westminster, its percentage of the votes plummeting from 26 to 14. Just as dramatic was the attempt by some leading unionists to suggest that Catholics might be permitted to join the party. The attempt was thwarted by the obduracy of the Orange Order, but that it had been made at all was seen as a sign of changing times.

So the 1960s started as the decade of hope. The retirement in 1963 of the Prime Minister, Lord Brookeborough, who was to many Catholics the personification of right-wing unionist opinion, and his replacement by Terence O'Neill, appeared to be another victory for moderation. The policies of the new premier encouraged this view. In 1964 he declared, 'My principal aims are to make Northern Ireland prosperous and to build bridges between the two traditions.'[14] In the same year the Irish Congress of Trade Unions (ICTU), to which most Northern workers were affiliated, was recognised by Stormont in return for the ICTU granting greater independence to its Northern Ireland Committee. In 1965 O'Neill and the southern premier, Sean Lemass, exchanged visits. As a direct result of this visit the Nationalist Party in Northern Ireland agreed to become the official opposition party in Stormont, effectively becoming part of the system they had refused to endorse since its creation.

Once again apparent moves towards conciliation were accompanied by warning signals, remembered in retrospect but underrated in the exuberant optimism of the 1960s, that basic attitudes had not altered significantly. There were echoes of the classic duel between liberal and right-wing Presbyterianism fought between Cooke and Montgomery in the 1820s when the Presbyterian General Assembly was picketed by Ian Paisley in 1966. In the same year the murder of a Catholic in the Malvern Arms public house revealed the continuing existence of the Ulster Volunteer Force (UVF), which presented itself as the loyalist equivalent of the IRA. The pressures for change in Northern Ireland had produced defenders of the status quo.

To some Catholics the changes which they were resisting seemed insubstantial and irritatingly slow. A series of measures – notably the closure of the main rail link to Derry, the decision to establish a new university at Coleraine instead of in Derry where a University College was already operating, and the establishment of a new growth centre at Craigavon – were seen as discriminating against the disadvantaged, and predominantly Catholic, west. In March 1967 the Republican Clubs, which represented an attempt by republicans to find a legitimate method of political expression, were declared illegal by the government, a move which seemed narrow and repressive even to many non-republicans. These developments seemed to confirm that reform would not come without pressure, and that, whether O'Neill wanted reform or not, the conservatism of his party would sabotage change. Housing allocation provided the issue for this pressure, and the success of the civil rights campaign in America suggested non-violent protest as the means. The Campaign for Social Justice in Northern Ireland, formed in Dungannon in 1964, developed through Housing Action committees in other parts of the province. In 1967 the broader-based Northern Ireland Civil Rights Association (NICRA) was formed to demand a range of internal reforms, including the removal of discrimination in the allocation of jobs and houses, permanent emergency legislation and electoral abuses. The campaign was modelled on the civil rights campaign in the USA, involving protests, marches, sit-ins and the use of the media to publicise minority grievances. It was followed with increasing interest by the news media, expanded what had been a local issue into an international one, and sparked off the most dynamic years in the history of Northern Ireland.

On paper the civil rights campaign had been a remarkable success. After two marches in 1967, to Dungannon in August and to Derry in October, the O'Neill administration had been forced to replace Derry City Council with a Development Commission, to establish an Ombudsman and to establish franchise arrangements similar to those in Britain. Certainly complaints remained, notably about the Special Powers Act, but promises were given that the schemes for allocating publicly owned houses would be clarified and the Special Powers Act reviewed. These successes ultimately split the civil rights movement.

Those, like the members of the People's Democracy (PD) who were moving towards a more radical position, believed that it would be foolish to abandon a successful campaign before it had achieved all its objectives. Others felt that both the reforms and the dismissal from office in December of William Craig, the Minister of Home Affairs, demonstrated the government's good intentions, and that a suspension on marches should be agreed to enable the passing of further reforms. The decision by the PD to march from Belfast to Derry in January 1969, and the violent opposition to the marchers at Burntollet Bridge, destroyed any hopes of non-violent protest. Many Protestants and liberal Catholics who had participated in the early campaigns now drifted out. The campaign became more radical, and as often happens during periods of rapid change, the agenda was increasingly determined by relatively small militant groups. The months leading up to the traditional celebrations were marked by riots in Strabane, Derry and Belfast. The annual August march by the Protestant Apprentice Boys of Derry was attacked. The violence of the police reaction in the Catholic Bogside produced two important responses. The Prime Minister of the Irish Republic, Jack Lynch, made his famous 'we will not stand by' speech, the strong language of which was intended to compensate for his inability to take strong action. The violence spread to Belfast. In August the Catholic Lower Falls area was invaded by a hostile mob, seven people were killed and more than 3,000 lost their homes. On 14 August the British government sent the army into Derry, and on the next day to Belfast. Ironically its initial function was the protection of Catholic families. More important, however, it restored the ultimate republican symbol of oppression – British troops on Irish soil. By January 1970 the Provisional IRA had been formed, and began a campaign of violence against the army. By 1972 it was clear that the local Northern Irish government, having introduced internment in 1971 as a last attempt to impose control, was unable to handle the situation. Invoking its powers under the Government of Ireland Act, the Westminster parliament abolished the Northern Ireland government in March 1972 and replaced it with Direct Rule from Westminster.

Northern Ireland 1921–69: external relations

....

Ireland is by natural design a complete geographical entity. This natural design enforced on the political life of Ireland at a very early date the ideal of national unity, and it is doing violence, not only to nature, but to the whole trend of the political life of the island to divorce politically at this late date in her national existence a considerable section of the northern part of the country from the motherland.

Stationery Office, Dublin, 1923

....

Northern Ireland's relationships with the southern part of the country and with Britain provided the issues which determined prime political allegiances. In simple terms this issue has been whether the Northern Ireland area should be included within the United Kingdom or within an all-Ireland state. The state of diplomatic relations between southern Ireland and Britain was reflected to some extent in the relationship between the two communities inside Northern Ireland, as were the interactions between the two parts of Ireland.

The relationship between the Northern Ireland and British legislatures was not defined in any great detail by the Government of Ireland Act 1920. Nevertheless some indisputable guidelines were laid down. One of these was the superiority of the Westminster parliament, to which Northern Ireland initially sent 12 representatives. The subservience of the Northern Ireland parliament precluded it from some areas of government, notably foreign affairs and defence, which remained the responsibility of Westminster. This meant that all dealings between the northern and southern parts of Ireland were outside the jurisdiction of Northern Ireland's legislature.

During the first decade after the 1921 treaty, both governments in Ireland were too preoccupied with internal affairs to court conflict with each other. Britain was determined to remain, as far as was possible, outside Irish affairs. The attitude of the Cosgrave administration, which remained in power in Dublin from 1922 until 1932, was relatively benign. In 1925 an agreement was signed by Britain and both Irish administrations which formally acknowledged the *de facto* partition of the island. From the 1920s north-south relations depended more on governmental changes south of the border than on those in Northern Ireland. The coming to power of Eamon de Valera and the Fianna Fáil party in 1932 had an immediate effect on these relations. Their aggressive policy of separatist nationalism immediately affected the Irish Free State's relations with Britain. De Valera's decision in 1932 to end the annuities which had been repaid to the British government since it had financed land purchase schemes for Irish tenants, produced retaliatory British tariffs on Irish cattle, which finally led to the raising of general tariff walls between the two countries. The new Irish constitution of 1937 introduced a distinctly Catholic and Irish flavour, recognising the 'special position of the Holy Catholic Apostolic and Roman Church as the guardian of the faith professed by the great majority of the citizens'. Northern Ireland was directly affected by these new changes. In 1933 de Valera had marked the new Northern policy by standing as an abstentionist for a seat in South Down. More important, Article 2 of the 1937 constitution stated unequivocally that 'the national territory consists of the whole island of Ireland, its islands and its territorial seas'. The trade war between Ireland and Great Britain ended with the trade agreement of 1938. But the challenge against partition was not so readily dropped.

Paralleling the deterioration of relations between Northern Ireland and the Irish Free State during the 1930s was a less spectacular but critical tightening of the bonds between Northern Ireland and the rest of the United Kingdom. This development particularly applied to the economic links between the two areas. Originally it was thought that taxes levied in Northern Ireland would adequately cover its expenditure, and even leave a surplus for an imperial contribution which was determined at £6.7 million for 1922–3. With the rise of United Kingdom social expenditure and a decline in Northern Ireland's industrial production, it soon became clear that such hopes were illusory. The Simon declaration in 1938 not only acknowledged Northern Ireland's entitlement to similar social standards as Great Britain, but that the Westminster exchequer must supply the necessary funds if a deficit occurred in Northern Ireland. This principle of parity was naturally welcomed in Northern Ireland. Its short-term effect was to widen further the standards of social services north and south of the border. It was some time before it became clear that such financial concessions might imply conditions and obligations from Westminster which had been avoided in the early years of the new state. The increase in Britain's financial involvement in Northern Ireland following the establishment of the welfare state led to the first British insistence that Stormont was obliged to adopt British standards in legislation. The Education Act (Northern Ireland) 1947 and the increase in family allowances in 1956 were two examples of British intervention to prevent the possibility of social services funds being distributed in a discriminatory fashion.

The immediate post-war years also saw statements in both southern Ireland and Great Britain about the position of Northern Ireland. Ironically enough, the declaration of an Irish Republic and its withdrawal from the British Commonwealth was carried, not by Fianna Fáil which had lost office in 1948, but by a coalition government under John Costello. Sheehy may exaggerate when he claimed that these actions 'set the seal on Irish disunity'[15] but they certainly aroused fervour among Northern Ireland unionists. The 1949 general election there, known as the Union Jack election, was fought largely on the issue of the union, thought by some to be in danger from a Labour government in Britain. The Ireland Act 1949 was designed to dispel such fears:

'It is hereby declared that Northern Ireland remains part of His Majesty's dominions and of the United Kingdom, and it is hereby affirmed that in no event will Northern Ireland or any part thereof cease to be part of His Majesty's dominions and of the United Kingdom without the consent of the parliament of Northern Ireland.'

This strong British guarantee, and the severing of the Commonwealth relationship between southern Ireland and Great

Britain, might have been expected to inflame passions between the two parts of Ireland and within Northern Ireland itself. There were indeed communal stresses in the North following the election, and the Republic launched an international anti-partition campaign. But by the early 1950s matters returned to normal, and a period of comparative stability was sustained for almost two decades. Britain became the main destination for most of the Irish Republic's exports, and for most of its emigrants. The economic dependency on Britain was conspicuous enough for the Danish sociologist, Anders Boserup, to claim that, in economic terms, the union between the Republic of Ireland and the United Kingdom was being restored. Nor was this all. The Republic of Ireland, quite apart from her relations with Britain, developed a much more outward-looking foreign policy from the 1950s, becoming actively involved in the UN movement, and eventually joining the European Economic Community in 1973.

It was within this new context of internationalism that the first few cautious steps of north-south cooperation began. Significantly, they were largely confined to economic interests which affected both areas. Thus in 1952 agreement was reached that both governments should take over the Foyle fisheries. This was followed by joint involvement in draining the Erne basin and in a hydroelectric development there. Between 1953 and 1958 the Great Northern Railway, which included the Belfast-Dublin line, was operated jointly by the two governments.

The meeting which took place in 1965 between the northern and southern premiers, Terence O'Neill and Sean Lemass, was a logical extension of these developments, but its symbolism was not lost in both parts of the island. They seemed to many to represent the new Ireland which had at last shaken off the past, men interested in prosperity rather than politics, in opportunities for cooperation instead of excuses for conflict. The effect inside Northern Ireland was considerable. The Nationalist Party agreed to become the official opposition at Stormont and the Catholic hierarchy appointed a chaplain to parliament. 'Twin towns' were established across the border, their citizens exchanging visits and experiences. Relations between north and south, and between both of them and Britain, had never been closer, and the prospects of a period of community harmony seemed good. They were to be destroyed by a mixture of majority tardiness and minority impatience. The events following from the civil rights campaign were to alter radically both relations inside Northern Ireland, and Northern Ireland's relations with her immediate neighbours.

Britain and the Irish Republic were not the only external actors in the Northern Irish conflict. In the 1990 census more than 40,000,000 USA citizens claimed that their ethnic identity was Irish, although their commitment to developments there was often sentimental rather than political. Nevertheless Irish-Americans had been enlisted by Irish politicians since Daniel O'Connell encouraged the formation of Friends of Ireland organisations and Hibernian Relief Societies in the 1820s to support his campaign for Catholic emancipation. In 1919 Irish-American sentiment was strong enough to persuade the USA House of Representatives to vote by 216 to 45 that the post-war peace conference should consider Ireland's claim to self-determination. But such interest was fleeting. As Andrew Wilson put it, 'by the mid-sixties it seemed that the long history of Irish-American involvement in the political destiny of their homeland had finally ended'.[16] The outbreak of violence in Northern Ireland in 1969 rekindled the involvement, almost exclusively in support of either constitutional nationalism or the revolutionary republicanism of the IRA. It gradually eroded over the next quarter century of violence. By the 1990s American influence – and that of the EU – was again to play an important part in urging an end to the violence and in supporting the moves towards a ceasefire and a settlement.

A varied inheritance

....

Partition does not depend upon a physical boundary which can be removed by political action; it depends upon very important differences in outlook between two groups of people; and though these differences may be accentuated by political division they will not necessarily disappear as a result of enforced political union. The real partition of Ireland is not on the map but in the minds of men.
J. C. Beckett, 1966

....

Division and violence are not Ireland's only historical inheritances. Three centuries living together in the same narrow ground has also brought familiarity. Despite the attempts during the Plantation of Ulster to keep the settlers and the native Irish apart, the two communities gradually came into increasing contact. Occasionally, and in growing numbers, they intermarried. One of the myths of the ideologues in Ireland is that of ethnic purity. The essence of the myth is that the two groups spring from separate loins and marry within their own people. Consequently the communities remain ethnically distinct. An extreme version is that Protestants and Catholics have physically different appearances. It is argued that the difference can also be identified by their names: Gaelic first names and surnames for Catholics, English and Scottish names for Protestants. Many people today persist in this view. Yet the names of political leaders mentioned daily in the political columns of newspapers demonstrate how untenable it is. The unionist Prime Minister who presided over the start of the Troubles, Terence O'Neill, carried the most Gaelic name in Ulster. The unionist security spokesman and Sinn Féin's chief negotiator in the coming political talks share the same name, although they spell it differently, as Maginnis or McGuinness. The two nationalist leaders whose talks began the overture to the IRA ceasefire, John Hume of the Social Democratic and Labour Party (SDLP) and Gerry Adams of Sinn Féin, have lowland Scottish names, Protestant names, the names of planters. The myth of purity is indefensible. Northern Ireland, like most places, is a community of mongrels.

History has bequeathed a varied inheritance. The common view that the Irish conflict is intractable because it is unchanging is demonstrably untrue. Since the Norman invasion by Henry II of England in the twelfth century, it is possible to discern significant shifts in the Irish problem. Until 1921 the political dispute focused on Ireland's attempt to maintain or secure independence from Britain. From 1921 the emphasis shifted to relationships within the island of Ireland, between what later became the twenty-six counties of the Republic of Ireland and Northern Ireland's six counties. Finally, since the outbreak of the current violence in 1969, relationships between Catholics and Protestants within Northern Ireland have played a much more dominant role in defining the Irish conflict.

3

THE PEOPLE OF NORTHERN IRELAND

I n 1976 Martyn Turner printed a cartoon entitled 'Portrait of a terrorist'. Instead of the customary stereotypes of mindless thugs or freedom fighters, Turner's 'terrorist' was a bemused, unthreatening teenager, average in every way. The cartoon had been inspired by a research study of prisoners which demonstrated that those involved actively in the Northern Irish violence were little different, in social background, intelligence and level of confusion, from the rest of the population.[1]

Figure 2 'Portrait of a terrortist' by Martyn Turner, the *Irish Times,* 1996

So what are the distinctive characteristics of the people who live in Northern Ireland? First, in an area of 32,595 square miles, there are 1,578,000 of them, according to the 1991 census, a rise of about a quarter since the foundation of the state in 1921, but still only 2.8 per cent of the population of the United Kingdom. Between 1951 and 1991 Northern Ireland experienced a net loss of 332,000 people, more than 8,000 per annum, through emigration, although there has been a small net inflow of people since 1991, mainly as a result of recession in Britain. Northern Ireland has the highest proportion in the United Kingdom (over 90 per cent) of people actually born in the region.

Figure 3 Northern Ireland's population 1821–1991

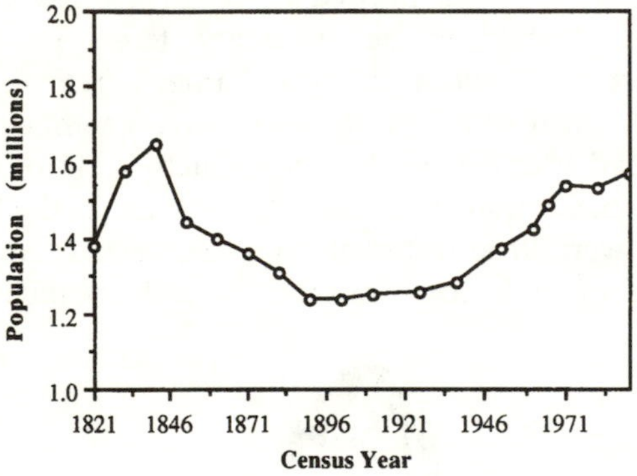

Source: Cormack, R., Gallagher, A.M. and Osborne, R., *Fair Enough? Religion and the 1991 Population Census*, Belfast, Fair Employment Commission, 1993.

There has been a drift from the rural west to the Belfast metropolitan area since the start of the twentieth century, a drift which still continues. Almost half the population live within 20 miles of the centre of Belfast. The other half live in rural areas or in small towns or villages. Outside Belfast only two towns, Derry and Newtownabbey, have populations of more than 50,000 people. About a third of the population live to the west of the River Bann, and this number has been rising since 1971.

The population is significantly younger than the average for the EU. With the exception of the Irish Republic, Northern Ireland has a higher proportion of under-15-year-olds, and a lower proportion of over-65-year-olds, than any EU country.[2]

Catholics account for about 40.6 per cent of the population – and may be as many as 43 per cent according to some commentators – an increase of about 10 per cent since the 1950s. The higher Catholic birth rate had traditionally been balanced by higher Catholic emigration and a tendency for Catholics to marry at an older age. There are some signs that these factors may be changing. The Catholic birth rate is diminishing, and Protestant emigration, especially among university students and postgraduates, appears to be increasing. These changes have to some degree maintained an equilibrium between the two communities. Relatively higher Catholic fertility rates are still reflected in the different age structures for the two religious groups. The most recent analysis of demographic trends, by Edgar Jardine, indicated that Catholics formed 52 per cent of Northern Ireland's 4–9-year-olds in the 1991 census. However, the proportion falls to 48.9 per cent of the 0–1 age group, a decline which has almost certainly continued since 1991.[3] Paul Compton argues that, while extrapolation of trends over the last 30 years would suggest that Catholics may become a majority of the population in about 50 years, this trend may have been arrested by the fall in the differential between Catholic and Protestant birth rates. Although the differential may fall in the shorter term, and may disappear by the end of the century, his conclusion is that neither group is likely to form a significant majority in the long term.[4]

Figure 4 Catholic proportion of the population 1851–1991

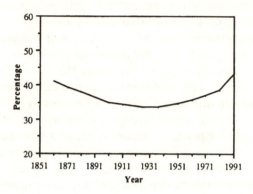

Source: Cormack, R., Gallagher, A.M. and Osborne, R., *Fair Enough? Religion and the 1991 Population Census*, Belfast, Fair Employment Commission, 1993.

In the 1991 census only 3.7 per cent of the population professed no religion. This stands in apparent contradiction with the Social Attitudes Survey conducted in 1989 which found that 12 per cent of the population claimed no religious affiliation.[5] The disparity may arise from the tendency to use the terms 'Catholic' and 'Protestant' to reflect ethnic identity as well as private religious observance. In Northern Ireland there is nothing incompatible in losing one's religious faith, yet still identifying oneself as Catholic or Protestant.

Figure 5 Church attendance in Northern Ireland 1968–89

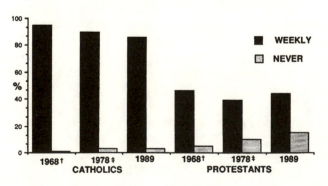

Source: *Social Attitudes Survey* compiled by V. Morgan, 1992.

One of the best known, if not the best, anecdote about Northern Ireland's divisions concerns a man who was stopped by a mob during the early years of the Troubles and asked to declare his religion. It was important to get the answer right, but he could not easily identify which side the mob supported. So he told them he was a Jew. The mob withdrew in confusion to consider this unusual outcome. Then the leader advanced and asked the question again, but in more direct form: 'Are you a Catholic Jew or a Protestant Jew?' The question was, of course, a perfectly sensible one. The mob had little interest in the man's views on the virgin birth or transubstantiation. They wanted to know which side he was on.

Figure 6 Church attendance by age 1991

	18–34 years %	35–54 years %	55+ years %	All %
Once a week	44	53	58	52
Once in two weeks	7	9	5	7
Once a month	9	8	10	9
Twice a year	9	6	6	7
Once a year	3	4	2	3
Less often	4	3	3	3
Never	22	17	16	18
No. of respondents	552	532	620	1,704

Source: *Social Attitudes Survey* compiled by V. Morgan, 1992.

It would have made matters easier for the mob if the Catholic and Protestant communities lived in more exclusive districts, as they do in Israel, Sri Lanka and many other ethnically divided societies. The prevalence of violence and intimidation after 1969 has certainly increased religious segregation, but less than might have been expected. Although some parts of Northern Ireland are religiously exclusive, many parts are not. Consequently, unlike some other apparently intractable conflicts, contact between members of the two communities is normal in many areas. 'They mingle,' as J.C. Beckett observed, 'with a consciousness of their differences between them.'[6]

··

*Let us suppose that you, a stranger, in going through our country-
side, have occasion to knock at a farmhouse door. Suppose you are
received graciously, invited to enter immediately, your request listened to readily, and yourself the centre of attention – you may be
sure that this is a Catholic household. For the Catholic is a charm-
ing and courteous person, open in manner and eloquent in speech.
His faults are those of volatility: 'easy come, easy go.' 'A glib person,' says the Protestant.*

*But there is another kind of farmhouse in Ulster. Knock at its
door and your request will be listened to with respect, and attended to with a few words. You will not be invited to enter: you will be
stood on the step. You will feel that you are at the circumference,
not the centre of attention. Only after long acquaintance will you
penetrate to the bosom of the house. That is a Protestant household. It reflects a difference of character which is historically a difference of race. The Ulster Protestant is a cautious, logical and
far-seeing person in speech and action, and he distrusts eloquence.
His virtue is that of stability. 'A stiff person,' says the Catholic.*

*These characters, Protestant and Catholic, are complementary.
They make the two halves of life. One takes a long view of life, the
other a short and roundabout one. One is thoughtful and individual,
the other is emotional and communal. One tends to a democratic
and progressive way of life, the other to a hieratic and static way.*

W. R. Rodgers, 1947

··

Members of both religious groups are represented to some
degree in almost every town, village and locality, creating a
mosaic of intermingled relationships with greatly varying levels
of social, economic and residential segregation and integration.
This is one of the defining characteristics of the Northern Irish
conflict. As A.T.Q. Stewart put it:

*'Most people, if asked to define the chief symptoms of the Northern
Ireland troubles, would say it is that the two communities cannot
live together. The very essence of the Ulster question, however, is*

that they do live together and have done for centuries. They share the same homeland and, like it or not, the two diametrically opposed political wills must co-exist on the same narrow ground.'[7]

They must also co-exist in a struggling economy. Northern Ireland has few natural resources, and has suffered severely since the 1960s for its dependency on traditional industries, especially ship-building and textiles. Unemployment rates have been generally about twice as high as the figure for Britain, often higher. Pay, income and disposable income are about 75 per cent of comparable British levels. The problems of economic peripherality were heightened by the outbreak of violence in 1969. The tourist industry was decimated. Inward investment dropped. Northern Ireland came to depend increasingly on public sector jobs, which rose by more than 25 per cent during the 1970s. Until 1994 it was the only region in the United Kingdom sufficiently disadvantaged to benefit from the European Community's regional redistribution of funding. The exceptionally high reliance on jobs created by British and European funding has, in the view of many, created a dependency culture, but one which applies to all classes from the unemployed to the professional middle classes. In some ways the people who have benefited most from public subsidy are Northern Ireland's middle classes, not the poor.

Figure 7 Economic activity for men by year and religion 1971 and 1991

	Catholic (%)		Protestant (%)	
	1971	1991	1971	1991
Economically active	78.4	72.4	79.8	71.9
Economically inactive	21.6	27.6	20.2	28.1
All	100.0	100.0	100.0	100.0

Note: 1971 comprises men aged 15 years and over: 1991 comprises men aged 16 years and over. (These rates are different from those derived from the population aged 16–64.)
Source: Cormack, R., Gallagher, A.M. and Osborne, R., *Fair Enough? Religion and the 1991 Population Census*, Belfast, Fair Employment Commission, 1993.

Catholics have been under-represented in the workforce since 1921, and discrimination was one of the main triggers for the Troubles. The most recent research shows that the Catholic proportion of the economically active population has been rising, mainly as a result of the introduction of fair employment legislation since the 1970s, and especially since 1990. While Catholics represented 36.7 per cent of the over-35 economically active population, the percentage was 43.9 per cent for those under 35, perhaps a healthy sign for the future. Catholic unemployment rates, however, remained stubbornly and significantly higher than for Protestants. In 1995 Catholic men were still almost twice as likely to be unemployed, although the differential was diminishing slowly.[8]

Figure 8 Economic activity for women by year and religion 1971 and 1991

	Catholic (%)		Protestant (%)	
	1971	1991	1971	1991
Economically active	35.2	43.9	36.4	45.0
Economically inactive	64.8	56.2	63.6	55.0
All	100.0	100.0	100.0	100.0

Note: 1971 comprises women aged 15 years and over; 1991 comprises women aged 16 years and over.
Source: Cormack, R., Gallagher, A.M. and Osborne, R., *Fair Enough? Religion and the 1991 Population Census*, Belfast, Fair Employment Commission, 1993.

The roles of men and women reflect Northern Ireland's general conservatism. Protestant women are more likely to be economically active, 45 per cent against 43.9 per cent of Catholic women.[9] Women's level of participation in the market place has increased in recent years, but still lags behind British rates. Catholic women are also one-and-a-half times more likely than Protestants to be unemployed.

Figure 9 Unemployment rates by age 1996

	Males				Females				Both sexes			
	(%)		(%)		(%)		(%)		(%)		(%)	
	P	Base	RC	Base	P	Base	RC	Base	P	Base	RC	Base
16–24	15	233	30	198	11	180	21	112	13	413	26	310
25–34	13	357	24	277	9	280	8	235	11	637	17	512
35–44	8	325	24	228	5	266	9	162	6	591	18	390
45–64/59	10	473	16	267	5	282	6	133	8	755	13	400
All 16+	11	1,430	23	990	7	1,067	11	633	9	2,497	18	1,653

Source: *Labour Force Survey: Religion Report*, NISRA Monitor, Belfast, NISRA, 1996.

Many of Northern Ireland's institutions are also conditioned by religious differences. Shared worship between different Protestant religious denominations is not uncommon, but rarely includes Catholics. Primary and secondary education is strongly segregated by religion for both children and teachers, with less than 2 per cent of children attending the newly formed integrated schools. The two universities are fully integrated, although increased preference among Protestant students for British universities is believed by some to have produced a relatively high Catholic presence at the University of Ulster and Queen's University, Belfast. The two morning newspapers, the *Irish News* and the *Newsletter*, cater for the two religious communities, while the evening *Belfast Telegraph* has readers from both. Not so policing. Catholic participation in the RUC was always disproportionally low, a situation exacerbated by the Troubles, and stood at 7.4 per cent in 1994.[10] It is notable that, despite Northern Ireland's abnormal political violence, the province is relatively law-abiding. In 1969, before the violence started, Northern Ireland had the lowest per capita prison population in western Europe. The normal crime rate, excluding politically motivated crime, is still low. People feel safer walking the streets at night than in Britain, and express less concern about crime.[11] Their confidence is justified. Rates of victimisation for burglary, assaults and thefts are substantially lower than in England and Wales.

Informal social intercourse across the religious divide is determined primarily by two factors – the level and quality of integration at local level, and social class. Residential integration between Catholics and Protestants, however, was adversely affected by 25 years of violence, Liam Clarke claiming in 1994 that 'the separation of the two communities in the north is more complete than anyone in 1969 could have imagined'.[12] This is certainly true, but even more remarkable is that cross-religious contact continues routinely at many levels. The arts and many voluntary and vocational organisations draw support from across the community, regardless of religion. Some leisure activities and sports are church based, and provide only limited opportunities for cross-community contact. Others are a positive barrier to it. The Orange Order, in particular, combines religious, political and social activities into a powerful, and of course exclusive, reinforcement of Protestant identity. It would be a mistake to exaggerate the social influence of religious or quasi-religious organisations in Northern Ireland. Most people have only occasional or superficial contact with them. But social life in Northern Ireland is rarely conducted in ignorance of religious identity.

The potential of sport to create cross-sectarian social opportunities must be measured against its demonstrable ability to reflect society's divisions. The most authoritative study of sport in Northern Ireland pointed out that 'sport can be an integral element in the creation and exacerbation of political conflict'.[13] Gaelic football, hurling and camogie are fostered by the Gaelic Athletic Association as expressions of Irish culture, and attract few Protestant participants. Conversely rugby football, although organised on an all-Ireland basis, is an almost exclusively Protestant sport in Northern Ireland, and the Schools Cup Rugby competition had its first Catholic participant in 1996. Other sports, including golf, boxing and athletics, are common property in many areas. The most popular and global sport of all, soccer, is widely played by both communities and the Northern Ireland international team has always had Catholic and Protestant players. Yet the playing of international matches in what Catholics regard as a Protestant venue, the playing of the national anthem before games, and the chanting of sectarian slogans during them, amount to an appropriation of the team by Protestants.

They account for the fact that in 1990, 91 per cent of Catholics wanted the Irish Republic to win a competition in which Northern Ireland also participated; 62 per cent wanted Northern Ireland to come second, suggesting both an equivocal affiliation with the local team and a belief that the Republic's team in 1990 promised a better chance of success.[14]

The opposing symbols used to distinguish Catholics and Protestants in Northern Ireland are widely visible – the Irish tricolour or the Union Jack, wall murals, republican and Orange songs, Gaelic or 'English' games. Some of the public institutions which unite other communities – voluntary organisations, some charities – have also become victims of these divisions, and are seen and presented as a badge of identity in Northern Ireland. In a society divided by ethnic conflict, the badges of identity, even apparently neutral ones, are often interpreted as the property of one side or the other.

4

THE NORTHERN IRELAND PROBLEM

The Home Rule struggle is a struggle between two nations, the Protestant and the Roman Catholic, or as, to avoid the semblance of ministering to religious bigotry, they had better perhaps be called, the Unionist and the Nationalist.

W. F. Moneypenny, 1912

Northern Ireland has long been a favourite laboratory for testing theories about the causes of conflict. The resulting explanations have been varied and contradictory. The use of religious affiliation to differentiate the communities, and the prominence of clergymen as political leaders, has encouraged a popular view that the conflict is essentially religious – a view shared by only a small number of academic commentators, notably Bruce, who forthrightly declared that 'the Northern Ireland conflict is a religious conflict'.[1] Others have adopted racial or ethnic interpretations to explain the apparent immutability of Northern Ireland's differences, often assuming that ethnic identity was primordial and immutable. Since the eighteenth century David Ricardo, Richard Cobden, John Bright, John Stuart Mill and others were inclined towards economic explanations, and Marx and Engels at one point believed Ireland's social inequalities made it a likely trigger for a general social revolution. As late as the 1970s Marxist analysts dominated the literature on Northern Ireland, attracted by the apparent willingness of protagonists in the conflict to act against their own economic self-interest: some believed that the sectarian conflicts were in fact class conflicts in disguise; others pointed to the Orange Order as the mechanism which united disparate class interests among Protestants into a controlling bloc. These explanations were unsatisfactory in explaining the forces which drove prisoners to starve themselves to death, or why attraction to, or revulsion from, a united Ireland had little to do with the economic advantages of the two constitutional arrangements.[2]

The essence of most nationalist analyses is the need to remove a British presence from Northern Ireland. The classic unionist position depends on stressing differences between the two parts of Ireland, and the links with Britain, as follows:

> *'Around the word Ulster a new separate image has grown in people's minds of a modern, progressive industrial community. We want to make the image clearer still so that the world will picture us as we are: an entity entirely separate and distinct from the South but as much a part of the United Kingdom as is Scotland.'*
> **Brian Faulkner, 1960**

Some Marxists have attempted to address the basis of ideological explanations of the conflict, from both nationalist and unionist positions.[3]

Since each of these analyses carries its own prescription, the disputes are more than academic. It is not my intention to adjudicate between competing claims. This book focuses primarily on official policy approaches in relation to all aspects of the conflict. It is clear that these internal policies are influenced by external actors: the British government, the government of the Irish Republic, the USA and the EU. The first two in particular are intrinsic to the constitutional dispute which lies at the root of the conflict. Nevertheless my belief is that the essence of the problem lies within the northern part of Ireland and in the antagonisms between those who live there, since at least the early seventeenth century, and especially over the last 100 years. Whether the constitutional framework is the United Kingdom, or a united Ireland or some form of independence, the Ulster problem will remain until the two hostile groups can agree on acceptable arrangements by which they can peacefully occupy the same 'narrow ground'.

A multi-layered problem

The use of the term 'the Northern Ireland problem', with its implication that a solution lies around the corner for anyone ingenious enough to find it, is misleading. The most recent violence lasted for more than 25 years. The background conflict stretches back at least to the seventeenth century, and some believe the twelfth century; the very choice of date has a political connotation. Today the Northern Irish conflict is a tangle of inter-related questions. What should be the essential political context for the people of Northern Ireland? How can social and economic inequalities, especially in the field of employment, be remedied? How can the state accommodate religious and cultural differences relating to education, the Irish language and the broad spread of cultural expression? How can political disputes be conducted without resorting to violence?

It is not easy to weigh the relative importance of these questions. A range of opinion polls over the last 25 years consistently demonstrates that the majority Protestant community and the minority Catholic community place their emphases on different elements of the problem. Protestants are more likely to see the conflict in constitutional and security terms, and are primarily concerned about preserving the union with Britain and resisting the perceived threat of a united Ireland. Catholic views fall generally into two broad categories. The first perceives the issue as a nationalist struggle for self-determination, looking back to what they regard as the historical integrity of the island and the gerrymander of Partition; for many who share this view, the problem cannot be resolved by any measures short of British withdrawal and Irish unity. The other category, which also includes a number of Protestants, approaches it as a problem of corruption or unfair practices by successive unionist governments between the 1920s and the 1970s which, if removed, would create a society in which both Catholics and Protestants could live peacefully together. These two categories are not discrete. Nationalists who favour a united Ireland often point to the need to redress minority disadvantage while also arguing that reform is unattainable, even undesirable. Catholics who emphasise the need to remove unfair minority disadvantages within Northern Ireland may also have a general aspiration for Irish unity, or would at least be prepared to accept it.

There is some common ground between Protestant and Catholic analyses. Opinion polls indicate that they are both strongly opposed to the use of violence. Both would probably agree that the existence and nature of Northern Ireland itself lies at the core of the conflict. The trouble is that no formula has yet been found to satisfy Protestants' wish to remain part of the United Kingdom while meeting Catholics' aspirations to be more closely associated with the rest of Ireland. The situation is further complicated by an increasingly disinterested, perhaps uninterested, view towards Northern Ireland in both Britain and the Irish Republic. Opinion polls indicate that the British public has little enthusiasm for the union, a position apparently endorsed when Sir Patrick Mayhew, Secretary of State for Northern Ireland, declared in 1991 that Britain had no selfish strategic interest in the region. In the Irish Republic too, impatience with Northern republicans became more evident during the 1990s and may have contributed to the IRA's decision to call a ceasefire in 1994.

Amid these interwoven perceptions four issues have been particularly intractable: politics; inequality; violence and justice; and community relations.

A constitutional and political problem

Between 1921 and 1972, Northern Ireland's fundamental political division was between a minority which challenged the state's right to exist and a majority which believed that the emergency apparatus was necessary to maintain Northern Ireland's very existence against a recalcitrant minority. A change of government theoretically would have led to the abolition of the state and the introduction of a united Ireland. Elections were dominated by the constitutional issue. Consequently political allegiances and beliefs were petrified, and permanent unionist rule was assured.

Figure 10 Political support: Northern Ireland elections 1921–97

Election	Unionist UUP	DUP	Other	Nationalist SDLP	Sinn Féin	Other	NILP	Centre APNI	WP	Other
1969 S	61.1	–	6.3	–		18.8	8.1	0.0	–	5.7
1970 W	54.3	–	4.5	–		23.3	12.6	0.0	–	5.1
1973 LG	41.4	4.3	10.9	13.4		5.8	2.5	13.7	–	8.0
1973 A	29.3	10.8	21.8	22.1		2.0	2.6	9.2	–	1.0
1974 W	32.3	8.2	23.7	22.4		4.5	2.4	3.2	–	3.3
1974 W	36.5	8.5	17.1	22.0		7.8	1.6	6.3	–	0.2
1975 C	25.8	14.8	21.9	23.7		2.2	1.4	9.8	–	0.4
1977 LG	29.6	12.7	8.5	20.6		4.1	0.8	14.4	–	8.3
1979 W	36.6	10.2	12.2	19.9		8.2	–	11.8	–	2.1
1979 E	21.9	29.8	7.3	24.6		6.7	–	6.8	1.8	2.9
1981 LG	26.5	26.6	4.2	17.5		5.3	–	8.9	2.7	8.2
1982 A	29.7	23.0	6.7	18.8	10.1	–	–	9.3	1.9	0.7
1983 W	34.0	20.0	3.0	17.9	13.4	–	–	8.0	1.3	1.6
1984 E	21.5	33.6	2.9	22.1	13.3	2.4	–	5.0	1.6	0.3
1985 LG	29.5	24.5	3.1	17.8	11.8	–	–	7.1	2.6	1.8
1987 W	37.8	11.7	5.4	21.1	11.4	–	–	10.0	2.1	0.0
1989 LG	31.4	17.8	–	21.2	11.3	–	–	6.8	1.1	9.4
1989 E	21.5	29.9	–	25.5	9.2	–	–	5.2	–	5.7
1992 W	34.5	13.1	5.7	23.5	10.0	–	–	8.7	–	4.5
1994 E	23.8	29.2	3.0	28.9	9.9	–	–	4.1	0.3	2.1
1996 F	24.2	18.8	9.4	21.4	15.5	–	–	6.5	–	3.0
1997 W	32.7	13.6	4.2	24.1	16.0	–	–	8.0	–	1.1
1997 LG	28.8	15.6	7.2	20.7	17.0	1.0	–	6.6	–	4.0

S = Stormont; W = Westminster; LG = Local Government; A = Assembly; C = Constitutional Convention; E = European Parliament; F = Forum election. Source: Election returns.

The civil rights campaign of the 1960s shook Northern Ireland's traditional party structures without fundamentally affecting its political allegiances. The old Nationalist Party had virtually disappeared by 1970, but most of its support had transferred to the SDLP. Unionist support, previously dominated by the Ulster Unionist Party (UUP), became more fragmented, primarily because of the emergence of Ian Paisley's Democratic Unionist Party (DUP), but was no less unionist. After a brief struggle with the Northern Ireland Labour Party (NILP), the new Alliance Party of Northern Ireland (APNI) emerged as the dominant force in the middle ground. On the face of things much had changed. Many of the party names were new. But the broad pattern of political loyalties within the three categories had altered very little since the civil rights campaign, and continued to be determined primarily by religious affiliation.

Constitutional politics in liberal democracies is about the management of differences, lubricated by compromise and moderated by the possibility of electors switching their party allegiances. Ethnic politics has a different function. Political success in most liberal democracies is determined by control of a floating centre vote. In Britain, for example, there is little political advantage for the Conservative and Labour parties to direct their political manifestos at, respectively, their extreme right or left wings. The electoral dividends would be minimal. Consequently the politics of the two major parties is usually determined by the need to court moderate rather than extreme opinion.

In Northern Ireland the situation has been reversed. Elections are less about casting your vote than voting your caste. Every election since the formation of the state has demonstrated that the centre has been decimated by sectarian politics. Parties seeking to draw both Catholic and Protestant support have never attracted more than 30 per cent of the vote – the NILP's share of the poll in 1962 – and that was more than double their support in elections before and since that date. The main problem for unionist and nationalist parties is not to attract support from the centre. Their main task has been to ensure that they did not lose support to more extreme opponents from their own tradition. In J.L. McCracken's words, 'there is no floating vote on the constitutional issue'.[4] An additional complication is that Northern Ireland, although deeply divided along sectarian lines, operates within the context of liberal democracy. Breaches of liberal democratic rules are closely observed by both governments and media in the United Kingdom, the Irish Republic, Europe and the USA. So any political agreement must be found within the context of considerable international attention.

Since the dissolution of the Northern Ireland parliament and the introduction of Direct Rule from Westminster in 1972, movement towards a political settlement has been frustrated by two disputes – about the constitutional context in which Northern Ireland should function, and the political arrangements which should govern executive power. For Protestants, Northern Ireland was the context which provided them with majority status. For Catholics the context was the island of Ireland. The demand by nationalists that the Irish Republic should have a role in the governance of Northern Ireland, and the refusal of unionists to allow any Dublin involvement, was the primary block to political settlement.

The other block concerned the political arrangements which would govern Northern Ireland internally. For unionists, Northern Ireland should have the same political system which operated in the rest of the United Kingdom. Governments should be formed by a majority of members, elected in a first-past-the-post election. For nationalists this approach would ensure permanent exclusion from power. Their argument was that majoritarian politics are inappropriate to deeply divided societies, and that some form of power-sharing, or grand coalition involving minority parties, was a *sine qua non* in any settlement.

These two disputes – about Dublin's involvement in Northern Ireland and power-sharing – formed both the framework for and obstacles to political discussion from 1972 to 1994. Since then they have been augmented by a third obstacle: whether parties associated with paramilitary organisations should be included in political negotiations before their weapons have been decommissioned.

A problem of inequality

For most nationalists the northern Irish state was an area artificially carved out from the island of Ireland to create and maintain a

Protestant majority. Some retained the objective of securing a united Ireland, by force if necessary, and the IRA conducted campaigns of violence in the 1920s, 1940s and 1950s. For the unionist majority the new arrangements and the union itself could be maintained only by the introduction of systematic discrimination against the Catholic minority (see pages 29-30).

Despite this, by the 1950s there were growing signs that some Catholics were prepared to accept equality within Northern Ireland rather than to insist on the more traditional aim of a united Ireland. The formation of the NICRA in 1967 appeared to reflect a new determination among Catholics to demand equal access to jobs, public housing and the franchise within the Northern Ireland state, as well as the removal of discriminatory laws. The success of the civil rights campaign, however, was soon overtaken by the spread of civil disorder, and by the introduction of Direct Rule in 1972. Direct Rule was intended as a temporary measure, until an agreed form of devolved government was established. It still continued in 1997.

These years have seen a number of policy initiatives aimed at addressing minority grievances, which will be reviewed in detail later. Direct Rule had removed legislative and executive power from local politicians. It also provided an opportunity to tackle minority disadvantages in housing, employment, educational provision and the fair operation of the franchise. Paradoxically, the removal of local democracy in Northern Ireland may have accelerated the systematic removal of minority inequalities. Any attempt to remove minority grievances in a more democratic local setting would have been severely hampered by the sectarianism which is a feature of all ethnic politics.

Nevertheless, on virtually every indicator of socio-economic disadvantage, Catholics still experience higher levels of need or disadvantage than Protestants.

- Overall unemployment rates are 18 per cent for Catholics and 8 per cent for Protestants, and the differential is especially great between Catholic and Protestant males (23 per cent compared to 11 per cent).
- More than twice as many Catholic households as Protestant are dependent on social security.

- Twice as many pupils in Catholic schools (37 per cent) were entitled to free school meals as pupils in other schools (19 per cent) in 1994–5. Entitlement to free school meals is regarded as a robust indicator of social deprivation.
- More Catholic pupils leave school lacking any formal qualification (11.9 per cent) than Protestants (8.4 per cent). Around 35 per cent of Catholic pupils attend grammar school – important as the most efficient institutions for feeding students into the higher education system – compared to 42 per cent of Protestant pupils.
- Fewer Catholics are home owners, and more are dependent on public authority housing. Catholics are more likely than Protestant tenants (10 per cent compared to 3 per cent) to suffer from overcrowding.
- Healthcare provision for the two communities is more difficult to quantify. Levels of disability, higher in Northern Ireland than in Britain, are higher for Catholics than Protestants in Northern Ireland. An analysis of ill-health, conducted by electoral wards, confirmed that the 12 most advantaged wards were in predominantly Protestant areas, and the 12 least advantaged were predominantly Catholic.[5]

Figure 11 Unemployment rates (all economically active) 1996

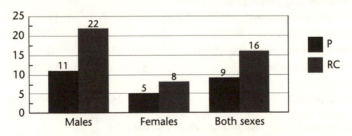

Source: *Labour Force Survey: Religion Report*, NISRA Monitor, Belfast, NISRA, 1996.

So, despite significant improvements since the 1970s, there is ample evidence of Catholic disadvantage across a broad range of social and economic indicators. There is also evidence that Catholics perceive themselves to be disadvantaged.[6] A major study of attitudes asked a large sample population which single change was most needed to end violence. While Protestants emphasised political grievances, the highest percentage of Catholics (33 per cent) demanded the establishment of equal opportunities for all members of the community.[7]

Figure 12 Occupational concentrations (all in employment stating occupation)

	Males		Females	
SOC Major Group	P (%)	RC (%)	P (%)	RC (%)
1 Managers and administrators	19	18	6	6
2 Professional occupations	9	11	9	10
3 Associate professional and technical occupations	5	4	8	12
4 Clerical and secretarial occupations	9	7	27	24
5 Craft and related occupations	22	26	4	4
6 Personal and protective service occupations	8	6	16	16
7 Sales occupations	6	5	11	11
8 Plant and machine operatives	14	16	6	5
9 Other occupations	8	7	13	12
Base (= 100%)	1,250	753	979	588

Source: 1993 *Labour Force Report: Religion Report*, PPRU Monitor, PPRU, 1994.

A problem of violence and justice

The conflict in the north of Ireland has been exceptionally persistent. No generation since the Plantation of Ulster has escaped its heritage of violence. In Belfast alone there were nine periods of serious rioting between 1835 and 1969, and many other years where some disturbances have been recorded.[8] The recent violence was the longest and most sustained of all. It was uninterrupted, except for variations in form and intensity, from 1969 to 1994.

This persistent antagonism has primarily been between two internal groups rather than between hostile neighbouring countries. The distinction between internal conflicts and international wars needs to be emphasised. In internal conflicts the combatants permanently inhabit the same battlefield; even during periods of tranquillity their lives are often intermeshed with those of their enemies; it is not possible to terminate hostilities by withdrawal behind national frontiers. As a consequence, ethnic conflict is often characterised by internecine viciousness rather than by the more impassive slaughter of international wars.

During the early 1970s many observers believed that the upsurge of violence in Northern Ireland could lead to one of two outcomes: either the belligerents would be shocked into an internal accommodation, or they would be propelled into genocidal massacre. Neither occurred. The initial rioting in 1969 between Catholics and Protestants, during which eight people were killed, was soon replaced by more structured violence after the arrival of the British army and its confrontations with the Catholic community. The emergence of the Provisional IRA, strengthened by the introduction of internment in 1971, converted the violence to more organised confrontation between the IRA and the British army, with interventions from loyalist paramilitary organisations. During the 1990s the pattern shifted again, with loyalist paramilitaries causing more deaths than any other group in the years immediately preceding the ceasefires. All three actors were both perpetrators and victims of violence. The violence reached a peak in 1972, when 468 people died. In subsequent years, a succession of particularly dramatic events periodically raised the casualty rate: the killing of 13 Catholics by paratroopers on Bloody Sunday 1972; the loyalist Ulster Workers' Council (UWC) strike in May 1974; the activities of the 'Shankill butchers' in the mid-1970s; the IRA hunger strikes in 1981; and the killing of 11 Protestants at the Cenotaph bombing at Enniskillen in 1987. By the 1990s the violence had gradually declined to an annual average of below 100. Between 1969 and the declaration of the ceasefires by republican and loyalist paramilitary organisations in 1994, the Troubles had claimed 3,173 deaths in Northern Ireland, and a total of 235 in Britain, the Irish Republic and the rest of Europe. Thousands of people were intimidated from their homes, and thousands more injured.

This violence, while very persistent, was controlled by both social and military constraints.[9] The social constraints include both formal institutional features and informal social controls within local communities. The decision of the Irish Republic not to intervene in Northern Ireland, despite the claim in its 1937 constitution that the state included all 32 counties of the island, removed one potentially escalatory element. The operations of both the British security forces and paramilitary organisations were also limited by strategic difficulties and political obstacles to the use of greater force. The violence was further controlled by limits imposed on the protagonists by themselves, such as the refusal of the British security forces to 'take their gloves off' in their pursuit of the IRA, as so often demanded by unionist politicians. A similar self-imposed constraint was the decision by paramilitary groups not to wage more persistently a general campaign of violence, which may have arisen from a realisation of their own military limitations, or from limits on their conduct imposed by their own supporters. All these controlling factors, although important, were secondary to the presence of a large army. The army's arrival in 1969 certainly altered the nature of the violence and added new tensions and grievances, but it also reduced the number of direct confrontations between Protestants and Catholics and limited the spread of sectarian violence. As the war between the army and the IRA came to dominate Northern Ireland during the 1970s, the sectarian riots which had been the main motor of violence in its early years became less common. Most republicans and loyalists, while far from disinterested, were content to observe the struggle between the military and paramilitary as a surrogate for their own struggle, rather than to become directly involved.

The controls on violence certainly prevented a collapse into anarchy. Nevertheless, 25 years of violence raised tensions between the two communities and obstructed the search for political accommodation. The result has been an increased level of intimidation and migration and consequently greater residential segregation. This has been most marked in parts of Belfast and Derry, but also in some border areas in Armagh and Fermanagh, where there was a wide perception among Protestants that the IRA was attempting to establish republican supremacy by targeting Protestants. Demographic changes since the 1960s have led to higher proportions of Catholics in southern and western areas of the province, greater Protestant percentages in the east and an increasingly Catholic inner Belfast. These population movements have reduced the practicality of repartition as a means of tackling the Northern Ireland problem. They also have implications for electoral boundaries, for the political control of local authorities and for allocation policies in planning and housing.

Violence causes stark and obvious distress for its victims. The problems created by security operations may initially be secondary, but soon become tangled with the other issues dividing the communities. Emergency legislation and procedures were not novelties in Northern Ireland. A Special Powers Act had first been introduced in 1922, and renewed annually until 1973 regardless of the level of background disorder. It was inevitable that the prevalence of violence after 1969 would affect legal and policing procedures. There was practically a standing army on the streets after 1969. Witnesses were sometimes intimidated from giving evidence against paramilitaries. Police were constantly under armed attack. Public opinion on the state's handling of these problems was divided, and fluctuated during the years of violence. According to most opinion polls, it was generally accepted that normal procedures were inadequate for dealing with such an abnormal situation. There was concern, however, that the barrage of special powers infringed individual rights, that emergency powers were not exercised impartially, and that the surveillance apparatus installed by the British army collected information not directly related to security concerns. The administration of justice, especially emergency laws, since the 1970s has added another coat to the already ingrained varnishes which obscure and comprise the Northern Ireland problem.

A problem of community relationships

People in Northern Ireland are born into communities which have often been structurally and sometimes residentially divided since the Plantation of Ulster. The divisions are ratified and reinforced by different social patterns and mutual suspicion. Ninety-seven per cent of children still attend schools which are overwhelmingly segregated by religion and, as Murray has described, have substantially different experiences in them.[10] Nevertheless, social contact between Protestants and Catholics takes place regularly in most districts of Northern Ireland, in many workplaces, in higher education, and in social and leisure activities. It is true that relationships are not often made in ignorance of religious affiliation, but they are often made despite this.

Perhaps more surprising is that most people declare themselves to favour increased cross-religious contact. In 1990, as many as 67 per cent of Catholics and 57 per cent of Protestants believed that the government should encourage integrated schooling; 79 per cent and 66 per cent respectively favoured greater mixing in residential areas; even 54 per cent and 34 per cent were in favour of more mixing in people's marriages, usually the most serious taboo in ethnically divided societies. All of these aspirations stood in contrast with actual practice. According to Gallagher and Dunn, they may have been 'based more on hope than experience';[11] nevertheless, if aspirations carry any weight, they indicate that Catholics and Protestants in Northern Ireland may have more in common than divides them.

Figure 13 Support (%) for mixing or separation of Catholics and Protestants

	More mixing		Keep things as they are		More separation	
	RC	P	RC	P	RC	P
People's marriages	54	34	38	49	5	15
Residential areas	79	66	17	29	-	2

Source: *Social Attitudes Survey*, compiled by A.M. Gallagher and S. Dunn, 1991.

The obstacles frustrating natural relationships across the religious divide are formidable. A society cannot hope to function fairly and peacefully if there is a central split about its very existence. A substantial body of evidence indicates that Catholics and Protestants perceive themselves as belonging to distinct groups, and perceive the conflict to be rooted in these differences. Psychological factors, including real and imagined fears, are serious barriers to conciliation. Northern Ireland harbours a culture of intimidation. Nevertheless there are policy approaches available to manage pluralism, either by aspiring towards the erosion of differences and the creation of an integrated community, or by protecting and respecting expressions of cultural difference within an agreed framework.

Figure 14 Religion of respondents' neighbours, friends and relatives

Percentage saying that all or most of their... (%)

	Catholic		Protestant	
	1989	1993	1989	1993
... neighbours are of the same religion	62	62	67	67
... friends are of the same religion	63	57	72	67
... relatives are of the same religion	82	83	89	91

Source: *Social Attitudes Survey*, compiled by A.M. Gallagher 1995.

The main actors in the conflict

Unionists

Unionists are the successors of those who opposed Home Rule in the nineteenth century, and eventually settled for the state of Northern Ireland. The main unionist parties are the UUP, which formed all governments from 1921 to 1972; and the DUP, which is more populist, more anti-nationalist, but less popular in electoral support. Both are opposed to the involvement of the Irish Republic in Northern Ireland, and have been unwilling to share executive power with non-unionist parties. They also share a suspicion of Britain's commitment to the union. The DUP holds all these positions more extremely than the UUP, and is also more preoccupied with the power of the Catholic Church. In 1997 the leader of the UUP was David Trimble, and Ian Paisley led the DUP. Two new loyalist parties emerged during the 1990s – the Progressive Unionist Party (PUP) and the Ulster Democratic Party (UDP). Despite their origins in, and continuing association with, loyalist paramilitary organisations, they have consistently taken more moderate positions on negotiation than the mainstream unionist parties. They gained a combined 3 per cent of the vote for the 1997 General Election, against 32.7 per cent for the UUP and 13.6 per cent for the DUP.

Nationalists

The basic tenet of nationalists is the aspiration to unify the island of Ireland. The main constitutional party is the SDLP, which contests the nationalist vote with Sinn Féin, generally accepted to be the political arm of the IRA. The SDLP has accepted that unity must await the support of the majority in Northern Ireland. Sinn Féin, having argued until the 1980s that force was necessary to achieve their historical mandate to remove the British presence, moved towards a more political role during the 1990s. After a series of talks with the SDLP, and secret ones with the British, Sinn Féin persuaded the IRA to declare ceasefires in 1994 and 1997, and subsequently attempted to become involved in all-party negotiations.

John Hume led the SDLP in 1997, and Gerry Adams Sinn Féin. In the 1997 General Election, the SDLP took 24.1 per cent of the popular vote, and Sinn Féin 16 per cent.

The paramilitaries

The republican paramilitary organisations, of which the IRA is by far the most important, believe that force is necessary to remove the British from Ireland. Initially they saw themselves as defenders of the Northern Catholic minority, but later spread their military activities throughout Northern Ireland, Britain and Europe. They declared a ceasefire in August 1994, broke it off in February 1996 by resuming a bombing campaign in Britain and declared a second ceasefire in July 1997. There is disagreement about whether loyalist violence was essentially a reaction to republican violence, but certainly the pattern of violence by the UVF, the Ulster Defence Association (UDA) and the Ulster Freedom Fighters (UFF) generally shadowed IRA violence. Between 1992 and 1996, for the first time, loyalists killed more victims than republicans. The UDA, UVF and UFF declared ceasefires two months after the IRA ceasefire in 1994.

The United Kingdom

The official British position is that Northern Ireland is part of the United Kingdom. This is shared by all political parties, although the Labour Party has in the past leaned towards support for Irish unity when the majority in Northern Ireland supported it. Until 1993 most political talks aimed to restore a devolved government, with power shared between unionists and nationalists. The 1985 Anglo-Irish Agreement between the British and Irish governments accepted that the Dublin government had the right to be consulted on Northern Irish affairs. Secret talks between the British government and Sinn Féin led to the 1994 ceasefire, but moves to all-party talks were slowed by British insistence on the IRA decommissioning its arms.

The Irish Republic

Articles 2 and 3 of the Irish constitution lay claim to all 32 counties of Ireland, modified by the Irish government's acceptance in the Anglo-Irish Agreement that any move towards unity requires the agreement of a majority in Northern Ireland. The same agreement assured the Irish government a role in Northern Irish affairs, which tended to be primarily an advocacy one for northern nationalists.

5

NORTHERN IRELAND 1969–94:
THE YEARS OF VIOLENCE

Policy is not made in a vacuum. Many of the limits within which policy-makers in Northern Ireland can manoeuvre are established outside the province. The levels of investment and employment, for example, are primarily determined by international economic trends. Policies aimed at attracting industry to particular areas of high unemployment are modified by the preferences of potential employers to locate elsewhere. Continuing high unemployment rates have in turn made the implementation of fair employment reforms more difficult.

Equally important is the effect of British policy on social change in Northern Ireland. Even before the introduction of Direct Rule in 1972, British social policy had profoundly affected political developments in Northern Ireland, most obviously through British insistence that the welfare reforms of the late 1940s should apply to the province. The continuing strength of this influence is currently illustrated in higher education policy. The dramatic increase in Catholic students entering higher education, 40 per cent of whom are from working-class backgrounds against 25 per cent of Protestants, is an important measure of improvement in minority conditions.[1] However, UK policy in the 1990s increased significantly the cost of higher education, and one of the incidental effects may reduce the number of Catholics entering universities. Thus Northern Ireland is affected by decisions made in London for reasons quite unrelated to the province. Broader economic trends suggest that this influence is unlikely to diminish. Northern Ireland's dependency on Britain and the EU has been steadily increasing as its economy declined, partly as a result of civil disturbances and violence, since the 1970s. By the 1990s public expenditure exceeded 70 per cent of gross national product in Northern Ireland, against just over 40 per cent in Britain. Northern Ireland does not operate in an autonomous policy setting.

Nor is Britain the only state involved in influencing policy. The constitution of the Irish Republic claims Northern Ireland as part of its national territory, and Anglo-Irish relations were affected by the dispute for decades. They improved significantly after the signing of the Anglo-Irish Agreement in 1985, which broadened the context in which policy was made. As Guelke pointed out, 'Britain and Ireland share the same objective of quarantining the conflict and preventing its intrusion into their domestic politics.'[2] The Agreement provided the Irish government with a formal avenue of influence into Northern Ireland, and the resulting improvement in Anglo-Irish relations laid the foundations for later joint governmental action through the *Downing Street Declaration* (1993), *Frameworks for the Future* (1995) and the *Joint Communiqué* (1996).

Beyond Britain and Ireland, the Irish Diaspora in Australia, Canada, New Zealand, but principally in the USA, has had an erratic influence on Irish affairs. It can be traced at least to the 1820s when Daniel O'Connell encouraged Irish-Americans to form Friends of Ireland organisations and Hibernian Relief Societies. By 1919 the Irish-American influence was sufficiently strong to deliver a 216/45 vote in the USA House of Representatives that the post-war peace conference should consider Ireland's claim to self-determination. The interest among Irish-Americans subsequently diminished, but revived after the outbreak of violence in Northern Ireland. It was overwhelmingly republican in sympathy, and indeterminable amounts of money were channelled to support the newly formed Provisional IRA. Noraid was formed in 1970 to provide funds for the families of IRA prisoners and, it has been claimed, for IRA operations.[3] Since 1974 the Irish National

Caucus has sought to apply American diplomatic and economic pressure to British policy in Northern Ireland. The caucus lobbied against the extradition of IRA suspects from the USA, but its main influence within Northern Ireland was through its campaign to persuade American firms and investors that they should apply the MacBride Principles to their investments in Northern Ireland. These were modelled on the Sullivan Principles which had been applied to American investment in South Africa, and included an insistence on equitable employment practices, the removal of provocative emblems from the workplace and recruitment drives to attract under-represented groups. The campaign, which also aimed to influence investors from public and private pension funds, had considerable impact, and was one of the major covert influences on the passing and composition of the 1989 Fair Employment bill in Northern Ireland. In addition to Noraid and the Irish National Caucus, a group of powerful Irish-American politicians, known as the Four Horsemen, sought to encourage constitutional nationalism rather than militant republicanism by persuading successive American administrations to become involved in Northern Ireland. It has been argued that these external influences, especially those from the USA, have legitimised violence and 'made the conflict more intractable'.[4] The opposite case might also be made, especially during the 1990s, that some of these powerful interests have generally encouraged and supported moves towards a settlement, and that the USA and the EU were particularly influential in the negotiations leading to the IRA ceasefire and in providing economic support for the subsequent peace process.

Even within the narrow confines of Northern Ireland, policy-makers do not operate as a monolith. Policies have been determined by the interplay of different interests and influences, emphasising at different times security concerns, social reforms or political initiatives. The 25 years of violence in Northern Ireland have produced a wide range of security initiatives, with varying levels of success. In an attempt to coordinate government policy on community relations a Central Community Relations Unit (CCRU) was set up in 1988 within the government machinery to monitor all policy for its impact on community relations.

It soon confirmed that very few aspects of public policy, even such apparently neutral services as public transport, health and agriculture, have been untouched by the central community split.

Most official community relations initiatives since 1969 have been determined, not by government policy, but by factors outside its control. The ability of paramilitary organisations to disrupt normal life, to undermine political discussions from which they were excluded, and to maintain a campaign of violence for 25 years, show how little control government has had over events. Not all influences were so negative. The reconciliation work carried out by a wide variety of individuals and organisations, expressed through voluntary and community groups, the main churches and political action, helped to keep the fabric of society together. The Corrymeela Community, set up in 1965 to promote reconciliation, continued to provide a forum for discussion and contact throughout the Troubles. The Committee on the Administration of Justice (CAJ) has monitored human rights issues and criticised abuses in the administration of justice since its formation in 1980, a role particularly important during such a protracted period of extraordinary legislation. Since 1976 the Peace People have seriously challenged the use of paramilitary violence and the state's emergency apparatus. The work of the Community Relations Commission in the early 1970s, and the Community Relations Council in the 1990s, helped to promote public debate and asked awkward questions of both government and the paramilitary organisations. In times of violence these voices were particularly important, pointing out the dangers of accommodating the unacceptable, and the need to search for a fair and permanent settlement.

A harsher judgment is that moderate demands for compromise and an end to violence have only had marginal influence on political developments. Opinion polls consistently reflect more moderate positions than general elections, which are invariably contested along sectarian lines. Ethnic politics is conservative politics, fuelled by fear of conspiracy, compromise and betrayal. The apparent gap between popular feelings and political positions has channelled moderate campaigners towards more specific objectives, and they have achieved some notable results. The movement to establish integrated schools, for example, started in the 1970s by All Children Together (ACT), eventually won government support and funding by sheer persistence and effective lobbying. The leaders of the four main churches – the Roman Catholic, Presbyterian and Methodist and the Church of Ireland – have occasionally acted in concert to mediate effectively on particular disputes. After the 1994 ceasefires, organisations like Families Against Intimidation and Terror (FAIT) continued to draw public attention to the persistence of paramilitary punishment shootings and intimidation. In the main, moderate pressures have been more effective in achieving such targeted objectives than in affecting general political patterns.

The rest of this chapter will concentrate on official approaches and the policy initiatives introduced over the last 25 years. These will be followed along five main tracks:

- the search for political accommodation
- the reduction of inequality
- improvements in human rights and the administration of justice
- dealing with violence, and
- the encouragement of conciliation and cultural diversity.

The search for political accommodation

The collapse of the Northern Ireland administration in 1972 and its replacement by Direct Rule from Westminster had a profound impact on both the Catholic minority and Protestant majority in Northern Ireland. For Catholics it represented the end of 50 years of Protestant domination. While most of them wanted some connection with the Irish Republic, up to two-thirds had been willing to accept a power-sharing arrangement within Northern Ireland. The reasons were varied, but a major consideration was the perception that unification might raise Northern Ireland's unemployment rates and reduce its living standards. Public opinion surveys indicated that some form of Irish unity was the preferred constitutional arrangement for between 40 per cent and 55 per cent of the Catholic population. Respondents have been more flexible when asked what they considered as acceptable political options, rather than their preferred ones. A 1990 *Belfast Telegraph* poll is typical. It indicated that most Catholics were willing to settle for any of four options, ranging from a united Ireland to a power-sharing government within Northern Ireland.[5] A small but constant minority of Catholics was not prepared to accept any solution short of a united Ireland. Sinn Féin's support in elections, although small – less than 2 per cent in the Irish Republic and vacillating in Northern Ireland from 13.4 per cent in 1983 to 17 per cent in the 1997 Forum elections – has been solid. It accounts for between 30 per cent and 40 per cent of Catholic voters in Northern Ireland.

For the Protestant majority, Direct Rule ushered in a period of political uncertainty. Although 75 per cent of Protestants were willing to admit Catholics into power-sharing, almost all were opposed to moves towards a united Ireland. The *Belfast Telegraph* poll found that only 2 per cent of Protestants preferred a united Ireland to other constitutional arrangements for Northern Ireland, with 90 per cent selecting some association within the United Kingdom. Most Protestants oppose any involvement of the Irish Republic in the affairs of Northern Ireland, although there has been a growing acceptance since the Anglo-Irish Agreement in 1985 that Dublin's influence was here to stay. This recognition is more widespread among supporters of the UUP (the largest party in Northern Ireland with 32.7 per cent of the vote in the 1997 Westminster elections) than in the more extreme DUP (which won 13.6 per cent of the 1997 vote). Both parties were opposed to power-sharing with nationalist parties.

Between 1972 and 1985 the essential strategy of all British governments was to build up the political middle ground by such measures as the reintroduction of proportional representation for provincial elections. Their aim was the empowerment of an assumed silent majority, followed by the creation of a power-sharing executive comprising moderate unionists and nationalists and the centre parties. Apart from 14 weeks in 1974, the strategy failed. The ethnic magnet becomes more powerful in times of violence, and support for the centre parties was weak. Between 1972 and the ceasefires of 1994 there were seven attempts to reach a political and constitutional settlement.

Attempts to reach a political agreement: 1973–93

1973–4

The Power-Sharing Executive, which lasted for three months, remains Northern Ireland's only experience of a government shared by Catholics and Protestants. It attempted to construct a devolved system based on power-sharing between Protestants and Catholics, and on a Council of Ireland to regulate affairs between the two parts of Ireland. It was opposed by the DUP and most of the UUP, but eventually was brought down by a Protestant workers' strike in May 1974.

1975–6

A constitutional convention was called to enable elected representatives from Northern Ireland to propose their own solution. The majority unionist parties proposed a return to majority rule, modified by a committee system with some inbuilt minority guarantees. This was rejected by both the British and the minority SDLP.

1977–8 and 1980

Two attempts to set up devolved institutions were initiated by two Northern Ireland Secretaries of State, Roy Mason and Humphrey Atkins. Neither made much progress. They were opposed, for different reasons, by the SDLP and the UUP, and both simply petered out. As a measure of the cultural gap between the two sides, two bars were set up in Stormont during the Atkins talks of 1980, one serving only non-alcoholic beverages. Students of national stereotyping may guess which bar was designed for which political party.

1982–4

Rolling devolution, introduced by James Prior, was perhaps the most ingenious proposal, again involving an elected assembly and a committee system. This envisaged a gradual return to power by elected representatives, but only if the proposed powers had 'widespread acceptance', defined as 70 per cent agreement. In other words, the amount of power devolved to local

77

politicians depended on their ability to agree, and would roll along at the speed of progress determined by them. It was boycotted by the SDLP because it did not guarantee power-sharing.

1985
The Anglo-Irish Agreement was signed by the governments of the United Kingdom and the Irish Republic. It did not involve local politicians and was bitterly opposed by unionists for giving Dublin a voice in Northern Ireland's affairs.

1990–3
The Brooke and Mayhew initiatives sought to introduce phased talks, involving the Northern Irish parties first and the Dublin government at a later stage. Although considerable agreement was reached between the parties, the approach petered out in preference for secret negotiations, later admitted, between the British government and Sinn Féin.

All the initiatives failed to produce a political accord for two main reasons: the unwillingness of Catholics to accept any settlement which did not involve them in power at ministerial level; and Protestants' unwillingness to accept either executive power-sharing or the involvement of the Irish Republic as the protector of the Catholic minority within Northern Ireland.

These initiatives incorporate two distinct policy approaches. Most of them were confined to talks between constitutional parties, with the exclusion of Sinn Féin, and were brokered by British governments. The other approach, represented by the 1985 Anglo-Irish Agreement and the 1993 Downing Street Declaration, was for the British and Irish governments to go over the heads of the local parties to create a paramount agreement. The Downing Street Declaration, for the first time, incorporated both the political and security elements of the Northern Ireland problem, and offered the prospect of tackling both elements simultaneously. The effects of the IRA and loyalist ceasefires will be discussed later.

Alongside the official initiatives by government, a series of mediation and facilitation attempts have been made since the

1970s by a range of academic, community and religious groups. Occasionally these meetings utilised the 'other hat' approach, convening meetings of 'community leaders' who were also known to be close to the paramilitaries. Some of the meetings involved elected politicians, others community activists and paramilitary leaders. These included a meeting in 1974 between a group of Protestant clergymen and the Provisional IRA in Feakle, County Clare, which led to a brief IRA ceasefire and furious criticism from unionists, and secret talks in Duisburg, West Germany, in 1988 to explore the possibility of talks between the constitutional parties. The launch of the Opsahl Inquiry/'Initiative '92 – A Citizens' Inquiry' invited the people of Northern Ireland to present their ideas about ways out of the violence, at a time when official talks appeared to have stalled. It is difficult to evaluate the impact of this and other independent initiatives, but the resulting public hearings and the Opsahl Report revealed a remarkably varied range of political views, and helped to maintain a political discourse during a political vacuum.

All unofficial approaches before 1994 suffered from two weaknesses. First, how to handle the bewildering set of preconditions imposed by participants; and second, the knowledge that, even if a level of agreement were reached, it had been reached outside the power structures and lacked any effective means of implementation. Despite this, most people would agree that the ceasefires declared in 1994 were the most significant move towards peace since the violence started in 1969, and that two of the most significant mediators in bringing the republican and loyalist paramilitants close to mainstream politics were two clergymen, working without official sanction or support.

The reduction of inequality

The first serious civil disorder in Northern Ireland in 1969 underlined the need to address minority disadvantage. The Cameron Report (1969) – the first public investigation into Northern Ireland's civil disturbances in 1968 and 1969 – suggested, perhaps optimistically, that its causes lay in material rather than constitutional grievances:

'Much of the evidence of grievance and complaint that we heard, when analysed, was found, as might be expected, to be concentrated on two major issues – housing and employment. "Jobs" and "houses" are things that matter and touch the heart of the ordinary man more than issues of "one man, one vote" and the gerrymandering of ward boundaries.'[6]

Since then the progress towards the reduction of structural inequalities between Protestants and Catholics has been erratic. By a series of electoral reforms completed by the early 1970s long-standing gerrymandering practices and discriminatory practices in the local government franchise were abolished and electoral grievances were effectively removed from the political agenda. There were other successes too, and failures.

Housing

In 1969 an unusually high proportion of Northern Ireland's population lived in houses rented from public bodies, and sectarian patronage was widespread. By 1972 the power of allocation had been removed from the local councils and the Northern Ireland Housing Trust. They were replaced by an appointed centralised body, the Northern Ireland Housing Executive (NIHE), which was given responsibility for all public housing allocations. The extent to which the NIHE was established to remove discrimination in housing has been disputed, but whatever the reason, the problem of systematic unfair housing allocation was effectively solved. The number of complaints about the distribution and addition of housing diminished significantly during the 1970s and 1980s. In 1991, according to the most recent independent review of housing conditions, Catholics and Protestants occupy houses of broadly similar quality, 'although in the public sector, the properties occupied by Catholics tend to be in a much worse state of repair than those occupied by Protestants, especially in Belfast'.[7] On balance, housing is a rare example of a major grievance which has been virtually removed from the political agenda through changes in government policy and practice.

Employment and unemployment

Job distribution was the second major minority grievance identified in the Cameron Report, and has continued to be a serious
source of grievance. Discrimination against Catholics in both
public and private sectors had led in the 1960s to a workforce
highly stratified by religion. Catholics were much more likely
than Protestants to be unemployed, to be employed in lower-
paid jobs and were likely to be paid less for equivalent work.[8]
The civil rights campaign in the 1960s highlighted these grievances and pressure from Westminster led to the Downing Street
Declaration of 1969 which declared that 'every citizen of Northern Ireland is entitled to the same equality of treatment and freedom from discrimination as obtains in the rest of the United
Kingdom'. The Fair Employment Act 1976 aimed to encourage
more equitable employment practices, and a Fair Employment
Agency (FEA) was established to receive individual complaints of
discrimination and monitor equality of opportunity. The initial
emphasis was on persuasion rather than enforcement, but
tougher measures were later introduced. Since 1982 government
contracts have been restricted to firms awarded certificates from
the FEA.

A further Fair Employment Act in 1989 required companies to
monitor the religious composition of their workforces, and to
engage in affirmative action if the two communities did not
enjoy fair participation. Defaulting employers became ineligible
for government contracts. The act extended the definition of discrimination to include indirect discrimination. A specialist Fair
Employment Tribunal (FET) was set up to hear individual complaints of discrimination in employment. Following the passage
of the act there has been a marked increase in the number of
individual cases alleging religious or political discrimination,
indicating both the effectiveness of the legislation and the continuing need for it. Well over £1 million was awarded by FETs
against public bodies and private companies between 1992 and
1994, with 500 further cases in the pipeline. Eighty per cent of
the awards have gone to Catholics.[9] Most larger employers in
Northern Ireland have now introduced more formal and strin-

81

gent interviewing regimes, if only to protect themselves against civil actions. Many of them, notably such traditionally Protestant firms as Shorts Brothers, have significantly raised their proportion of Catholic workers by actively recruiting in Catholic schools and newspapers, by relocating part of their training facilities and by negotiating with their employees the removal of sectarian flags and symbols from the workplace.

Figures 15 and 16 Attitudes to likelihood of Catholics and Protestants getting a job

Percentage saying that the chances of Protestants and Catholics getting a job are...

	Catholic				Protestant			
	1989	1991	1993	1994	1989	1991	1993	1994
...the same	30	29	41	42	60	62	61	57
...different	60	59	55	55	30	30	32	38

If the chances are different, which group is more likely to get a job? (%)

	Catholic				Protestant			
	1989	1991	1993	1994	1989	1991	1993	1994
Protestant	89	82	86	88	34	26	28	30
Catholic	1	2	2	–	43	49	41	42
Don't know/ depends	10	16	12	12	22	25	31	28

Source: *Social Attitudes Survey*, compiled by A.M. Gallagher 1996.

As a result, significant improvements have been made in reducing Catholic disadvantage in some categories of employment, notably the professions and the civil service, although a study of employment in the civil service indicated that the proportion of Catholics in the senior grades was still very low.[10] The first monitoring figures from the Fair Employment Commission, established by the Fair Employment Act 1989, indicated that, for those in employment, the ratio of Catholics to Protestants is close to the Catholic/Protestant ratio in the adult population, at least in those jobs – 60 per cent of the total – which are monitored. The main area of remaining imbalance was in large private companies, in which only 29.6 per cent of male employees were Catholics, although current levels of appointment were closer to the Catholic proportion of the population.[11]

The same cannot be said of unemployment differentials. Catholics, especially Catholic men, are much more likely to be unemployed than Protestants. The ratio of male Catholic unemployed to male Protestant unemployed has stood at 1:2.5 over the last 30 years, falling to 1:2.1 in 1994. Whatever the reasons for this – and they are furiously disputed[12] – there is no doubting its political importance. Not only is this objectively a problem, but it is perceived to be a major cause of Catholic grievance. The Continuous Households Survey indicates that inequalities are seen by more than a third of Catholics as the main obstacle to a solution. The unemployment differential continues to be regarded as an important indicator of the success or failure of the government's fair employment policy.

Education

Northern Ireland's primary and secondary schools were, until the 1980s, almost completely segregated along religious lines.[13] Until 1992 full recurrent costs, including salaries, were covered by government for all schools, but Catholic schools had to find 15 per cent of capital costs from their own resources. Despite this, differential funding was not regarded by Catholics as a major grievance, as it has been since the 1960s by black parents demanding desegregation in the USA. In practice the high level of educational segregation gave both religious communities considerable control over the management of their own schools. In addition, while black support for desegregation in the USA was driven by the inadequacy of black schools, Catholics in Northern Ireland did not perceive their schools to be inferior to those attended by Protestants.[14] In the 1990s, however, this issue has become more prominent. This has arisen almost completely from a growing interest in the possible connection between education and employability, rather than from concern about the effects of segregation on community relations. Catholic students perform less well on average than their Protestant counterparts, and more of them leave school without any qualification. Although the difference has been diminishing steadily, there is now a greater willingness to look at educational standards and curricula, notably the lesser emphasis on science in Catholic schools, as possible contributors towards higher Catholic unemployment.

Two changes in the procedures for funding schools were introduced to address these concerns. A more equitable process for determining the funding support available to individual schools replaced the system which had operated since 1947, and which had worked to the disadvantage of Catholic schools. In 1992 the Catholic Church was offered 100 per cent funding for their schools, removing the 15 per cent capital contribution previously required. In addition, a compulsory core curriculum was introduced, shadowing educational changes in England and Wales. This required all schools to teach science, a change which imposed more changes on Catholic than Protestant schools, and aimed to improve the prospects of Catholic school-leavers in the market place. It remains to be seen if these changes improve the employability of Catholic school-leavers. Social deprivation is a greater influence than curricular change in determining educational performance, and the much higher take-up of free school meals in Catholic schools (37 per cent) than in other schools (19 per cent) in 1996 confirmed that relative Catholic disadvantage continues to be reflected in the schools.[15]

Higher education presents a smoother record of improvement. In 1964 Catholics formed 21 per cent of Northern Ireland's university population. By the end of the 1980s, given the greater preference among Protestants for attending British universities, the Catholic percentage in Northern Ireland's two universities was at least in accord with its proportion of the relevant age cohort.[16] Some denominational differences continue in choices of university courses – Catholics over-represented in politics, social sciences and law; Protestants over-represented in agriculture, science and medicine. But the delivery of higher education

has been effectively removed from the agenda of minority grievances. Other sensitivities remain, and indeed have become more
public in recent years. As the Catholic proportion has grown in
Queen's University, Belfast and the University of Ulster, there
have been complaints from Protestants about the use of the Irish
language to give directions in Students' Unions, and from
Catholics about the playing of the national anthem during graduation ceremonies. In 1995 the decision to remove the anthem
from the graduation ceremony at Queen's University provoked a
furious debate in newspaper columns, and an extra-ordinary
meeting of graduates demanded the reversal of the decision.
Feelings can still run high as the orange groves of academe
become greener.

Improvements in human rights and the administration of justice

The spread of serious civil disorder from 1969 had severe effects
on the administration of justice. Internment without trial was
introduced in 1971 and its failure led both to the introduction of
Direct Rule and to a rapid rise in the level of violence. Following
the passing of the Northern Ireland (Emergency Provisions) Act
1973 the army's powers to stop and detain were strengthened,
jury trials were abolished and far-reaching changes in the rules
of evidence were introduced. Security became the dominant policy consideration. There were frequent legal challenges to interrogation techniques and to the gathering of security
information. Disputes about the treatment of 'politically motivated prisoners' – those arrested for suspected involvement with
paramilitary organisations – further undermined the rule of law.
Initially these prisoners were granted 'special category' status,
which placed them in compounds rather than cells, permitted
considerable autonomy within the compounds and allowed
extra privileges such as wearing their own clothes and having
extra visitors. In 1976 the government, expressing concern that
'special category' processes might increase commitment to terrorism, announced its intention to phase it out. An escalating
series of protests by prisoners culminated in hunger strikes by
republican prisoners in 1980 and 1981. Ten prisoners died before

concessions were made and the strike was called off, but not before political tensions had been seriously heightened and support for the IRA, both in Northern Ireland and elsewhere, revived.

Hillyard has argued that emergency laws, introduced to deal with communal violence, 'have now become normalised'.[17] The Northern Ireland (Emergency Provisions) Act was renewed every six months, and the Prevention of Terrorism Act every twelve months, both with little debate. Hillyard claimed that both the rule of law and the power of the legislature have been consequently diminished, and has argued that a 'repressive apparatus' has been constructed by the state.[18] Since then, further restrictions on legal rights have also given cause for concern. Despite the advice of the Standing Advisory Commission on Human Rights, established by government to monitor government policy on human rights issues, the fundamental precept that those accused of a crime have a 'right to silence' was overturned in 1988, and silence may now be construed as suggesting guilt. The ban on republican and loyalist paramilitary groups from speaking on radio and television, also introduced in 1988 but removed after the 1994 ceasefires, was a further restriction on individual rights.

Catholics and Protestants had different views about the state's increased powers. Catholics were 'less willing to endorse governments' right to keep secrets, surveillance of political dissidents, and strong application of police and other legal powers', while Protestants were more willing to curtail civil liberties during a period of civil disorder.[19] The explanation is uncomplicated. Catholics felt that they did not receive equal treatment from the police and the security forces, while Protestants believed that both communities were treated equally. Civil liberties, like everything else, reflect broader social and political divisions.

Dealing with violence

The search for political accommodation has been hampered by continuing political violence. Indeed the Northern Ireland administration's inability to deal with growing civil disorder in 1969 had led directly to the involvement of the British army.

Since the introduction of Direct Rule security policy has been in the hands of the British government, and security implementation has been the responsibility of the RUC and the British army.

Policing has always been close to the top of the minority community's grievances in the province, only varying in intensity from time to time. The Catholic proportion of the RUC probably never exceeded 12 per cent, and stood at 9.4 per cent in the early 1970s.[20] Following the spread of sectarian violence in 1969, a succession of official reports, notably the Hunt Report on policing (1969) and the Cameron Report on the 1969 riots (1969), criticised the partisan and unprofessional behaviour of the RUC and 'B' Specials. A series of reforms was introduced as a result of Hunt's recommendations, including the abolition of the 'B' Specials and a decision to disarm the RUC. In an attempt to neutralise the political control of policing, a Police Authority was created to assume responsibility for the RUC. The developing IRA campaign frustrated some of the Hunt reforms, notably the disarming of the police. Catholic reactions to these changes varied greatly throughout Northern Ireland. The 1991 Social Attitudes Survey indicated that 56 per cent of Catholics still felt that the RUC treated Protestants better than Catholics, and 69 per cent agreed that the police or army 'usually get away with it' when they commit an offence.[21] Catholic recruitment into the RUC continued to decline, mainly as a result of traditional suspicion and republican intimidation rather than through discrimination.

Figure 17 Belief that the RUC is doing a good job in controlling sectarian and non-sectarian crime

	Non-sectarian crime %	Sectarian crime %
Poor	75	48
Middle	91	83
Low income	82	67
High income	92	86
18–24 years of age	76	54
Over 65 years of age	90	83
Male	86	71
Female	84	72
Catholic	76	53
Protestant	92	84
Nationalist	67	42
Unionist	94	88

Source: *Social Attitudes Survey*, compiled by J.D. Brewer, 1992

The presence of an army among a civilian population raises even greater problems. Allegations of army misconduct, interrogation malpractices and undercover operations have been a constant feature of grievances, particularly from nationalists. Unionists often complain that security policies never amounted to more than *ad hoc* responses to IRA violence, apart from the late 1970s when a more aggressive campaign was conducted against the IRA. The argument was complicated by occasional periods when the security forces were criticised for their behaviour towards the Protestant community.

Most other interested parties, including successive governments, believed that a more rigorous military approach, to 'root out' the IRA, would have presented serious technical problems and risked further alienating the Catholic community, as happened when internment was unsuccessfully introduced in 1971. In addition, strong opposition from the Irish Republic, the USA and Europe would certainly have followed. The result was stalemate. Each set of combatants, the security forces and the paramilitaries, was able to frustrate the other, but unable to defeat it. Consequently security policy was subject to different emphases – the introduction of 'supergrass' trials in which witnesses were promised immunity in return for providing evidence; experimentation in prison regimes, including 'special status' for political prisoners convicted of 'political offences'; even an 'Ulsterisation' process which tried to replace the army by the RUC and the locally recruited Ulster Defence Regiment (UDR) as the main bodies responsible for law and order. None of these policies disguised the fact that, with the possible exception of a short period in the late 1970s, security policy had largely been one of containment, maintaining what the British Home Secretary Reginald Maudling called 'an acceptable level of violence'.

The policy of containment allowed republican and loyalist paramilitaries to become more firmly entrenched in many communities in Northern Ireland. Their involvement in organised violence, including protection rackets, intimidation and drug peddling, ensured that the 1994 ceasefires did not end paramilitary involvement in violence, and suggests that some vested interests may wish to maintain the absence of normal law and order.

Almost 3,200 people were killed between the army's arrival in 1969 and the ceasefires 25 years later. By comparison with most other violent ethnic conflicts this is a remarkably low figure. The presence of an army in a civilian setting has in itself attracted violence, but it has also been an obstacle to mass mobilisation and the uncontrolled violence of the sort seen in the Lebanon and Rwanda. The tension between the need to protect the innocent and the need to protect civil rights is an inevitable consequence of a permanent military presence. It is a matter of conjecture whether, without the military presence, the level of violence might have been far higher.

Figure 18 Deaths due to situation 1969–94

	NORTHERN IRELAND						OTHER PLACES			
	RUC	RUCR	Army	UDR/RIR	Civilians	Total NI	GB	Republic	Europe	Total other places
1969	1	0	0	0	12	13	0	0	0	0
1970	2	0	0	0	23	25	0	3	0	3
1971	11	0	43	5	115	174	0	3	0	3
1972	14	3	103	26	321	467	7	4	0	11
1973	11	3	58	8	171	251	2	6	0	8
1974	12	3	28	7	166	216	45	37	0	82
1975	7	4	14	6	216	247	10	7	0	17
1976	13	10	14	15	245	297	2	4	0	6
1977	8	6	15	14	69	112	0	4	0	4
1978	4	6	14	7	50	81	0	1	0	1
1979	9	5	38	10	51	113	1	6	2	9
1980	3	6	8	9	50	76	0	4	2	6
1981	13	8	10	13	57	101	3	1	0	4
1982	8	4	21	7	57	97	11	2	0	13
1983	9	9	5	10	44	77	6	4	0	10
1984	7	2	9	10	36	64	5	1	0	6
1985	14	9	2	4	25	54	0	4	0	4
1986	10	2	4	8	37	61	0	0	0	0
1987	9	7	3	8	66	93	0	6	0	6
1988	4	2	21	12	54	93	1	1	7	9
1989	7	2	12	2	39	62	11	1	4	16
1990	7	5	7	8	49	76	3	0	3	6
1991	5	1	5	8	75	94	3	1	0	4
1992	2	1	3	3	76	85	4	0	0	4
1993	3	3	6	2	70	84	3	0	0	3
1994	3	0	1	2	54	60	0	0	0	0
Total	**196**	**101**	**445**	**203**	**2,228**	**3,173**	**117**	**100**	**18**	**235**

Note: It is not easy to estimate how many deaths have followed the IRA ceasefire arising purely from 'the security situation', but by September 1996 the combined total (including those resulting from robberies, drug-related killings and deaths in the Irish Republic and Britain) was approximately 13.

Source: *Northern Ireland Omnibus Survey*, Police Authority, 1996.

The encouragement of conciliation and cultural diversity

The first community relations initiative in Northern Ireland following the outbreak of violence was the establishment of a Northern Ireland Community Relations Commission in 1969. Its achievement was to identify the two main approaches to community relations – whether to assimilate Protestants and Catholics, or to accommodate the differences between them.

During the 1970s social policies, like political policies, were loosely based on the hope that Northern Ireland had a large, untapped middle ground between unionism and nationalism, and that this 'silent majority' needed to be given confidence to make itself heard. To this end the government combined reform and support for moderate voices, including the mainstream churches and such reconciliation bodies as the Corrymeela Community, which facilitated contact between Catholics and Protestants. By the early 1980s the persistence of sectarian politics and violence raised questions about whether the middle ground alone could deliver an acceptable settlement.

The alternative approach was to accommodate the view that Northern Ireland had two traditions with different but equally legitimate cultures and aspirations, and to encourage both traditions to express their cultural separateness without embarrassment. The long-term aim was the evolution of a plural society which accommodated and respected differences. A number of changes, many of them conceded reluctantly after considerable pressure, signalled this policy shift: the introduction of 100 per cent financial support for Catholic schools; the granting of financial support from government for Irish-language schools; the acceptance by the authorities of Irish-language street signs for some areas; increased financial support for social celebrations, festivals and activities which were traditionally supported by either Catholics or Protestants. A Cultural Traditions Group was established with government support in 1988 to encourage the process, and a Community Relations Council was established to coordinate and encourage those working on the ground. The Council has, in collaboration with agencies and organisations in the community, encouraged mediation and training in conflict resolution. It has also engaged more directly in encouraging positive contact across the religious divide with schools, local councils, sporting and other bodies, as well as conducting more controversial anti-intimidation and anti-sectarian work.

The most visible signs of the move to pluralism were in the field of education. General concern that there might be a connection between segregated schooling and community conflict grew from the early 1970s. It was based on two basic hypotheses: the 'cultural hypothesis' – that segregated schools present children with two very different views of their cultural environment; and the 'social hypothesis' – that, regardless of whether or not the two sets of schools are similar or different, the fact of separation encourages mutual ignorance and validates group differences and hostilities. Underpinning both hypotheses is the suggestion that a higher level of contact between Protestants and Catholics would contribute to an amelioration of the conflict.[22]

These arguments have influenced government policy in two main ways. The first emerged from a small but growing public demand for the establishment of integrated schools where Catholic and Protestant pupils could be educated together. Public opinion polls during the 1970s consistently indicated that a high proportion of the population claimed to support the principle of integrated education, and a privately sponsored bill permitted the formation of integrated schools from the late 1970s. Government support remained lukewarm, and most of the early integrated schools which opened during the 1980s started outside the education system with the support of funds from private foundations. Public funding was only granted when schools had proved their viability. A more active support by government for integrated schools developed during the late 1980s, reflecting the emerging debate on cultural heritage and the particular interest of Brian Mawhinney, then the minister responsible for education. The Education Reform (Northern Ireland) Order 1989 finally accepted integrated schools as an integral part of Northern Ireland's public education system. By the start of 1997, a total of 33 integrated schools had been established.

The second set of changes in official policy on schooling addressed the experiences of the 98 per cent of pupils educated within Catholic or Protestant schools. The Education Reform

Order 1989 required that all pupils should be introduced to the concepts of cultural diversity and Education for Mutual Understanding (EMU). Doubts still remain about how effective the implementation of these directives has been.[23]

Pluralist approaches are not a panacea for divided societies. Indeed they can be positively dangerous unless accompanied by clear and effective legal procedures, and by sufficient sensitivity to arbitrate between competing rights. The flying of the Union Jack in the workplace, for example, may be presented as traditional by unionist workers, but is sometimes seen by nationalists and others as intimidatory or provocative.[24] In Northern Ireland the fondness for demonstrations and marches provides a predictable cycle of such confrontations. Orangemen claim the right to march, especially in the weeks leading up to their traditional celebrations on 12 July. Their claim is based on precedent – that they have marched certain routes for decades – and on what they regard as a basic right 'to walk the Queen's highway'. These are both territorial claims which may ignore changes in the demographic composition of a neighbourhood. Garvaghy Road in Portadown is such a place. Orangemen had walked the road for 188 years. But the Catholic residents who predominated in the area by the 1990s claimed the right to live undisturbed by a hostile culture. They regarded the march as triumphalist and wished to ban it. The clash between these conflicting claims led to seriously destabilising violence in 1995 and 1996, as had marches in other districts. It is a reminder that a reliance on pluralist approaches is unlikely to erode the ability of ethnic opponents to find opportunities for disagreement.

6

NORTHERN IRELAND 1994–7:
BEYOND THE CEASEFIRES

Until 1994 it seemed that the most likely route to a settlement in Northern Ireland would be through a process involving a gradual loss of public support for the IRA, the creation of a power-sharing government representing both constitutional traditions, and strong security policies to remove the remaining violence. Nationalist involvement in suppressing the IRA seemed essential to this course of action. The IRA turned the process on its head. Instead of the sequence beginning with political agreement, it began with the IRA decision to cease its campaign of violence in August 1994, and the loyalists following suit in October.

Figure 19 Martyn Turner, the *Irish Times*, August 1994

The ceasefires and after

Opinions differ about the motivation for the IRA ceasefire. Some argue that it was determined by war-weariness. Others suggest that the IRA would not have abandoned their long campaign without major, and secret, concessions from the British government. Perhaps a more convincing reason was the IRA's realisation that their violence was not only driving greater divisions between Catholics and Protestants in Northern Ireland, but was also alienating the population of the Irish Republic; the pivotal role of John Hume in initiating talks with Gerry Adams of Sinn Féin may have contributed to this realisation. Despite the conciliatory tone of the Downing Street Declaration by the British and Irish premiers in December 1993, the killings continued, and even increased; 50 people were killed during the six months after the Declaration, compared to 32 in the equivalent period in the previous year. The Dublin *Sunday Tribune* voiced a growing condemnation of IRA intransigence by the Dublin media just a month before the ceasefire: 'The IRA campaign, although not the only obstacle to this [peace] process, is now beyond all reasonable doubt the most substantial one. That is why the killing must stop.'[1]

The effect of the ceasefires was heightened by contrast with the violence and tension which preceded them. Fifty-one people were killed, most of them by loyalists, in the six months before the IRA ceasefire. Although the ceasefires did not end paramilitary violence in Northern Ireland, only two people were killed as a direct result of political violence in the six months following August 1994. As time passed and the enjoyment of the ceasefires held, there was a palpable determination not to jeopardise them. Pre-Christmas trade in Belfast rose by 30 per cent in 1994. The EU and the USA announced significant grants to buttress the peace dividend. People began talking politics across the religious divide – in shops, pubs and at work – as well as within their own community.

In February 1995 the British and Irish governments published *Frameworks for the Future*, their suggestions for political progress. It proposed a new Northern Ireland Assembly and a 'Panel of

Three', separately elected, 'to complement the work of the Assembly'. More controversial was the proposed establishment of a North-South Body, elected from and accountable to the new Assembly and the Irish Dáil. It would have executive, harmonising and consultative functions. The Irish government agreed to introduce and support proposals to remove the Republic's territorial claim to jurisdiction over Northern Ireland in the context of an overall settlement.[2]

This momentum started by the ceasefires peaked around February 1995. Subsequent progress was at best spasmodic. The main stumbling block was disagreement about the conditions necessary to allow Sinn Féin's participation in all-party talks. The British government and the unionists argued that the continuing presence of IRA weapons was at least an implied threat that they would return to violence if they did not get their way. They demanded that IRA arms should be decommissioned before talks started. Sinn Féin, supported by the SDLP and, more erratically, by the government of the Irish Republic, countered that the ceasefire was sufficient proof of IRA sincerity, that they had an electoral mandate (strengthened in June 1996 by the elections to the Forum), and that it was unrealistic to expect decommissioning from an IRA deeply distrustful of the British. A succession of formulae failed to come up with a compromise. In November 1995 USA President Clinton attempted to generate momentum by visiting Belfast and Derry. In December an international body on decommissioning (the Mitchell Commission) was set up to find a way out of the deadlock. The Mitchell Report was published on 25 January 1996. In its official response on the same day, the British government appeared to ignore its main recommendations in favour of a marginal recommendation for elections.

The IRA ended its ceasefire on 9 February by planting a bomb in Canary Wharf in London, citing as justification that the British government was not only failing to show sufficient urgency in starting political talks, but were actually setting up a succession of obstacles to them. The IRA's return to violence led to the first signs of political urgency since the ceasefires. Within a period of five weeks after the IRA bomb, John Major announced a date for all-party talks, the two governments launched a Joint Communiqué to get the talks back on the road and negotiations had started with the Northern Ireland parties about an election and negotiations. There was a sharp rise in support for Sinn Féin and the DUP in the June elections to a Northern Ireland Forum. The increased tension culminated in the confrontations between marchers and protesting residents in July 1996. It seemed that the opportunity provided by the ceasefire had been wasted.

Figure 20 Martyn Turner, the *Irish Times*, February 1996

This chapter will chart that troubled voyage of the peace process since 1994 along a number of parallel tracks: the continuing threat of violence; the path towards negotiations; the dismantling and continuation of the emergency apparatus; the economic support for peace; and developments on the ground.

Violence

When a ceasefire is declared to long-lasting ethnic violence, the most obvious and serious threat is the likelihood that it will collapse and that violence will return. Mutual suspicion between the antagonists does not evaporate overnight. They still have the weapons and soldiers necessary to pursue their objectives by violent means. The obstacles to reaching a negotiated settlement are formidable.

Figure 21 Martyn Turner, the *Irish Times*, October 1995

In Northern Ireland the declaration of the ceasefires did not bring an end to paramilitary violence in Northern Ireland. Punishment beatings continued as both loyalists and republicans carried on what they regarded as their policing role in a number of communities. People were expelled from the community and severely beaten for 'anti-social behaviour'. Alleged drug dealers were attacked in both communities, and at least seven were killed by the IRA during the months of the ceasefire.[3] The association of paramilitaries with such acts of violence as robberies and other violent crimes, often disowned by paramilitary sources as unauthorised or by mavericks, continued during and after the ceasefire. As late as January 1996, Mitchell McLaughlin, one of Sinn Féin's main spokespeople, protested that Sinn Féin was 'powerless' to stop the IRA engaging in drug-related beatings and killings.[4]

The continuing involvement of paramilitaries in violence may partly explain the failure to re-integrate into society those who have been engaged in violence for many years. In Gaza and Jericho, and in South Africa, the problem has been partly addressed by transferring ex-guerrillas into the regular police force. The transfer of ex-paramilitaries to policing functions was relatively smooth in these places because there was substantial support for local control of policing. The sectarian divide in

Northern Ireland, and the continuing reminders of the brutality of 'policing' by paramilitaries, probably rules this out as an acceptable option.

Far more important than any of these other violence-related problems was the growing entanglement between the decommissioning issue and the admission of Sinn Féin into full political negotiations. The requirement by the British government that the IRA must hand over its weapons as a precondition for Sinn Féin's admission to talks rapidly became the main stumbling block to progress. In January 1996, a month before the ceasefire ended, the great majority in Northern Ireland (95 per cent of Protestants; 68 per cent of Catholics) believed that the paramilitary organisations should hand over all or some of their weapons before talks took place, but almost a third of Catholics blamed the British for dragging their feet on political progress.[5] By December, Sinn Féin was not the only body questioning British intentions. An editorial in the Dublin *Sunday Business Post*, headlined 'Trouble brews as Major moves the goalposts', went on to declare that, 'rather than seeking ways to promote dialogue, he has constantly used the demand for a surrender of weapons by the IRA in order to prevent such a dialogue'.[6]

A great deal of ingenuity went towards finding a route out of the impasse:

- The British position in March 1995 (known as the Washington 3 conditions) required the decommissioning of paramilitary weapons ahead of political negotiations; soon after, the British suggested that they would settle for 'a start to be made on the decommissioning of weapons' rather than a complete handover (25 July 1995); later they hinted that they would accept 'the beginning of a credible process', rather than its completion (4 September 1995); later still, they accepted that an 'unequivocal' IRA commitment never to resume violence might be enough (6 December 1995);
- the Irish, again at various times, recommended the involvement of external mediators from Scandinavia (1 March 1995); six months later John Bruton, the Taoiseach,

declared that the onus should be placed on Sinn Féin to come up with a formula (21 September 1995);

- Sinn Féin argued that they should be distinguished from the IRA, and that there were no historical precedents for decommissioning (14 June 1995); an alternative line was that the IRA had already effectively decommissioned by taking their arms out of circulation rather as Royal Navy vessels were mothballed, but not destroyed, after a war (4 October 1995);
- Ken Maginnis, the Unionist MP, favoured an International Disarmament Commission led by 'a person of international repute' (6 March 1995); later the unionists went on to propose an 'elective process' as a possible alternative to prior decommissioning (12 January 1996); and
- the loyalist PUP helpfully suggested that the IRA retain only its 'defensive weapons' (17 August 1995); later this was supplemented by their proposal that the IRA should make a solemn commitment not to be the first to use arms in any future situation (30 September 1995).[7]

By December 1995 the failure to resolve the decommissioning issue had become such a brake on the movement to negotiations that the British government, under pressure from the Irish Republic and the USA, agreed to the establishment of the International Body on Arms Decommissioning chaired by Senator Mitchell. Its report detailed a set of principles to which participants in all-party negotiations must agree, including their commitment:

- to democratic and exclusively peaceful means of resolving political issues;
- to the total disarmament of all paramilitaries;
- that such disarmament must be verifiable by an independent commission;
- to renounce and oppose any effort to use force or the threat of force to influence the course of the outcome of all-party negotiations; and
- to abide by the letter of any agreement reached in all-party negotiations and to resort to democratic and exclusively

peaceful methods in trying to alter any aspect of that outcome with which they may disagree.

The Mitchell principles also required participants in talks 'to take effective steps' to end 'punishment' killings and beatings.[8]

The ending of the IRA ceasefire in February 1996 was cited by all sides as justification for their positions. Unionists claimed that it simply confirmed their warning that the IRA would resort to force to resist any developments they opposed. A senior London police source alleged that what 'some people call a ceasefire' had never been more than 'a period of terrorist preparation', and others pointed to the evidence that the IRA had been preparing for a resumption even during the ceasefire period.[9] Sinn Féin argued that constant British obstruction of moves towards talks had confirmed the IRA's worst suspicions of the British and forced them back to war. The journalist Mary Holland placed her emphasis on discontent within a number of IRA units:

'Their frustration stems from what they see as the slow pace of progress but also from a fundamental belief that Gerry Adams is willing to accept a compromise settlement within Northern Ireland which falls short of a united Ireland. On previous occasions since Ireland became independent, every move by the IRA away from violence and into constitutional politics has involved a split between the men of violence and the politicos. Provisional IRA was itself born from such a development.'[10]

Whatever the balance of blame, the ending of the IRA ceasefire did not lead to a resumption of the IRA campaign as it had operated up to August 1994 when the ceasefire was declared. Initially bombings were confined largely to Britain. London suffered a number of explosions and aborted attacks in early 1996, before the campaign was broadened in July to include Manchester, Germany and a raid in the Irish Republic during which a Garda officer was killed. The mood in Northern Ireland was 'one of dread tempered by hope',[11] at least while the IRA campaign avoided the province. In July responsibility for a hotel bomb in Enniskillen was apparently accepted by another republican organisation, but in October 1996 the IRA claimed its first attack, and first victim, within Northern Ireland for more than two years, on the British Army headquarters at Thiepval in Lisburn. Despite this evidence that the peace process was slipping away, there were some signs that it was still alive. The loyalist paramilitary organisations decided to preserve their ceasefire. Paramilitaries from both sides largely kept out of the confrontations which accompanied the Orange celebrations on July 1996. A year after the Docklands bomb in London there had not been a return of the full-blown Troubles.

Figure 22 Martyn Turner, the *Irish Times*, July 1996

These were straws clutched from the wind by optimists. Pessimists had a choice between haystacks. The confrontations between marchers and nationalist protesters in July 1996 invited comparisons with the civil disturbances and riots which sparked off the quarter century of violence in 1969. The traditional Orange parade from Drumcree church along the mainly nationalist Garvaghy Road in Portadown on 12 July, which had led to serious confrontations exactly a year earlier, was re-routed by the RUC. The Orange Order responded with a serious of pre-planned demonstrations, blocking roads, bridges and the airport and converging in increasing numbers at Drumcree in the days immediately preceding the parade. The protesters forced a number of Catholic families from their homes by intimidation. None of these was prevented by the police. On 10 July the RUC reversed its decision, escorted the parade down Garvaghy Road, physically removing local protesters from the road. That evening nationalist parts of Belfast were curfewed to prevent their anticipated protests. Civil society appeared to be in tatters.

The path towards negotiations

It is now known that secret talks had been held between the British government and Sinn Féin some time before the IRA ceasefire and had clearly helped to pave the way for it. Subsequently a range of pre-negotiation talks were initiated and proceeded at varying speeds. Although they often overlapped with each other, it may be useful to distinguish four main types of talks.

First were the regular meetings between the British and Irish governments introduced by the Anglo-Irish Agreement in 1985. The Agreement gave the Irish government the right to make proposals on policy and legislation, but in practice the meetings were often used to ventilate minority grievances in Northern Ireland. After the ceasefires, the two governments disagreed publicly about the pace of the peace process, the Irish government wishing to move to full talks between all the parties in Northern Ireland more speedily than the British. The difference between the governments about the pace of change was based on their different constituencies. For Dublin the main threat to peace was a resumption of IRA violence, and the best way to prevent it was to involve Sinn Féin in negotiations as full partners; a further complication was the replacement of Albert Reynolds by John Bruton as Taoiseach in December 1994, as the latter's Fine Gael Party was traditionally less sympathetic to republicanism. The British reluctance to move more quickly was rooted in their concern to keep the unionist parties on board, a concern which edged towards dependency as the government's domestic difficulties grew and its majority in the House of Commons diminished during 1995. Despite this and other differences, the regular meetings between the two governments provided a useful means of checking each other's reactions on Northern Ireland.

The second level of talks, introduced by the *Frameworks* document, concerned the relationship between the two parts of Ireland. In October 1994 the Dublin government set up a Forum for Peace and Reconciliation which met weekly and invited interested parties to address it. The Forum was ignored by the unionist parties, but addressed by other interests, including the main Protestant churches, in the Northern Protestant community. The Forum may also have played a useful political training role for interests such as Sinn Féin, which had limited experience in negotiation, but the Forum meetings were suspended immediately following the ending of the ceasefire by the IRA.

Third were talks within Northern Ireland. The government's initial policy was to move cautiously towards full negotiation through a process of stages, starting with separate bilateral talks with Sinn Féin and with the loyalist parties. These were described as pre-negotiation meetings, aimed at clarifying the conditions under which ex-paramilitaries might engage in full negotiations. Pressure was increasingly applied, especially to Sinn Féin, for the decommissioning of paramilitary weapons. These preliminary talks began with officials, and were later extended to include ministers. The pre-negotiation process, however, slowed down seriously during the second half of 1995 over the issue of decommissioning. It ended with the IRA bomb in London, after which both London and Dublin governments ended their official contacts with Sinn Féin.

Within days of the London bomb the British and Irish governments issued a joint communiqué announcing an agreed path to all-party negotiations. This included 'multi-lateral consultations' with Northern Ireland parties between 4 and 13 March 1996, the start of 'all-party negotiations' on 10 June and possibly a referendum. Sinn Féin's involvement in the talks would depend on the restoration of the IRA ceasefire and acceptance of the principles agreed by the Mitchell Commission. The elections to the Northern Ireland Forum confirmed that the main beneficiaries in times of sectarian tension are those parties which take the strongest and least compromising positions. Thanks in part to the complicated system adopted for the election, Sinn Féin significantly increased its mandate to 15.5 per cent of the vote, and the Official Unionists, who were the main advocates of the election, lost support to the DUP. The procedural wrangles during the early meetings of the Northern Ireland peace talks and Forum gave little indication that momentum towards agreement had been restored. The electorally strengthened Sinn Féin party was excluded from the peace talks, and the SDLP withdrew from the Forum after Drumcree, severely wounding its credibility. Attempts to start multi-party negotiations in early 1997 were still frustrated by failure to resolve the decommissioning impasse.

Much of the government's activity immediately following the ceasefires had been designed to lock Sinn Féin and the loyalist parties into normal political processes. Until the Forum elections in May 1996 there were signs that traditional political loyalties in Northern Ireland might be shifting. Unionist farmers, business interests and community activists were more willing to negotiate than their leaders. At the same time the Catholic middle classes were also showing less sympathy for traditional republicanism. An Independent Television News (ITN) poll following the publication of the *Frameworks* document found that 58 per cent of Protestants but only 49 per cent of Catholics believed that the *Frameworks* proposals would eventually lead to a united Ireland. While 56 per cent of Catholics would vote for Irish unity, 23 per cent would vote to stay in the United Kingdom, with the rest unsure.[12] This indicated that, despite the political alignment between the SDLP and Sinn Féin, some middle-class Catholics in particular were ambivalent about Irish unity. Polarisation hardened after Drumcree. An *Irish Times* poll in September 1996 revealed a move to more exclusive positions. Thirty-nine per cent of Catholics favoured a United Ireland against less than 1 per cent of Protestants. Almost a third of Protestants believed that Northern Ireland should be more closely integrated into the UK, a view shared by 3 per cent of Catholics.[13]

Throughout this period there was clear evidence of public support for negotiation. In the ITN poll 82 per cent of Catholics, and even 70 per cent of Sinn Féin supporters, found it acceptable that the union should not be altered without majority support in Northern Ireland. The initial opposition of the unionist parties to the *Frameworks* document continued, but the Official Unionists at least had to rethink their position in the light of opinion within the Protestant community. As McKittrick indicated, 'out in the Protestant community, things are stirring and attitudes are being re-examined, but this has not been reflected by the unionist MPs'.[14] Challenges to the unionists have come from community groups, from ex-loyalist prisoners, from elements in the business and farming communities and from the Church of Ireland bishops, who expressed concern about the hostile response of unionist politicians to the prospect of negotiations.[15]

The peace process was also affected by interventions from external actors. The fourth category of talks took the form of conferences sponsored by the EU, the USA and voluntary organisations like Foundations for a Civil Society. The most important external influence, however, was undoubtedly the USA. President Clinton was instrumental in welcoming Sinn Féin leaders into political respectability. The Americans lifted their ban on providing a visa for Gerry Adams, and one effect of Adams' subsequent visit was to exert pressure on the British government to accelerate their pre-negotiation talks with Sinn Féin. In November 1995 President Clinton visited Northern Ireland to encourage the process, and was received by enthusiastic crowds. Pressure by the USA on Britain to find a way out of the impasse over decommissioning led directly to the Mitchell Report. Given this high level of presidential commitment, there was an extremely hostile reaction in the USA to the ending of the IRA ceasefire and the bombings in England, both from the administration and the traditional supporters of Irish republicanism. Gerry Adams' visa was renewed on 2 March 1996 on condition that he pledged not to raise funds in the USA; on the same day the USA Congress adopted the MacBride Principles – a measure of the new American ambivalence about Northern Ireland. The USA itself had been directly affected by terrorist bombs, and republican supporters in America were less inclined, at least temporarily, to support the IRA.

The dismantling and continuation of the emergency apparatus

Close on the heels of the ceasefires were demands to dismantle the emergency apparatus erected during the Troubles. Within six months security ramps were removed and border roads with the Irish Republic, many of which had been closed by the army, were gradually re-opened. The strict security arrangements surrounding the international airport were systematically reduced. The military presence was reduced, but cautiously. Many of the restrictions on traffic through town centres were lifted, although most were retained as pedestrian zones.

Other emergency procedures were slower to change. Policing was one. In 1969, when the serious violence began, the RUC establishment stood at 3,044. By 1994 it had risen to 8,489, with a further 3,206 full-time, and 1,765 part-time, reservists. Even ignoring the RUC reserve, this was an increase of 178 per cent during a period when Northern Ireland's population increased by less than 2 per cent. To gain some impression of how large the RUC would have been without the violence, Northumbria, with a population close to Northern Ireland's at just under 1,500,000, has a police establishment of 3,600 officers, well under half the size of the RUC.

An additional complication was the continuing low proportion of Catholics in the force. When the RUC was set up in 1922, a third of the places were reserved for Catholics. The actual percentage probably never exceeded 12 per cent, and currently stands at less than 8 per cent. Matters have not improved significantly since the ceasefires. In March 1996 the RUC admitted that, of the 372 new recruits who had joined the force in 1994 and 1995, only 40 (10.8 per cent) were Catholics; and 106 of the recruits (28.5 per cent) were women. 'We have always accepted that we are under-represented in both Catholic and female officers,' the RUC stated, 'and have made it clear that we are taking every possible step to encourage applications from both groups'.[16] This posed a mathematical conundrum – how was the police force to be reduced to a more appropriate size while significantly increasing the number of Catholic officers?

The conundrum is also a political one. In a survey carried out for the Police Authority in March 1996, seven out of ten Catholics believed that the RUC should be reformed or disbanded, and the same proportion of Protestants believed that there should be no changes. This closely matched the findings of a poll conducted for the *Belfast Telegraph* two months earlier, when 74 per cent of Catholic respondents believed that changes were necessary for the RUC, but 71 per cent of Protestants believed they were not.[17]

Figure 23 Need for change in the RUC

Regarding the future of the RUC, do you think that it should be...

i By religion

ALL PERSONS AGED 16 AND OVER

	Total	Protestant	Catholic
Base = 100%	*2,558*	*1,571*	*987*
Allowed to carry on exactly as it is now	54	71	28
Reformed	29	23	38
Replaced by an altogether new police force or service	14	4	31
Disbanded	1	0	1
Don't know/Refusal	2	1	2

ii By area

ALL PERSONS AGED 16 AND OVER

	Total	Belfast	East of province	West of province
Base = 100%	*2,681*	*472*	*1,276*	*933*
Allowed to carry on exactly as it is now	54	49	62	44
Reformed	29	33	28	30
Replaced by an altogether new police force or service	14	13	9	22
Disbanded	1	2	0	1
Don't know/Refusal	2	3	1	3

iii By age

ALL PERSONS AGED 16 AND OVER

	Total	16-19	20-24	25-29	30-34	35-39	40-44	45-49	50-54	55-59	60-64	65+
Base = 100%	*2,682*	*227*	*219*	*250*	*275*	*261*	*218*	*221*	*202*	*184*	*169*	*455*
Allowed to carry on exactly as it is now	54	40	46	46	50	54	50	45	51	64	69	68
Reformed	29	27	32	34	29	27	33	43	36	24	19	24
Replaced by an altogether new police force or service	14	32	22	18	18	17	15	9	10	10	8	5
Disbanded	1	0	0	1	1	1	0	0	0	0	2	0
Don't know/Refusal	2	2	1	1	2	1	3	3	2	2	1	4

Source: *Northern Ireland Omnibus Survey*, Police Authority, 1996.

The government has shown little willingness to respond to this growing division. In March 1996 the Police Authority announced the findings of its Community Consultation study, which had involved a series of 13 information seminars, letters to 3,500 private and public bodies as well as every RUC officer and civilian staff member, and a public opinion survey.[18] It recommended that there should be no change in the name, uniform or badge of the RUC, and suggested changing the oath of allegiance to the British monarch to an affirmation. These changes were condemned as 'mere window-dressing' by the SDLP and Sinn Féin, and the chairman of the Authority who had launched the study and subsequently been dismissed, David Cook, claimed that the original version of the study had been watered down.[19] Two months later the government's White Paper on Policing Structures also rejected any need for substantial structural changes. The breakdown of the IRA ceasefire and the increased sectarian tension in 1996 both underlined and undermined the need for reform. In January 1997 the government accepted with unusual readiness the main recommendation of the Hayes Report on the police complaints system. The report stressed the need for an independent complaints system, and recommended the appointment of a Police Ombudsman, through whom all complaints about the police – not just those on conduct – should be made in the first instance. Elsewhere a more cautious approach prevailed. Also in January 1997 the new Chief Constable, Ronnie Flanagan, supported plans for modernising the RUC. These included setting targets for recruiting more Catholics and women, promoting a neutral working environment and enhancing community awareness training. They did not include major changes in staffing levels. The plans would be phased in 'over a number of years'.[20] If pressures to reform the police force were increasing, especially from the minority community, the evidence indicates that there was little appetite to embrace them.

Nationalist confidence in the police was further weakened by the events at Drumcree in July 1996. Whatever the operational justification, the failure of the RUC to move against Orange law-breaking and road blocks in the days before the march, its decision to force through the parade despite the earlier decision to ban it, and its willingness to clamp down on nationalist areas on the same day, confirmed to many nationalists that the police force, and perhaps the state which directed it, had demonstrated partiality in the enforcement of the law. Both Sinn Féin and the SDLP questioned if the same policing decisions would have been taken if the march had been a republican one. Attempts to balance this perception by stronger action against loyalists are more likely to alienate both sides than to persuade them that the RUC is a balanced police force.

Equally resistant to change was the range of emergency laws introduced since 1973. The broadcasting ban was removed shortly after the ceasefire, but most of the other restrictions continued. The CAJ launched a campaign entitled 'No Emergency – No Emergency Law', demanding the repeal of sections of the Prevention of Terrorism Act and the Emergency Provisions Act, as well as the system of Diplock courts. The ending of the IRA ceasefire did not end the dispute between those who wished to keep the emergency structures and those who had advocated their removal. For the former the renewed IRA campaign justified their caution. For the latter, the caution had contributed to the renewal of violence.

Economic support for peace

It has been estimated by the Northern Ireland Economic Council that as many as 40,000 jobs in Northern Ireland depended on security-related work – police, soldiers, security guards, even construction workers – during the early 1990s. If these jobs disappear, the resulting discontent could threaten the emerging peace process, hence emphasising the need for a peace dividend to compensate for the conflict deficit. This paradox, that peace was accompanied by economic dangers, is not peculiar to Northern Ireland, but also applied to South Africa and the Middle East. Northern Ireland has two major advantages in dealing with this problem – the EU and the Irish-American connection. Within months of the ceasefires the EU announced an additional grant of £240 million to support the peace process, and insisted that it should be directed to areas especially affected by violence. Irish-America too has contributed both grants and additional American investment in Northern Ireland and the border counties, including a major investment conference in Washington DC in May 1995. Even after the IRA ceasefire ended, the EU launched an aid package amounting to £29 million for the border counties,[21] implicitly making a distinction between the ending of the ceasefire and the continuation of a peace process.

Just as the ceasefire had led to a dramatic increase in trade and tourism for Northern Ireland, its ending threatened to reverse the trend. North-South trade rose by 14 per cent between 1994 and 1995, and the trade balance between Northern Ireland and the Republic narrowed significantly in the first nine months of 1995.[22] Trade in Belfast, which had risen by 30 per cent in the months following the declaration of the IRA ceasefire, suffered a serious setback when it ended in 1996, the Belfast Chamber of Commerce reporting that 'numbers coming to shop in Belfast from the south are down by at least 50 per cent'.[23] Tourism had especially benefited from the ceasefires. The number of tourists to Northern Ireland rose from 270,000 to 430,000 between 1994 and 1995. It started to fall immediately after the Docklands bomb in February 1996. The Northern Ireland Tourist Board reported that the number of enquiries received in the first quarter of 1996 was down by 27 per cent on the same period in 1995, and the violence in July further frightened off actual and potential visitors.[24] The Europa Hotel in Belfast experienced a fall in business in the year following the ending of the ceasefire. Guests from 'down south' had accounted for 22 per cent of the hotel's business. 'Now it's around 7 per cent' its manager reported.[25]

Economic factors appear to have been marginal in determining the progress of the peace process. Nevertheless they were able to exert some influence on occasions. The decisions to call off rival and potentially violent demonstrations in Derry on 10 August 1996, for example, were influenced by the argument that confrontation would have an adverse effect on jobs and investment in the city.

Developments on the ground

The 1994 ceasefires were greeted with public euphoria, and the benefits in terms of business, tourism and general well-being were immediately evident. The general expectation was that the ceasefires were permanent. Nevertheless, as the move towards all-party negotiations stalled, Catholics were more inclined to blame the delay on the conditions set by the British government, while Protestants blamed the unwillingness of the IRA to decommission their arms. So the battle lines were already set when the ceasefire ended.

The Docklands bomb was received with almost universal shock and anger, and protest meetings across the province attracted large crowds from both communities. But alternative scapegoats were available. As tensions increased throughout 1996, the balance of blame increasingly took a sectarian tinge. The Forum elections in May seemed to confirm a return to more polarised politics. So did the reactions to the Drumcree confrontations in July. A survey carried out just a week before the Drumcree parade found that the most popular view about marches, if first and second choices were combined, was that they should be determined by an independent body. But the first preference of more than 75 per cent of Catholics – that the residents should decide – was only the third choice of Protestants, almost half of whom thought that all parades should be allowed.[26] The announcement by the government after the Drumcree incident that it would set up an independent body begged the question why this had not been done a year earlier. The resulting publication of the North Report on parades and marches in January 1997 recommended that a five-member Parades Commission replace the RUC as the statutory body empowered to make decisions about disputed parades. The Report's impact was somewhat blunted both by the government's failure to implement the findings immediately and by the highly polarised response to the proposals.

One of the most consistently liberal commentators on Northern Ireland, Barry White, was moved to pessimism a week after Drumcree, believing that the Orange 'victory' would remove any pressure on unionists to make concessions:

'We have no common nationality to rediscover, and the two mother

countries we look to regard us as aliens. The lesson of last week was that if we can't learn to tolerate our differences, and find some way of accommodating our conflicting aspirations, we'll destroy ourselves, either in an all-out conflagration or a slow death.' [27]

It is impossible to gauge the extent to which the strength of protest against the London bombs contributed to the IRA's initial decision to confine its new campaign to Britain and Europe, and to hold back from returning to violence in Northern Ireland. It seems probable that it had some effect. The hard truth, however, is that public opinion had as little effect on the calling of the cease-fire as it had on its ending.

So, in the months following the ending of the IRA ceasefire, Northern Ireland experienced both a political stalemate and a lim-ited, in IRA terms, war. There was little enthusiasm for the North-ern Ireland Forum or the talks. The multi-party talks were stranded. IRA violence had spread from Britain to Northern Ire-land. The loyalist ceasefires were under threat.

Within the nationalist family the common stance of Sinn Féin and the SDLP was coming under increasing strain. The return of IRA violence put the final stamp on Sinn Féin's exclusion from multi-party negotiations, and dealt a severe blow to those advocat-ing a political strategy. The SDLP was not only frustrated by the continuing IRA violence, but uneasy about Sinn Féin's improved performance at the Forum election. In January 1997 John Hume responded to a proposed pre-election pact from Sinn Féin with two conditions: a complete end to IRA violence and to Sinn Féin absentionism from attending parliament. Gerry Adams angrily rejected them. In the May 1997 Westminster elections, Sinn Féin consolidated its gains in the Forum election, and raised its per-centage of the vote to 16.

On the unionist side, the Ulster Unionists had enjoyed holding the electoral balance in Westminster from late 1996, but their per-formance in the Forum elections was disappointing. Perhaps more important, they were left holding the tail of their own Drumcree tiger, with the prospect of its annual re-awakening during the marching season. Only the DUP seemed comfortable in its intran-sigence. The election of a Labour government in 1997, with a substantial majority, raised unionist apprehensions about a new political initiative.

The IRA was also boxed in. Its war had not delivered its objectives. The ceasefire had failed to get Sinn Féin into talks and its ending had severely depleted its revenue, especially from the USA, as well as halting the early release of republican prisoners. The IRA had reason to doubt that its supporters would tolerate another war, perhaps confirmed by an exceptionally high number of arms finds, often made with the help of informers. The return to a limited form of violence, rather than full-scale war, revealed its dilemma. On the one hand, the declaration of another ceasefire would mean accepting conditions which had not improved since 1994, indeed they had been available since Sunningdale in 1974. On the other, was another sustained period of violence likely to be more successful than the last one? 'If an IRA bomb explodes any minute now,' asked journalist Fionnuala O'Connor in December 1996, 'what is that bombing meant to convey?' Her answer: 'The IRA's problem is that they no longer know. The problem for everyone else is that confusion in the ranks of bombers and among their leadership does no-one any good.'[28]

Without strong guidance, the current was more likely to move the situation towards greater violence than towards a period of calm, unless a new initiative could jolt the peace process back into motion. The irony is that the declaration of a second IRA ceasefire on 19 July 1997 followed on the heels of a period of high instability. The IRA had killed two policemen in Lurgan on 16 June in an apparent attempt to raise tensions before the marching season. The decision to force an Orange march through the Garvaghy Road on 6 July had once again led to street violence and apprehension about the marches scheduled for 12 July. The Orange Order's agreement to postpone or divert four potentially violent marches had defused the immediate danger without removing the background tension.

The origins of the second ceasefire predate the events of the summer. By late 1996 Sinn Féin leaders had articulated four preconditions for a second ceasefire – a firm date for Sinn Féin's entry to talks; a timetable for those talks; confidence-building measures (largely a euphemism for the accelerated release of prisoners); and no decommissioning until a settlement had been reached or was in sight. John Major's dependence on unionist political support had prevented progress under a Conservative administration. But the 1997 British general election brought in a Labour government under Tony Blair, with a comfortable majority and a new energy. Mo Mowlam, the new Secretary of State for Northern Ireland, resumed direct communication with Sinn Féin in May 1997. Despite the murder of the two RUC men and the tensions surrounding the July marching season, agreement was reached on all four points. The government agreed that Sinn Féin might enter talks six weeks after a ceasefire, allowing substantive talks to start in September 1997. May 1998 was set as the date for the completion of the talks. Assurances were given on 'confidence-building measures'. Decommissioning remained as the final and most difficult problem, not least because unionists threatened to pull out of inter-party peace talks unless weapons were handed over before and during substantive talks. On 24 June the British and Irish governments published their joint paper on decommissioning, passing the responsibility to an independent commission to be chaired by the former Canadian defence chief, John de Chastelain. Tony Blair announced that political talks would start at the same time as the new body met. Sinn Féin had overcome their last obstacle. Martin McGuinness was able to announce that 'The IRA have said that they will not decommission a single bullet and I have not heard any statement saying that they have changed their position'. The ceasefire was restored on 19 July. It was not greeted with the same joy as the 1994 ceasefire. A *Belfast Telegraph* headline on the same day caught the mood of caution. 'Hopes for peace,' it declared, 'but no euphoria.'

A clash of cultures

Many people think of the Northern Ireland conflict as a conflict between two cultures – unionism against nationalism or, more often, Protestantism against Catholicism. A stronger case can be made that the central cultural division, especially since the declaration of the 1994 ceasefires, is between a culture of violence and a culture of co-existence. The result of the interplay between these two tensions ultimately determines whether any peace process succeeds or fails.

By culture is meant the body of moral, political and social norms which arises from what is regarded as a norm by society. It has both a behavioural and an attitudinal aspect: that is to say, the norms arise from attitudes in society and from social behaviour. The norms are mutable. Their nature is often determined by those forces living on the margins of society which wish to challenge generally acceptable modes of behaviour. The liberal democratic culture, for example, defines itself partly by its response to those who wish to use the norms of liberal democracy to challenge it. The use of violence to achieve political objectives is the most testing challenge of all.

A culture of violence is one where violence has radically altered social norms, at least temporarily. It has both active and passive consequences, often simultaneously. The most active manifestations of a culture of violence follow the declaration of war. Soldiers are conscripted into the army, and national success depends on the ability of the establishment to convert ordinary decent people into people who are trained and willing to kill. In this instance a culture of violence is sanctioned by society to achieve what it perceives as a common good. But a culture of violence is not always sanctioned by the establishment. At certain times in certain societies the routine procedures for maintaining law and order fail, and society is forced to accept violence imposed by sub-groups within its boundaries. Chicago during the 1930s provided an environment where accepted methods of law enforcement proved to be temporarily ineffectual against organised crime. Exceptional measures became necessary to protect the community.

This is an active demonstration of a culture of violence. The culture of violence is also manifested passively. Those who oppose it, even by the act of opposition, are also subject to it. Hence many people react to the culture of violence by seeking either to deny or to escape it – through emigration, or internal migration (as, for example, the middle classes' gravitation to suburbs when inner cities become too violent), or mentally turning off. In Northern Ireland, for example, there was a measurable decline in the willingness of people to watch the local television news during the height of the Troubles.[29] These denials are also part of the culture of violence.

The opposite of a culture of violence is ... what? In practice, for most people, the opposite of violence is the absence of violence, a non-state rather than a positive one. It is not easy to move from a culture of violence, especially a long-entrenched one, to a culture of co-existence – a state where conflicts are resolved in ways that are generally acceptable through discourse, compromise, politics. For many, the ending of violence is a sufficient objective. Only when it is achieved do its limitations, and the obstacles towards a more stable peace, become apparent.

Consider peace processes – all peace processes – within this framework. They may best be understood as the state of tension between a culture of violence and a culture of co-existence. The relative strength of each – in South Africa, the Middle East, Northern Ireland – is likely to be a main determinant of its pace and ultimately of its success or failure. This is not to neglect the importance of other factors – the parts played by neighbouring countries, the economic infrastructure which may buttress or buckle under the process, the management of policy. Indeed, external intervention can play a critical positive or negative role in determining the outcome, by providing economic or diplomatic support, for example, or by military intervention. In some conflicts external factors may have exceptional importance, as when India invaded Sri Lanka in 1983, or Russia intervened in Chechnya in 1994. It is suggested, however, that these influences are essentially secondary, and will not determine the final destination of the peace process. The *kulturkampf* – the struggle between the cultures – is the central factor.

Apply this to Northern Ireland. A culture of violence has certainly evolved during the quarter century of violence – it would have been surprising if it had not. People's lives have been directly affected by violence. It has eroded investment, employment and industry. In a population of around a million and a half, very few do not have a relative or close friend who has suffered from the violence. More than 3,400 have died, in Northern Ireland and abroad; almost ten times that number have been wounded. In some localities the dominant role model became the paramilitary hero, the hunger striker, even the racketeer connected to the paramilitary organisations. The child who did not aspire in those directions was the deviant.

In comparison the culture of co-existence was weak. The peace movements briefly flared only to dim through their failure to connect to the decision-makers in and out of government. An entire generation, many of whom left Northern Ireland and are now working in Europe and Britain, has no memory of the years before the violence. Would they have left in any case, as a result of market forces, or are they too victims of the culture of violence, in their case negatively? Statistics suggest that a 'Troubles factor' does operate, with more than 40 per cent of undergraduates from Northern Ireland electing to study in British universities. But cultures are by definition organic, not static. After the ceasefires there were some signs that a stronger culture of co-existence may be emerging in Northern Ireland. It suffered setbacks from the ending of the ceasefire and the sectarian violence of July 1996.

The move from a culture of violence to one of co-existence creates difficulties for leaders of both the minority and majority communities. The political problem facing both is the presence of alternative actors, political and paramilitary, offering simpler and more extreme choices. How is one to move towards change while maintaining mass support?

The initial minority campaign for civil rights in the 1960s, initiated by leaders from the middle classes and channelled mainly through the SDLP, has been largely successful. All the statutory instruments of deprivation, and many of the material ones, have been removed. The leaders, while not denying that problems remain, argue that they no longer justify the use of violence, if they ever did, and that remaining grievances should be treated through conventional political, legal and other procedures. These grievances seem more serious, and the gains less obvious, to those at the bottom of the socio-economic ladder. They look for more radical moves towards social equality or fundamentalist nationalism. The efforts by Gerry Adams and the Sinn Féin leadership since the late 1980s to lead their supporters towards more constitutional approaches ran into similar problems to those earlier confronting the SDLP. Failure by Sinn Féin to achieve political and constitutional gains will confirm the belief among traditional nationalists that their objectives, both socioeconomic and constitutional, cannot be achieved through negotiation, but only by force.

Unionist leaders who desire a negotiated settlement face similar fundamentalist pressures. If the Ulster Unionists become involved in another Drumcree confrontation, they run the risk of encouraging loyalist violence and further alienating British and overseas opinion; if they move towards compromise, the risk is that the party will split as it did in 1974, and the DUP will be waiting to seize any electoral advantage.

The need for speed is perhaps the most important lesson of the ceasefire and its ending. The opportunities for agreed change are infrequent and their rejection, far from returning the problem to the situation immediately preceding the opportunity, moves it to a more intransigent level. Unionists, distrustful in any case of negotiations with Sinn Féin, will feel that their distrust was justified by the IRA's resumption of violence. Nationalist willingness to negotiate a settlement within Northern Ireland has been jolted by doubts about the impartiality of the RUC.

Measured against this internal stalemate are changes within both the United Kingdom and the Irish Republic. It is difficult to see economic advantage for either in demanding Northern Ireland as part of its national territory. Even more important, their emotional ties to Northern Ireland have diminished dramatically in the last generation. British and Irish interests are not identical, but have never been so close since the creation of the Irish state. To put it more positively, for the first time both neighbouring states are simultaneously willing to reach a disinterested settlement, one which is primarily determined by the will to lock in peace and create long-term stability for Northern Ireland, rather than to look for electoral or any other advantage. It is a rare coincidence which may not last for ever.

Figure 24 Cartoon by Martyn Turner

Source: *Pack Up Your Troubles*, Belfast, Blackstaff, 1995.

MINORITY RIGHTS: AN AUDIT

The five policy approaches separated in Chapter 5 for the sake of analysis are the strongest of the threads which make up the quilt of the Northern Irish conflict, but they are neither definitive nor separate. Policy in any one area affects all the others. Perhaps the most intimate connection was the relationship between a strong or weak security policy and attempts to reach a political settlement. A strong approach to security often led to suspicion and protests from Catholic nationalists. A policy of restraint produced complaints from Protestant unionists. The usual outcome was a compromise policy of military containment, which maintained the violence at an 'acceptable level'. Most people lived normal lives. Normal crime continued at a low level. The incentive to compromise, in order to reach political agreement, remained weak.

This may explain why many people in Northern Ireland, as those in all durable ethnic conflicts, regard the central dispute as sterile and immutable. Witness Richard Rose's gloomy observation: 'Many talk about a solution to Ulster's political problem but few are prepared to say what the problem is. The reason is simple. The problem is that there is no solution.'[1]

Snapshots of change and the drag effect

Contrary to popular misconceptions, the Northern Ireland question has not remained static. It has continued to evolve during the last quarter century, each change of direction creating new problems and possibilities. Some examples from the last 25 years:

- Aspirations within the Catholic minority have shifted backwards and forwards between a demand for reform within Northern Ireland and a demand for reunification with the Irish Republic.
- Direct confrontations between Catholics and Protestants, a feature of 1969 and 1970, were replaced by organised violence between the IRA, the army and loyalist paramilitaries. Paradoxically, the ending of IRA violence in Northern Ireland in 1994, coupled with dilatory moves towards political negotiation, appears to have re-activated sectarian feelings and sparked off the July riots in 1995 and 1996.
- The issues in dispute have altered; different generations of paramilitaries are driven by different and more complex motives.
- There has been a significant rise in residential segregation over the last 25 years.
- Each side has been prepared to enter negotiations at different times.

How are these changes to be audited? How is progress to be measured? It is sometimes difficult for those working in the eye of the storm to recognise change taking place around them.

One way to measure progress, or regression, in a durable conflict like Northern Ireland's is to imagine a series of freeze-frame photographs. The foregrounds would capture the atrocities – internment in 1971, Bloody Sunday in 1972, the hunger strikes in 1981, the war memorial bomb in Enniskillen in 1987, the Shankill and Greysteel killings in 1993. A more careful study would show that the background has been subtly changing. Northern Ireland is now a more fair society, and this change has been achieved gradually, almost imperceptibly.

Some of the more blatant discriminatory practices were removed many years ago. Franchise abuses were ended by

1969. The allocation of housing – a major issue in 1969 – has effectively been removed from the roster of grievances. All schools, including Catholic schools, are now funded on a completely equal basis. Children attending primary schools must now be introduced to the concepts of cultural pluralism and education for mutual understanding. The employment differentials between Catholics and Protestants have been substantially reduced. There is no longer an officially sanctioned system of discrimination. The principle of political, social and cultural parity is now much more widely accepted. Nevertheless, serious problems still remain, among them the religious composition of the police force, the continuation of emergency legislation – including its effects on prisoners and alleged miscarriages of justice – and the continuing higher Catholic unemployment rate.

Both communities have been affected by these changes. On the Protestant side, there has been a growing distrust of all British parties and by 1996 an acceptance, however reluctant, that the Dublin government would have a role in talks about Northern Ireland's political future. In the Catholic community the freeze-frame photographs would record erratic enthusiasm for a united Ireland, swinging against it as it became more closely associated with the IRA's campaign of violence, and back again when Sinn Féin was excluded from talks and the RUC was perceived to favour Orange marches in 1996. Neither picture would have been predictable a decade before.

The rate of change appeared to accelerate after the 1994 ceasefires. It seemed inconceivable then that unionists would have agreed to Sinn Féin's involvement in political negotiations. Indeed, within a few weeks during December 1994, their insistence on a testing period for a ceasefire dropped from six years to three months. Equally dramatic was the speed with which some republicans seemed to be moving towards an acceptance that a majority in Northern Ireland as well as in the island of Ireland – the traditional republican position – would be necessary for any constitutional change. The very speed of these changes heightened public expectations that a political settlement could be reached. The irony was that failure to move with sufficient urgency from ceasefire to negotiation coincided with one of the rare occasions when both communities appeared willing to search for an agreement.

The freeze-frame photographs reveal the importance of what might be called the drag effect. As protagonists find new areas for disagreement they often tacitly move towards resolutions of previous sticking points. Resolutions are dragged along in the wake of change, the real advance taking place behind the lines, concealed by the sound and fury at the new battle front. The signs of the drag effect are the issues which aroused passion in the past but which are now quietly accepted. In the debate before the Fair Employment Act 1989, for example, employers strongly opposed the requirement to monitor the religious composition of their workforces. They argued that workers would resist or defy the demand to record their religious affiliation. Apparent mass conversions to Islam or Buddhism were forecast. They were wrong. In 1989 only 64 per cent of Catholics and 42 per cent of Protestants accepted the need to monitor. By 1993 the percentages had risen to 91 and 64 respectively, and religious monitoring had become part of the social scenery.[2]

A number of other fiercely contested positions are now similarly accepted: the principle of fair employment and fair access to housing; equal funding for all schools; the inability of either the IRA or the British army to win a military victory; the Dublin government's involvement in negotiations; the need for endorsement of any political agreement by a majority in Northern Ireland. These may appear undramatic or obvious to younger people. Thirty years ago these principles were at the very centre of political disputes.

It is necessary to add a cautionary note. A major assessment of employment and housing, carried out by Smith and Chambers for the Standing Advisory Commission on Human Rights in 1987, concluded that there was unmerited complacency about the level of change:

'A common view among the liberal successors to the unionist establishment in Belfast is that, following the reforms of the 1970s, the public services and the main social and economic institutions are as fair as they can be in a divided society in

which the two communities occupy distinct geographical and social territory, and that equality of opportunity for Protestants and Catholics has nearly been achieved; on this view, any remaining inequality of condition is a reflection of historic discrimination which has now been put right, and will gradually disappear without further corrective action. This view is emphatically contradicted by the weight of evidence collected in this book.'[3]

This view, while accepting that inequalities in housing and education had been significantly reduced, was based on a number of factors including the persistently higher Catholic unemployment rate, a relatively lower Catholic standard of living and the ineffectiveness of the Fair Employment Act 1976. Smith and Chambers hoped that their evidence 'will provide a bench-mark against which future progress can be judged'.[4] Their survey was conducted in 1987 and some, though not all, of their criticisms have been caught up by subsequent events: the replacement of the Fair Employment Act 1976 by tougher legislation in 1989; the introduction of equal funding for Catholic and Protestant schools and the curricular reforms of the 1990s; and the effectiveness of the FETs in remedying individual complaints of discrimination.

When the smoke has cleared, three remaining grievances continue to dominate majority-minority relationships – employment, cultural expression and the constitutional issue. The review of the Fair Employment Act 1989, due in 1997, will be carefully scrutinised to assess its success in encouraging fair employment and in reducing the unemployment differential between Catholics and Protestants. Equally pressing is the need for effective mediation and legal procedures in order to avoid confrontations between marchers and local residents during the marching season. The key remaining question, however, is also the original question: within which constitutional framework should Northern Ireland be located?

The Universal Declaration of Human Rights

A more objective measure for auditing change are the 30 articles of the UN's Universal Declaration of Human Rights. It would be a travesty of the truth to suggest that human rights abuses in Northern Ireland are close to the level of abuse in totalitarian states, because developments are subject to the permanent scrutiny of democratically elected representatives and free media. Nevertheless the case of Northern Ireland has given, and in some cases continues to give, cause for concern and occasional congratulation.

Article 2: *Everyone is entitled to all the rights and freedoms ... without distinction of any kind, such as race, colour, etc.*
The absence of any legislation against racial discrimination was a serious gap in Northern Ireland until the passage of the Race Relations (Northern Ireland) Order in August 1997.

Article 3: *Everyone has the right to life, liberty and security of person.*
Twenty-five years of civil disorder, and more than 3,000 deaths, have offended the most basic human right of all – the right of people not to be killed. Some blame for this should be aimed at the failure of successive governments to reduce minority grievances and reach a political settlement. Nevertheless, since well over 80 per cent of victims were killed by members of paramilitary organisations, this underlines the point that the protection of human rights does not depend solely on the actions of the state.

Article 5: *No-one shall be subjected to torture or to cruel, inhuman or degrading treatment or punishment.*
The intelligence structures and techniques established by the army and police in Northern Ireland led to growing concern during the 1970s about a range of security practices. Bodies ranging from Amnesty International to the European Court of Human Rights were highly critical of army and police interrogation of prisoners. The semantic juggling of the Compton and Parker reports, which preferred the terms 'ill-treatment' and 'inhuman

treatment' to the plainer word 'torture', had little immediate effect, but the hostile international response led eventually to a series of procedural reforms. By the 1990s allegations of torture or ill-treatment had decreased significantly.

Article 7: *All are equal before the law and are entitled without any discrimination to equal protection of the law.*
The first academic study into the administration of justice in Northern Ireland found that 'there is a small but cumulative measure of (perhaps unconscious) sympathy with Protestants and Loyalists'.[5] Despite the increased paraphernalia of emergency legislation which has been instituted since then, allegations of bias within the judicial system have greatly diminished. However a succession of successful appeals by Irish people which overturned previous convictions in British courts has raised serious questions about the partiality of police and judicial procedures in other parts of the United Kingdom. Within Northern Ireland the principle of equality before the law is still frustrated by the Diplock court system, which distinguishes between, for example, security-related murders and 'ordinary' murders.

The operation of policing in a divided society still gives cause for concern. The dominance of Protestants in the RUC is seen by some Catholics as indicating bias. They cite the police response to Orange and republican protests in July 1996 as an illustration that the RUC expresses different levels of tolerance to republican and loyalist parades, thereby not providing 'equal protection of the law'.

Article 9: *No-one shall be subjected to arbitrary arrest, detention or exile.*
Internment without trial was introduced in Northern Ireland in August 1971, and is now generally regarded as both an abuse of human rights and a political misjudgment. The Emergency Provisions Act 1973 extended the army's right to stop and detain suspects, and was renewed at regular intervals for the next 22 years. The Prevention of Terrorism Act, introduced for the whole United Kingdom in 1974, further extended the period for which suspects might be detained to seven days, despite the fact that 75

per cent of those detained were released without charge. Both measures are essentially emergency laws, and their continuing presence raises a question about whether human rights are being infringed.

Article 11 (1): *Everyone charged with a penal offence has the right to be presumed innocent until proved guilty according to law...*
The removal of the 'right to silence' for people charged with a crime severely undermines the presumption of innocence, and has been criticised by the UN Human Rights Committee and the UN Committee Against Torture.

Article 13 (1): *Everyone has the right to freedom of movement and residence within the borders of each state.*
The Prevention of Terrorism Act 1974 allowed the government to exclude from Great Britain, from Northern Ireland, or from the United Kingdom as a whole, persons thought to be involved with Northern Irish terrorism. In addition, the UK has been unable to ratify the freedom of movement rights in Protocol 4 of the European Convention on Human Rights. These actions have been criticised for establishing what amounts to internal exile, and exclusion orders were still operated by the Secretary of State in 1996.

Article 19: *Everyone has the right to freedom of opinion and expression...*
Sinn Féin and a number of other specified republican and loyalist organisations were excluded from radio and television airwaves from 1990 until shortly after the declaration of the IRA ceasefires. This broadcasting ban, apart from creating the risible convention whereby representatives of these organisations were muted on television while actors spoke their lines, was a *prima facie* abuse of the right to freedom of speech.

Although Article 19 unconditionally supports the right to express opinions freely, it overlooks the intimidatory effects of sectarianism. In deeply divided societies, the removal of political symbols from the workplace has encouraged a broader and more representative range of job applicants, and extended rather than diminished human rights.

Article 20 (1): *Everyone has the right to freedom of peaceful assembly and association.*
The right to assemble, apparently absolute, takes on a more sinister tone if the purpose of assembly is to intimidate ethnic opponents. The traditional routes of sectarian processions have raised questions about whether historical tradition or local negotiation is the more appropriate method to determine the most peaceful routes for marches, especially after some local demographic patterns have altered substantially and local residents have expressed opposition to marches. The potential of parades to lead to violence and intimidation continues to be demonstrated on an annual basis.

Article 26 (3): *Parents have a prior right to choose the kind of education that shall be given to their children.*
One of the most significant extensions of human rights has been the provision of schooling on equal terms to different groups. Catholic schools have been awarded equal funding to schools attended by Protestants. The authorities have increasingly accepted the establishment of religiously integrated schools, and schools which use Irish as their language of instruction.

Have attitudes changed?

....

The true Partitionists are those who would (in a political sense) remove Ulster from what anyone who glances at a map of Europe will recognise as a national geographical, social and economic unit, namely the British Isles.

William Carson, 1957

....

All of us are born into a variety of communities – families, local communities, religious communities, cultural groups, economic communities – the mix varying between individuals. Our identities are partly determined by the characteristics and beliefs of these communities. In a society divided by nationalist or ethnic tensions, identities are also partly determined by the need to mark out the distinction from one's ethnic opponents. Energies are devoted to emphasising the differences between groups rather than the features they hold in common. When tensions run high, the simple test is: are you for us or against us? There is little space for those caught in the middle.

In some respects 25 years of violence have exaggerated these differences in Northern Ireland. Demographic segregation between Catholics and Protestants has increased. Some families have moved to live among their co-religionists, either in the face of direct threats or from fear. Despite this, in most areas, the two communities live in daily contact with each other. Northern Ireland does not experience the high levels of segregation of many other conflicts such as Israel, South Africa or even some inner cities in North America or Europe. The resulting mixture of contact and separation greatly complicates feelings about identity or allegiances. Far from creating conditions where both communities live comfortably among their own people, allegiances in Northern Ireland reflect constant uneasiness. Northern Catholics often aspire to Irish unity, yet sometimes feel alien and are regarded as alien in the south. Northern Protestants almost unanimously want closer union with Britain – hence are unionists – but almost unanimously distrust the British.

The complexity of attitudes and relationships often surfaces during public events. An example is Remembrance Sunday, the day on which the dead from past wars are remembered in the United Kingdom. The ceremony is also held in Northern Ireland, because it is part of the United Kingdom. The dead are remembered by processions, church services, the laying of wreaths of poppies on war memorials (a reference to the poppies blooming on the battlefields in Flanders during the First World War). In the weeks before Remembrance Sunday badges in the form of artificial poppies are sold on the streets to raise funds for old soldiers. They are worn on the days up to and including Remembrance Sunday. Or, to be more precise, they are predominantly worn by a section of the population. For many Catholics the simple act of wearing the poppy is complicated by its political associations with Britain.

The recent experience of a Catholic teacher who has lived in Northern Ireland all her life illustrates the point. Until recently she, like many Catholics, had not bought or worn poppies, nor attended Remembrance Day ceremonies. To wear a poppy would have been an unnatural activity, something vaguely Protestant. Then, in 1987, the IRA planted a bomb at the War Memorial in Enniskillen, during the Remembrance Day ceremonies. People were blown to pieces during a memorial service for their dead. Whatever inherited reservations the Catholic teacher had about wearing poppies were wiped out by the Enniskillen bomb. Since then she has worn it every year. Last year it was her turn to read the lessons at mass on Remembrance Sunday. She removed the poppy during the reading. She is not sure why, but is embarrassed by her own decision. If she reads at mass again next year, she will wear the poppy.

The story has two points. First, like an increasing number of Catholics, she had begun wearing what in her youth had been regarded as a Protestant badge. Second, inherited loyalties are deeply rooted. The confusion between her two instincts indicates that old habits die hard. It also indicates that some of them are dying.

It is not easy to gauge the rate at which attitudes are changing. During the last quarter century the direction of major events has been less influenced by public opinion than by paramilitary violence and the decisions of a government sitting in Westminster. None of the legislative or administrative changes had a local mandate, for no local assembly existed to approve them. The most dramatic of the changes, the 1994 IRA ceasefire, far from reflecting greater tolerance, followed a period of unusually high tension.

Some of the most obvious indicators of good community relations provide ambiguous clues about the extent to which attitudes have changed:

- Church membership figures remain high – 87 per cent against 66 per cent in Britain. The proportion in Northern Ireland who claim to attend church at least weekly was 52 per cent in 1992, against 14 per cent in Britain.[6] Both figures suggest that general attachment to religious identities remains high.

- Intermarriage may be infrequent, but few families do not have ancestors from the other side. One of the ironies of the Troubles was that, despite the constant violence, the increased demographic segregation and community alienation, marriages between Catholics and Protestants have fluctuated considerably over the last 30 years, and there appears to have been an increase during the 1980s. According to the *Northern Ireland Social Attitudes Survey* the figure stands at around 6 per cent of all marriages, but this disguises considerable geographical variation. It is also an underestimate if compared to figures from the Catholic churches. These estimate that 20 per cent of all marriages in Down and Connor, the diocese which includes Belfast, were between Catholics and Protestants in 1991.[7]
- Church-based organisations retain an important social function, but are now seriously challenged by secular alternatives such as sporting facilities, commercial entertainment and charity fundraising; loyalties have become more fluid.
- Integrated schools are attended by a small percentage of children, but are the fastest growing educational sector, with 33 schools by the end of 1996 and three more planned for 1997. Twenty-five years ago – indeed 15 years ago – no such option existed, nor was there a discernible demand for it.
- Irish language, music and culture have much higher profiles in 1995 than would have been thought possible ten years earlier: the BBC schedules Irish-language broadcasts and Gaelic sports; there was a *ceili* in Belfast City Hall on St Patrick's Day 1995; Irish-language schools are in receipt of public funding; the funding was given public support by a group of Shankill Road Protestants.[8]
- One point, however, indicates that attitudes remain fundamentally unchanged. Voters are still rejecting political parties which aim to appeal to both traditions, and mainly vote along sectarian lines. In the 1997 Westminster elections, only 8.3 per cent of the electorate voted for centre parties.

Figure 25 Choice of national identity 1968–94

Choice of national identity 1968–1994 for Protestants and Catholics (%)

	Protestant					Catholic				
	British	Irish	Ulster	N. Irish	Other	British	Irish	Ulster	N. Irish	Other
	%	%	%	%	%	%	%	%	%	%
1968	39	20	32	–	9	15	76	5	–	4
1978	67	8	20	–	5	15	69	6	–	10
1989	68	3	10	16	3	10	60	2	25	4
1991	66	2	15	14	3	10	62	2	25	1
1993	70	2	16	11	3	12	61	1	25	2
1994	71	3	11	15	–	10	62	–	28	–

Notes: Northern Irish identity offered as an alternative from 1986. Other includes 'Anglo-Irish' and 'sometimes British, sometimes Irish'. Respondents who said they had 'no religion' are excluded from this analysis.
Source: *Social Attitudes Survey*, compiled by K.Trew, 1996.

So attitudes remain suspicious, or at least cautious. An opinion poll in December 1993 found that 37.5 per cent of those polled believed that political attitudes in the ranks of the professional and middle classes had progressively hardened in the previous three months, while only 25.6 per cent disagreed.[9] This followed a period of exceptional violence, when even greater pessimism might have been expected. But while evidence of major attitude changes or of a growth in genuine tolerance is thin on the ground, there have been substantial changes in behaviour and practice. The absence of local democracy in Northern Ireland has enabled reforms to be made which would almost certainly have been defeated or diminished by a locally elected assembly. However, since the reforms were implemented, there has been much greater acceptance that they are here to stay, and also that they are fair. The enforced reforms – in fair employment, the distribution of educational resources, cultural rights – are not only operating, but in themselves have shifted attitudes. The shift has not been towards a greater tolerance, but towards reluctant acceptance of minority rights. Northern Ireland's experience shows that there is no need to wait until attitudes become more tolerant before introducing reforms. Changes in attitudes can be driven by changes in behaviour, and both can be encouraged by institutional reforms.

There are indications that most people still aspire towards a more integrated society. Eighty-two per cent of Catholics and 66 per cent of Protestants would prefer to live in a mixed neighbourhood. Ninety-four per cent of Catholics and 87 per cent of Protestants would prefer to work in a mixed workforce.[10] Not only has the middle ground refused to collapse, but the number and quality of concrete cross-community contact appears to be increasing.

Shifting minorities

Since Harold Jackson's description of the double minority in 1971 *(Two Irelands: The Problem of the Double Minority)*, the nature of Ireland's minorities has undergone some significant shifts. These include at least three changes in the balances between competing interests: the balance between the Protestant-British bloc and the Catholic-Irish Republic bloc; the balance between Catholics and Protestants in Northern Ireland; and the balances within each of the two communities.

There has been a shift in the balance between each of the two traditions in Northern Ireland and the external states to which they looked for support or protection. Most Protestants regard Britain less as an external champion than as another part of the same United Kingdom to which they also belong. Most Catholics regard the southern part of Ireland as part of their shared culture and heritage. In the past, Northern Ireland's Protestants were confident that all British governments shared their view of the union. The Irish Republic assumed a special responsibility for the Catholic minority, the relationship having been formalised and accepted by the United Kingdom since the Anglo-Irish Agreement in 1985. While this latter relationship broadly continues, many Protestants have lost confidence in Britain as a guarantor of their position within the United Kingdom. This leaves an imbalance of confidence, at least until the Irish government feels it can alter its special relationship with Catholics and reach out with more sympathy to the Protestant community as well. This would require a move away from its historical traditions comparable to Northern Irish Unionists making their party more appealing to Catholics.

The balance between Protestants and Catholics within Northern Ireland has also shifted. In the past it was held in equilibrium because the higher Catholic emigration rate cancelled out the higher Catholic birth rate. Between 1937 and 1961, for example, more than 55 per cent of those who emigrated from Northern Ireland were Catholics, but the Catholic birth rate at the time was about 50 per cent higher for Catholics than Protestants. Both factors have changed since then. The birth rate in the Catholic community has fallen by 20 per cent during the 1980s alone, much faster than the reduction for Protestants, and this process has continued into the 1990s to a point where Catholic and Protestant fertility rates are almost equal.[11] There are some indications that middle-class Protestants are emigrating in larger numbers. According to a 1994 analysis by Coopers and Lybrand, which has been contested, a continuation of these trends could lead to a Catholic majority in Northern Ireland within a quarter century.[12] This trend has been given added political significance by the increased residential segregation resulting from violence. The Coopers and Lybrand poll found that 37 per cent of electoral wards in Northern Ireland were highly – more than 90 per cent – religiously exclusive. Belfast and Derry are particularly segregated by the rivers Lagan and Foyle. The 'peace lines' in Belfast were erected as much from public demand for protection as the demands of security policy. The segregation has been accelerated by middle-class Protestant departure from both cities to suburbs outside the city boundaries. In the 1997 local government elections, unionists lost control of Belfast City Council for the first time, and both Derry and Belfast elected nationalist mayors. The confidence of the Catholic minority has increased, especially among the young, for reasons ranging from demographic changes and greater equity to political changes since the Anglo-Irish Agreement.[13] At the same time Protestant confidence has been eroded. Social reforms, especially in connection with fair employment, were regarded as advantaging Catholics, and the same political changes which have pleased Catholics were viewed by Protestants as the start of a British sell-out. The determination of the Orange Order to march through the Catholic Garvaghy Road from 1995 to 1997 was partly specific to the locality, but also arose from a more general feeling that too many concessions had been made to the minority since the 1960s, what David Trimble described as 'a litany of retreat, surrender and concessions'.[14] The irony is that unionists were increasingly using the same rhetoric that nationalists had been using for decades, about the legitimate expression of cultural identity. The Catholic minority is behaving less like a minority, and the Protestant community more like one.

So is a nationalist majority ultimately inevitable? All is not as simple as it appears. There is consistent evidence of considerable Catholic ambivalence towards Irish unity. Colin McIlhinney, who conducted the Coopers and Lybrand poll, pointed out:

'You can't make a naive translation from a simple head count to a voting figure. Our polls were finding substantial numbers of Catholic middle-class AB 1 groupings, people in management or white-collar jobs, who are saying that a united Ireland isn't their first preference.' [15]

This indicates that perhaps the most significant changes of all are happening within the two communities themselves, and especially inside the Catholic community. The minority aspiration towards a united island, for example, has fluctuated considerably during the 25 years of the current violence. By the late 1960s most Catholics were more concerned with reforming Northern Ireland than uniting with their co-religionists in the Irish Republic; none of the six demands of the NICRA campaign mentioned Irish unification. The arrival of the British army in 1969, and the growth of violence between the army and the Provisional IRA, restored the rhetoric and paraphernalia of traditional republicanism. Opinion polls since the mid-1980s appear to indicate another reversal, with a minority of Catholics – 36 per cent according to the latest Social Attitudes Survey – indicating that unity was their constitutional preference. In 1994 this trend was dramatically reversed yet again, the pro-union support among Catholics declining to 25 per cent.[16] So Catholic concerns since the 1960s have shifted back and forth along a spectrum between nationalism and reform, the position determined by a number of background factors, including the level and type of violence and the prospects of political accord.

In some ways the sum of these changes questions the extent to which it is still useful to talk of a Catholic minority at all. It is increasingly necessary to make a distinction between different groups of Catholics. The socio-economic conditions of middle-class Catholics have improved significantly since the 1960s, bringing them more into line with middle-class Protestants. However, there is evidence of a growing bifurcation between the conditions of middle-class and working-class Catholics. For middle-class Catholics, more open access to professional jobs and the relatively low cost of housing in Northern Ireland has led to a considerable growth in disposable income, and a reduction in real and perceived disadvantage. But working-class Catholics are still more likely than their Protestant counterparts to be unemployed or to earn low incomes. The distinction is underlined by the disproportionately high support for Sinn Féin among poor and unemployed Catholics. The growing gap between the rich and the poor is a feature of the Protestant as well as the Catholic community. The real differential for both Catholics and Protestants at the bottom of the economic scale is increasingly based on economic rather than religious factors.

This by no means exhausts the discussion about minorities in Ireland, or in Northern Ireland. There was no legislation against racial discrimination in Northern Ireland until August 1997, when the passage of the Race Relations (Northern Ireland) Order, whose terms included the Irish travelling community, ended the anomaly. The preoccupation with the sectarian problem has distracted attention from other issues at least as deserving of concern. Prominent among these is the gender issue. The economic and social disadvantages facing women in Northern Ireland are arguably greater than those facing Catholics, at least following the reforms of the last two decades. The plain truth is that the sectarian issue has had more political muscle in Ireland

and abroad. It seems at times that any society has a finite amount of energy available for addressing minority grievances at a given time. Reform energy in Northern Ireland has been mainly directed towards redressing the disadvantages of the religious minority. The gender minority, which is actually a majority, has lost out.

8

NORTHERN IRELAND: BROADER LESSONS?

I t is dangerous to generalise about ethnic conflict and its resolution, or to transplant lessons from one setting to another. There is a paradox at the core of every ethnic conflict. Each setting is essentially parochial, with its own history and social characteristics, but the phenomenon is universal. Any approach to conflict resolution must pay respect to its local characteristics while searching for its general features.

With that in mind, what has the Northern Ireland experience to contribute to general understanding and management of ethnic conflict? Is the experience only understandable in terms of Irish history and culture? In what ways does its evolution – from its historical origins, through civil protest to paramilitary violence, the various attempts to reach agreement, the ceasefires and the uneasy threat of continuing violence – match or differ from the cycle of violence in other conflicts?

Cycles of change

Ethnic conflicts never stand still. They are affected both by their own dynamic and by policy interventions. The official response to early discontent is particularly critical in determining the future direction of the conflict. When the violence takes on its own momentum, sometimes the only available policy is containment, in an attempt to prevent total collapse.

It is a mistaken assumption that all conflicting parties want to reach a settlement at any given time. The war in Bosnia during

1993 and 1994, for example, demonstrated that the willingness of Muslims, Serbs or Croats to engage in negotiation depended primarily on their fortunes on the field of war and the resulting territorial gains or losses. By definition, these conditions never coincided for all three parties. During the Northern Ireland conflict, opportunities when all the main parties were prepared to negotiate were infrequent. In practice, each side's position was partly determined by the attitude of their opponents. Expression of an interest in negotiation from one party may in itself be sufficient cause to raise opponents' suspicions. Sometimes one party may propose negotiation only because they know that their enemies cannot accept, thus achieving a short-term reputation for moderation. The result is a pendulum-like swing, with ethnic rivals proposing talks in turn, but rarely at the same time. Windows of opportunity, when all parties are simultaneously prepared to negotiate, are rare, and of limited duration. Yet it is usually during such relatively infrequent opportunities that a settlement is reached.

The opportunities, and appropriate responses to them, vary according to a number of factors, notably the extent to which the violence is entrenched. Consequently policy initiatives at the early stages, when violence is threatening but not yet endemic, are particularly important. In the late 1960s NICRA, which articulated early grievances, identified six priority demands. By 1970, following the start of violence in 1969 and pressure from Britain, five had been conceded. The concessions did not prevent the growth of violence. Speedy though the response had been, it was not speedy enough. By the time concessions had been made, minority demands had already shifted from content to process. It was no longer sufficient for reforms to be granted to an aggrieved minority by a magnanimous majority. Catholics were already insisting that they should participate fully in the government which determined the reforms, rather than simply benefit from its largesse. It is impossible to exaggerate the speed with which demands become radicalised when conflicts become violent.

The later stages of violence present different problems. If ethnic violence continues for a long period it often becomes detached from the reasons which originally caused it. Not only do the issues in contention change, but different generations of fighters become engaged in the struggle. The second and third generations of activists are often driven by different motives from their predecessors, and younger recruits are sometimes more extreme and uncompromising. Violence can become so endemic in some districts that the true deviants are those adolescents who do not participate in paramilitary activities, rather than those who do. This reality limits the approaches available to those wishing to negotiate a way out of violence. The 1995–6 negotiations in Northern Ireland, for example, were made possible by the declaration of the IRA ceasefire, an event not widely anticipated nor an obvious result of government planning. Willingness to seize unexpected opportunities is an underrated political skill.

It was during these two phases of Northern Ireland's conflict – the years immediately preceding the progression from civil protest to community violence in 1968–9, and the 18 months following the 1994 ceasefires when the ending of the war failed to lay the foundations for making the peace – that swift and inventive initiatives were needed and were not found. During the 1960s unionists were unable or unwilling to recognise the shift in Catholic attitudes away from traditional nationalism, and to introduce the reforms demanded by the civil rights movement. During 1994–6 mutual distrust pushed the peace process into the doldrums. The IRA refused to decommission its arms, endorsing unionist fears that the ceasefire was a tactical and temporary ploy, and that the threat of weapons would continue to undermine talks. The British insisted on a series of tests before Sinn Féin could fully enter negotiations, and little effort was made to dismantle the security apparatus – the release of prisoners, the reform of policing, the ending of emergency legal procedures. However understandable each fear, the end result was that the delays fuelled already deep suspicions, and certainly contributed to the ending of the ceasefires in 1996. The failure convinced the IRA that the British, satisfied with the ending of violence, were not interested in negotiations. The ending of the ceasefires simply confirmed unionists' forecasts.

A contrast might be made with the speed of developments in South Africa between Nelson Mandela's release from prison in

February 1990 and the signing of the National Peace Accord in September 1991; full transfer to majority government followed in April 1994. It is of course possible that time will reveal constitutional and administrative errors resulting from the rapidity of change in South Africa. The point is that, without the speed, the necessary radical changes would not have been accomplished. Obstacles to an agreed settlement were numerous – the mobilisation of Afrikaaner resistance, high levels of violence, moves towards Zulu secession, demands within the ANC for more radical changes. Fear festers during times of fundamental change. Decisive action by brave leaders can accomplish more in months than can otherwise be accomplished in years.

Ending the war: tumbling the dominoes

The process of moving out of violence can start at any of a number of alternative points. Imagine the set of factors required to end ethnic violence – a ceasefire, agreement to negotiate, the intervention of a mediator, etc. – as a circle of dominoes standing like the stones at Stonehenge. The ending of violent conflict requires all the dominoes to topple. The process can be triggered by moving any one of the dominoes forward, creating a momentum which collapses its neighbour, and so on to the next one, and the next. What are the dominoes, and what triggers can tumble them?

The removal of minority disadvantage

Some violent conflicts assume ethnic manifestations because of discrimination against minorities; indeed few ethnic conflicts lack economic, political and cultural grievances. The successful and long-term management of pluralism is impossible unless these are addressed. The removal of minority disadvantage rarely ends violence by itself, because violence often takes on its own justification and momentum, but it is an essential precondition for moving towards the cessation of violence and political accommodation. The gradual reduction of minority disadvantage in Northern Ireland during the 1970s and 1980s – in housing, the franchise and education – removed grievances which would have made a political settlement even more difficult than it is. The obstacles are not always material ones. The ambiguous nature of cultural identity can just as easily provoke groups to violence, whether it takes the form of a dispute about primary ownership of an Indian temple or the Dome of the Rock in Jerusalem, or the right to official use of a minority language. In Northern Ireland violence has been sparked by the flying of flags, the playing of anthems, marches and demonstrations. Ethnic groups often regard the protection of their culture as a basic right, but may not accord the same right to opponents. When one group sees the other's expression of cultural identity as an expression of cultural dominance, violence becomes almost inevitable, so the addressing of minority grievances must incorporate the dangerous and sensitive search for parity of esteem.

The removal of violence

Violent action by the state can, of course, suppress ethnic violence; indeed, the presence of a large army limited its effects in Northern Ireland. But state suppression often produces only short-term gains, with the violence breaking out again later. Ceasefires by belligerents are more rare, and successful negotiation is difficult while one of the negotiators is still engaged in violence. Nevertheless, political talks often begin despite continuing violence, as they did in El Salvador, the Basque region and the Middle East. The initiation of talks with paramilitary organisations, however painful, is justified less by their electoral mandate than by their ability to frustrate negotiations from which they are excluded. The declaration of ceasefires enhanced the atmosphere for political negotiation in South Africa and Northern Ireland.

In Northern Ireland, however, the ceasefires only moved the process slightly forward, and the difficult issue of decommissioning soon put a stop to further progress. The IRA was not willing to give up its arms until some movement towards negotiations was evident. Some of the other actors, including the British government and most mainstream unionist parties, were unwilling to negotiate under the threat of a renewal of violence if the IRA did not get its way. In 1996 the Mitchell Principles introduced an ingenious procedure for resolving the issue. These were a set of principles to which all negotiators had to agree before admission to talks, including agreement to exclusively peaceful means of resolving political issues, to total and verifiable disarmament of all paramilitaries and to abide by any agreement reached in all-party talks. The Mitchell intervention came too late to maintain the IRA ceasefire, but played a part in its restoration in 1997, and may prove to be a useful device for tackling the decommissioning issue when it arises in other places.

Political compromise

Political discussions aimed at reaching a compromise between the belligerents are perhaps the most obvious first step towards ending violence. Don Horowitz has argued that electoral systems should be constructed so as to reward compromise and penalise ethnic voting.[1] Such mechanisms aim to encourage and reward cooperation and compromise. They may evolve unconsciously in a plural society through a range of internal or external influences – greater prosperity, modernisation, increased cosmopolitanism, international pressures, even generational changes.

Before negotiations can start about political compromises it is necessary either to end the violence or to get the fighters or their surrogates to the table. The IRA ceasefire in 1994 was partly based on an expectation that Sinn Féin would be involved in the subsequent negotiations. Certainly failure to secure this contributed to their ending in 1996. More generally, paramilitary participation in negotiations is usually justified on pragmatic rather than principled grounds – that they have the capacity to disrupt any agreement reached by more moderate negotiators – but it brings its own problems. There is no obvious correlation between military and political skills, nor any reason to expect paramilitaries' skills to run to negotiation. If paramilitary leaders feel uncomfortable or inadequate while negotiating, they may be tempted to return to the methods with which they are more familiar. If Northern Ireland's experience is anything to go by, many of the paramilitaries are well aware of the need for political education, and keen to participate. The more effective the skills of the negotiators in presenting their objectives, the more likely the success of the negotiations.

External intervention

Sometimes well-timed interventions by the international community or sponsor states can be the trigger which starts the process towards peace, or the sanction which terminates force. Few ethnic conflicts are divorced from external support and encouragement. These can have either a negative or positive influence. External involvement can sometimes make things worse, as the Indian intervention in Sri Lanka demonstrated. On the other hand, foreign forces have controlled many ethnic conflicts, and overseas friends can play essential roles in providing economic support in the post-violence phases of conflict. The economic support of the EU and the USA has greatly enhanced the Irish peace process, and the USA played a major role in moving the peace process towards negotiation.

Most often the process requires a combination of more than one of these triggers to create momentum. Then the momentum itself, by providing the opportunity for the opposing communities to work together, can become an agent in the process.

All the standing dominoes are part of the problem. Some of them are more weighty and more likely to create momentum than others. But none of them should be dismissed. Sometimes the most unpromising initiative can deliver the goods. At certain times there is a chance of moving one of the dominoes, while the others are apparently deeply entrenched. In such circumstances it makes sense to adopt a pragmatic approach, and to concentrate efforts according to opportunity and circumstance. The lesson? Push where there is give.

Making the peace: hard choices

When ethnic conflict becomes violent, it raises hard questions about the very nature of the state and the relationships within it.

147

The Northern Ireland experience illuminates three of the most fundamental choices which must be confronted if ethnic differences are to be successfully managed. These are:

- whether it is ever possible to resolve ethnic conflict or if conflict regulation is a more realistic objective;
- whether ethnic minorities can or should be assimilated into the general culture, or their differences recognised through pluralist institutions; and
- whether minority aspirations can be better satisfied by secession or by internal constitutional reforms.

Conflict resolution or conflict regulation?

In the main, most people regard ethnic conflict as dysfunctional, as evidence that something has gone wrong in the social body. The role of sociologists and political scientists, in this view, has been to identify the fault and point out how it might be fixed. There is, however, an alternative tradition, presented by Georg Simmel almost a century ago. It sees conflict as a natural element of social intercourse, and argues that it is as pointless to attack it as to attack the ageing process. Conflict is neither good nor bad, but intrinsic in every social relationship from marriage to international diplomacy. Whenever two or more people are gathered, there is conflict or potential conflict. The real issue is not the existence of conflict, but how it is regulated.[2]

The fundamental question posed by this analysis is whether it is ever possible to resolve conflict, or more realistic to recognise that conflict is a social norm rather than an aberration, and plan accordingly to accommodate differences. It suggests that the term 'conflict resolution' has long passed the stage where it is merely unhelpful or confusing. It has become positively harmful. Conflicts can rarely be resolved. Very often the best one can hope for is a compromise, a move towards a more civilised approach to the management of differences.

To reach this compromise a distinction needs to be made between conflict – opposing interests and aspirations – and violence – the means sometimes used to advance one set of interests or achieve particular aspirations. The use of violence marks the failure of normal approaches to conflict management – political exchange, negotiation, compromise.

Applying this argument to the conflict in Northern Ireland, it suggests that all the ideologically determined 'solutions' – a united Ireland, full integration with Britain, an independent Northern Ireland – aspire towards an unrealisable permanence. None of these could guarantee stability. A united Ireland carries the risk of creating a substantial Protestant minority, concentrated in one part of the island and entrenched against the new arrangements. Full integration with Britain is unacceptable to everyone, including the British, except a minority within the unionist community. An independent Ulster is the least feasible option of all, for political and economic reasons. This leaves as the only serious option a compromise arrangement which seeks to satisfy through negotiation the aspirations of all interests in Northern Ireland. It would need to carry a battery of strong and enforceable guarantees for all parties including protection of minority rights, a charter on human rights, rewards for political cooperation, sanctions against majoritarianism and the frequent monitoring of employment patterns.

Internal guarantees are not enough. When negotiations to settle any ethnic conflict move to discuss the protection of minorities, attention needs to be given to the need for an external review body with sufficient weight to monitor developments and to enforce fair treatment for all. The EU or the UN may carry the necessary authority to perform this function in relation to Northern Ireland. In other conflicts the most appropriate body will depend on local considerations, but must be acceptable to all parties.

Assimilation or pluralism?

Violence is only the tip of the conflict iceberg. Its main bulk is formed from the tensions and differences below the surface. The best way to prevent conflicts spilling into violence is to address minority grievances during periods of relative tranquillity.

What broad strategy options are available, and what light does the Northern Ireland experience throw on them? If one assumes that certain policy approaches to plural societies – genocide, apartheid, the removal of human rights – are morally unacceptable, governments faced with ethnic minorities have two broad strategic approaches available to them: policies of assimilation or policies of pluralism.

Policies of assimilation emphasise the integrity of the national unit and approach minority issues as individual rather than group problems. The background philosophy is that, if all are treated equally before the law and fairly in other respects, there is less need to recognise and protect the rights of particular groups. Underlying this approach for many of its advocates is the hope that fair government will diminish group differences in time, leading eventually to assimilation of different ethnic groups into a corporate citizenship. If cultural diversity is not fully respected, however, assimilation may amount to the establishment of a dominant culture, to which other groups are expected to conform. Examples of countries which have adopted broadly assimilative approaches, at least until the 1960s, are France and the USA.

Policies of pluralism emphasise the need to accept that some ethnic differences are unlikely to disappear and that separate groups should be given both parity of esteem and substantial control over their own affairs. In their most extreme form, pluralist approaches may recognise that ethnic and other differences between groups are so strong as to justify dividing the states into smaller states, as has happened between Belgium and the Netherlands, in the Indian sub-continent and, more recently, in Czechoslovakia and the former Yugoslavia. A less dramatic approach is to establish a decentralised federal state with relatively weak central structures, and with considerable powers devolved to the regions. Regional devolution has operated successfully in Switzerland for centuries, and more recently in the Basque region. It is more difficult in countries where ethnic groups do not live in geographically separate districts, but even there a form of what might be described as administrative devolution may be possible. This incorporates structures based on

ethnic, religious or other differences into the system of government, and devolves to each ethnic group considerable control
over its own resources. In the Netherlands and other consociational
democracies where religious or ethnic groups are demographically
mingled, for example, separate institutions – schools, universities,
trade unions, hospitals, political parties and even radio and television channels – are allowed to reflect these divisions.

Northern Ireland can show examples of both assimilative and
pluralist policies operating in parallel. Government policies have
been predominantly assimilative, at least until the 1980s. The
introduction of electoral reforms, the Fair Employment Act 1976
and the move to a centralised administration of housing set out
to protect individual rights before the law. There were also pluralist structures functioning alongside them: almost all children
attended predominantly Catholic or Protestant schools; certain
sports were almost exclusively played by one or other community; organisations like the Orange Order, the Apprentice Boys of
Derry and the Ancient Order of Hibernians catered exclusively
for one tradition; the Irish language, music and folklore were
largely, but not exclusively, the province of Catholics. The recent
encouragement of cultural diversity through the establishment
of integrated and Irish-language schools alongside the existing
segregated system, and increased encouragement of cultural
diversity, represent a further shift towards pluralism. Not that
this shift is without its dangers. Pluralism can be used to support
separatism, and the need to protect cultural identity has been
cited as a defence of paramilitary violence. Cultural diversity
only improves matters if it incorporates tolerance towards different traditions, and aims to move from tolerance to acceptance.

There is still some distance to travel, in both directions. The
clashes in 1996 and 1997 between the Orange Order's right to
march through nationalist areas and the determination of the
residents to prevent them will be repeated until both parties can
negotiate an agreed approach to the issue. They were caused by
hope of change and fear of change. Debate among demographers
about the current and likely future balance between Catholics
and Protestants in Northern Ireland is complicated by a number
of uncertain factors: the declining Catholic birth rate; the growth

151

in Protestant migration from Northern Ireland; the ambivalence in both communities on the constitutional debate. But one factor is incontestable. Whether Catholics or Protestants form a majority in 50 years' time, neither will be sufficiently large to enforce effective dominance over the other. The mixture of assimilative and pluralist policies described above reflects the confused mixture of emotions and identities experienced by many people in Northern Ireland. The mix will, and should, constantly alter to follow the barometer of changing community attitudes. If they improve, the segregated elements may be relaxed. If tensions grow, people may take comfort from their separate institutions and culture.

A similarly flexible approach might also apply in other divided societies. Although assimilative and pluralist policies represent intellectually different philosophies, there are good arguments against moving too hastily towards formal separation. In plural societies where ethnic groups do not live in geographically distinct territories, careless moves towards partition or regional devolution may cause apprehensions and encourage mass population movements. Some states which introduced administrative devolution have found that it is easier to construct separate structures than to dismantle them. The Protestant and Catholic churches in the Netherlands, for example, became the essential props on which the state depended, a role it was difficult to alter when church membership declined in the 1970s. There is also a danger in responding too rapidly to the first signs of disagreement and institutionalising divisions on the basis of short-term changes. Consequently it often makes sense to maintain elements of both assimilative and pluralist policies in divided societies, even if they occasionally sit uneasily beside each other. In dealing with pluralism, pragmatism is always preferable to dogma.

Secession or accommodation?

The demand to secede from an existing state is the most radical possible constitutional expression of ethnic difference. It indicates that a dissident group within the state has no confidence that its aspirations can be met within existing boundaries and has determined to create its own state. The attractiveness of this alternative, especially for long-standing colonial or nationalist conflicts, is demonstrated by the rise in member states of the UN from 72 at its foundation to 186 in 1997. But the experience of secession, most notably in the former Yugoslavia, has not always been successful.

Northern Ireland was the product of a botched attempt at secession. The desire of the majority in Ireland at the start of the twentieth century to separate from Britain and establish independence was frustrated by a concentrated minority in the northern part of the island. The island was partitioned in 1921. Since then, this minority, converted into a majority within Northern Ireland, has itself been frustrated by a substantial minority within the new jurisdiction. Ireland does not provide a convincing exemplar for secession.

Further experiments in applying the principle of self-determination are unlikely to be any more successful. The Catholic minority is not territorially compact, but dispersed in pockets throughout Northern Ireland. Re-partition would require large population transfers, including substantial districts of Belfast and the eastern part of the province. Further, there is no popular desire for re-partition, nor any political will for it in Britain or Ireland. More importantly, there is no likelihood that re-partition would remedy the present political or constitutional problems, or improve the prospects for the minorities abandoned on the wrong side of the newly constructed frontier.

The alternative way forward is through agreed arrangements which accept the likely continuation of Northern Ireland as an entity in the immediate future. This has external and internal implications. Externally any settlement must pay proper regard to Britain's historical attachment to and responsibility for the unionist population, and show a similar respect for the Irish Republic's historical attachment to and responsibility for nationalists. Within the region of Northern Ireland the rights of both communities must be accorded equal weight.

The two governments have already moved substantially towards a common acceptance of each other's role through the signing of the 1985 Anglo-Irish Agreement. This acceptance has been strengthened since 1985 through closer administrative coop-eration, the 1993 Downing Street Declaration and the joint publi-cation of the *Frameworks for the Future* document in 1995. This is not to claim that there are no differences of interest, but that these have diminished and are unlikely to frustrate a settlement. The final obstacles to settling the conflict will come from inside North-ern Ireland, not from Britain or Ireland.

Many ethnic conflicts, especially those based on ethno-national-ist differences, are strongly influenced by forces operating outside the main area of violence. They may have both a positive and a negative effect on the conflict itself. International sanctions on South Africa and Serbia were a major influence in pushing for a set-tlement. Diaspora populations have supported protagonists, not only in Northern Ireland, but in Sri Lanka, the Baltic countries, the Middle East, Armenia and many other conflicts. It may be difficult to make the argument convincing to Greek and Turkish Cypriots, or to the Kashmiris, but the experience of Northern Ireland demon-strates that, if the external powers interested in the outcome of the conflict can reach agreement, they can apply pressure and provide openings for internal negotiations.

Understanding conflict: preventing violence

There has been an increase of international interest in ethnic vio-lence, and in how it might be prevented from starting in the first place. The then Secretary General of the UN, Dr Boutros Boutros-Ghali, pointed out the obvious consequence in 1993: 'It is in fact easier, and cheaper, to prevent war than to end a war once it has started. This preventative capacity is based largely on research and access to information that can help us anticipate events more effectively.'[3]

Much of the current activity has latched on to early warning – the compilation of data which might facilitate the identification of endangered societies or regions – and work by Singer, Gurr, Harff and others has greatly refined the comparative analysis of interna-tional trends.[4] It is important to monitor patterns of violence, but prevention only starts at that point. In addition to providing early warning, there is an urgent need to know more about early response – what military, humanitarian and other relief capabilities are available regionally and locally to respond to violence? What economic, social, legal and educational policies most effectively encourage a more fair and equitable pluralism? Can diplomacy be improved to prevent disputes escalating into violence?

Comparative studies of functioning plural societies may help to answer these questions. General comparisons, however, have only limited value. It is pointless to seek direct comparisons between Northern Ireland and the new racism in European cities; between either of those and the problems of indigenous people in Australia or Latin America; and between any of these three and violence in the Balkans. And where are the comparisons to be found for inner-city conflict in the USA?

Comparative analyses of ethnic conflict are likely to become more necessary if ethnic violence continues to spill across national frontiers and challenge regional stability. But unless the comparisons are carefully chosen, the outcome will not increase our understanding of ethnicity and how it sometimes becomes dysfunctional. The need is to disaggregate the apparently universal phenomenon of ethnicity, and find more narrow and more closely comparable cases with common characteristics. This requires not only an agenda to approach ethnic conflict or conflict resolution, but a series of agendas. There is need for a process which will identify comparable groups of conflicts. These might include:

Conflicts with shared regional characteristics

Ethnic conflicts within the same geographical regions, while individual and distinct, may share characteristics which distinguish them from other regions. These regions include Latin America (although this may be too large a geographical area and require further sub-division), South Asia, the Balkans and the Islamic republics which had previously been part of the Soviet Union.

Elements of conflict grouped around common problems

It makes a great deal of sense to isolate particular themes within ethnic conflict, and to approach these comparatively: the prob-

lems of indigenous peoples; the protection of linguistic and religious minorities; how political mediation has been conducted;
the governance of divided cities; the reduction of discrimination;
the role of education in encouraging mutual understanding. It is
equally important to address the common problems affecting
particular interests and groups in society – peace-keepers, police,
judges, politicians. These more targeted comparisons are more
likely to identify groups of cases which speak more closely to
each others' needs.

Conflicts located within a continuum of violence

Reference has already been made to the need to focus research
activity within different phases of a cycle of ethnic conflict,
including the successful management of conflict in such plural
societies as Switzerland or the Netherlands. The point is that we
need to understand better the dynamics of conflict and violence,
and to find policy approaches appropriate to each stage.

The sheer variety and complexity of ethnic violence at times
may overwhelm those dealing with its consequences. The isola-
tion of realisable objectives is essential, not least to preserve sani-
ty. Most of all is the need to resist the temptation to despair, to
believe that a situation cannot be improved, to fear that, as Rose
wrote about Northern Ireland, there is no solution. The last word
rests with Erskine Childers and Brian Urquhart: 'The scale of the
phenomenon [the eruption of violent conflict calls for highly
sensitive international machinery. Such machinery is needed in
the first place to foster creative dialogue about increasingly common problems; to make it respectable to search for solutions.'[5]

9

FINDING OUT MORE ABOUT NORTHERN IRELAND

There has never been a shortage of myths about the Irish conflict, and the renewed demand for information since 1969 has added to the total. Some of them are based on an element of truth. During the early 1970s, for example, the evening cluster of visiting reporters in the bar of the Europa Hotel in Belfast did lend some support to the popular view that its bar provided a more frequent source of news stories than the dangerous streets outside.

The research scene has changed considerably since those early days. It is difficult to imagine an ethnic conflict anywhere in the world which has been more thoroughly researched. Basic data have become more readily available to researchers. A body of theory, as distinct from polemic, has emerged. More subjectively, the depth of scholarship has also improved. The province's academic institutions have become more concerned with the problems, and better equipped to tackle them. A much greater level of sophistication in the presentation and synthesis of data – notably illustrated in work by Ó'Maoláin (1993) and Flackes and Elliott (1988 and 1995) – has made the information more accessible. The most far-reaching change has been the shift during the 1990s towards the provision of electronic sources of information.

The growth of interest both inside Northern Ireland and elsewhere is reflected in a variety of associations, centres, study groups and other forms of research collaboration. At every level, from undergraduate dissertation to major research project, a more serious approach to the conflict has been adopted.

At all these levels remains the problem of where a research study might be started. This chapter will review the information available to those seriously interested in the Northern Ireland conflict – undergraduates, postgraduates, journalists, established academics and policy-makers. The aim is to suggest possible starting points for inquiry, and to identify signposts and references to sources of information.

Basic references: bibliographies, chronologies and registers

The preliminary information required by social scientists varies little between different settings. What research is being carried out, and by whom? Has it been published, and when? Is it possible to establish reliably when particular events took place? Until the early 1970s these questions could not be answered without considerable inconvenience. However, as the amount of social research increased, so did the research tools required to carry it out.

An invaluable starting point for background research is Flackes and Elliott (1988 and 1995). It contains a reliable chronology and a dictionary of politics, politicians and election results, as well as useful essays on systems of government and the security system; its list of abbreviations is indispensable for those unfamiliar with Northern Ireland. Mansbach (1973) covers events during the previous half century. Many books have selective chronologies, and time acts as a judicious editor. Brennan and Deutsch (1993) and Bew and Gillespie (1993) have written two chronologies covering most of the duration of the Troubles, with useful indices and appendices. For subsequent events the *Irish Times* publishes a useful summary at the turn of each year, and its Saturday edition includes a review of the week's main events.

Three registers of research into the Irish conflict have been published since the current violence began in 1968–9.[1] These provide snapshots of the state of research in 1972, 1981 and 1993, and together they are a useful research tool for a longitudinal comparison of the patterns of conflict research over the period of violence. The number of projects detected in the three registers, for example, were respectively 175, 517 and 605. Each research project in the 1993 register, excellently edited by Ó'Maoláin, has up to ten keywords and an extensive cross-referencing 'keyword' index. An update of the Register, funded by the CCRU, has been agreed for 1997. The Economic and Social Research Institute in Dublin also produces, on an irregular basis, a register of the social and economic research being conducted within Irish institutions, but does not include research conducted overseas; the most recent edition appeared in 1994. A similar geographical limitation applies to the *Current Research in Britain* series.[2]

Research registers are primarily concerned with the present and the future, and are designed to inform researchers about other scholars working in similar fields. To find out what books, pamphlets, articles and ephemera have been printed in the past, one must go to the numerous bibliographies on the conflict. These are necessarily parasitic publications, each one absorbing its predecessors, so some earlier bibliographies now have only limited value. The most comprehensive bibliography within the social sciences (Rolston *et al.* 1983) covers publications relating to Northern Ireland published between 1945 and 1983, and its 5,000 items can be searched through the Conflict Archive on the Internet (CAIN) web pages (see page 167). An update is badly needed, although CAIN has recently completed a bibliography on 2,000 items mainly relating to the Northern Ireland conflict. The catalogues of the Linen Hall Library (available for sale from the Linen Hall), the Irish collections of Northern Ireland's Education and Library Boards, and the two universities are all good bibliographical starting points, and the Community Relations Council has a reference library with around 1,600 titles, to which it has a bibliographic listing. Postgraduate theses on conflict-related themes are normally available in the libraries of both Northern Ireland universities. Undergraduate dissertations are more difficult to track down, and require visits to individual departments; this is occasionally worth the journey.

Official statistics and publications

The quality of official publications, and the scope of official statistics, has improved enormously since the 1980s. *The Ulster Year Book* includes a general description of broad social and economic trends, but most of Northern Ireland's official statistics are produced by the Northern Ireland Statistics and Research Agency (NISRA). NISRA's responsibilities include the conduct of the Census of Population and the registration functions of the General Register Office, and it provides and manages professional statistical staff working in the various departments of government and some non-governmental bodies. Up-to-date information on NISRA is available on the Internet (http://www.nics.gov.uk/nisra/).

The Guide to Northern Ireland Statistics gives the best overview of NISRA publications, and includes information on the frequency, price and source of over 100 statistical publications. It also provides details of UK and European publications containing information on Northern Ireland. An update of the *Guide* is available for 1994 and another planned for 1997. NISRA produces *Focus on Northern Ireland*, in conjunction with the UK Office for National Statistics, as part of a series providing statistical portraits of each UK region.

NISRA's *Northern Ireland Annual Abstract of Statistics* (AAS), which has been published since the early 1980s, presents statistical data on a wide range of demographic, social, legal, economic and financial features relating to Northern Ireland, and is indispensable for serious researchers; ten-year runs are given for most of the statistical series. The AAS also contains a useful 'Contacts Points' section which details the main suppliers of official statistics in Northern Ireland. This section includes details of the burgeoning list of statistical publications produced by various government departments and statistical branches. Many government departments now issue their own publications. The Department of Education, for example, issues a *Basic Education Statistics Data Card* and an *Annual School Census* and now has a Statistics and Research Branch which has produced a *Statistical Bulletin on the Transfer Procedure Results* (1996), and *Free School Meals* and *Low Achievement* (1996). It also publishes a Research Series, mainly on research commissioned by the Department. The monthly analysis of unemployment statistics produced by the Department of Manpower Services also has interest for social scientists. The most research-relevant publications of the Department of Health and Social Services (DHSS) are *Social Security Statistics* and *Personal Social Statistics*. NISRA itself conducts and commissions social research and publishes the NISRA Occasional Paper series. The CCRU has funded approximately 80 research projects on community relations and conflict, and will supply details on request.

There has been a recent trend to include Northern Ireland in a number of British and European surveys. *Regional Trends*, produced by the UK Office for National Statistics, gives a wide range of comparable statistics for Northern Ireland and other UK regions; it also contains a European chapter with a limited number of statistics for all EU regions, including Northern Ireland. The Statistical Office of the European Union (Eurostat) maintains a database (Regio) of regional information, biased heavily towards demography and agriculture, and proposals are being considered to market it commercially. Within the United Kingdom, the longest running public sector sample survey is the *Family Expenditure Survey* (FES), for which results have been available annually since 1967. The *Continuous Household Survey* (CHS), which commenced in 1983, allows comparisons with *Britain's General Household Survey*. NISRA publishes its own monitor series on both the CHS and an enhanced sample of the FES, and the raw data are available in the Economic and Social Research Council (ESRC) archive at the University of Essex. NISRA also publishes annual reports on the religious composition of the *Labour Force Survey* (LFS). The LFS is the main survey for internationally comparable labour market statistics throughout the EU, and is conducted in all EU states. Northern Ireland features as part of the UK, but benefits from an enhanced sample.

The largest social survey is the *Northern Ireland Census of Population*, published after each Northern Ireland census since 1926; statistics for the area of Northern Ireland are available from earlier censuses since 1821. The Census Office has published a series of topic reports, including one on religion, from the 1991 census. The Registrar-General, at his discretion, will consider requests for unpublished and small-area statistics.

Annual reports from a number of public bodies contain material relevant to the conflict. Particularly useful for researchers into the conflict are those produced by: the Chief Constable of the RUC, whose reports present terrorist-related and 'normal' crime by region; the Independent Commission for Police Complaints; the NIHE, which also publishes *Northern Ireland Housing Statistics*; the Northern Ireland Commissioner for Complaints; the Northern Ireland Economic Council; the Community Relations Council; the Equal Opportunities Commission; the Consumer Council for Northern Ireland; and the Standing Commission on Human Rights, which now has the responsibility of reviewing the Fair Employment Act 1989.

For those interested in employment and unemployment patterns the reports of the Fair Employment Commission (previously the FEA) are essential reading. Over the years its analyses of Northern Ireland's workforce by religion and its investigations of the employment practices of specific companies – taken together with the work of the FETs, which judged alleged cases of individual discrimination – amount to an extraordinary body of information on a society undergoing change.

The media

Newspapers and periodicals are the starting point for most social research, and for some the complete race. It is appropriate, therefore, to consider the value of the media for researchers. To some extent this depends upon whether they are interested in the events reported in the newspapers, or in the way the media report them. Those wishing to look at the coverage of the violence by Northern Ireland's three daily newspapers will find a terrain which has been largely uncharted, but two studies by Curtis (1984) and Rolston (1991) are critical of general media coverage, and Darby (1983) has examined different perspectives on the Troubles through the work of political cartoonists. An entertaining and illuminating way to trace the evolution of the conflict is through the cartoons of Ireland's leading cartoonist, Martyn Turner, which have been published in a succession of books.[3]

The use of magazines and newspapers as a source of information on events in Northern Ireland since 1969 is complicated by their variety. *Fortnight*, produced regularly in Belfast since 1970, continues to provide the most thoughtful chronicle and analysis of events.[4] Within the province, the *Belfast Telegraph* has the largest daily readership and, as the only evening newspaper, attracts both Catholic and Protestant readers. In 1994 the readers of the other two local daily newspapers, the *Irish News* and the *Newsletter*, were respectively 87 per cent Catholic and 80 per cent Protestant. The *Belfast Telegraph* has now set up an Internet page which is updated on a daily basis and includes news, business and sporting stories. So have the *Irish News*, the *Irish Times* and *An Phoblacht*. All can be accessed through John Coakley's Guide to Irish Politics Resources (http://www.ucd.ie/~politics/irpols.html). In recent years the Dublin-based *Irish Independent* has developed a keener interest in the North, and the *Irish Times* has consistently devoted much space to events in Northern Ireland. It is the most reliable newspaper of record on Northern Ireland, publishing every major document and speech relating to the Northern Ireland situation. Local newspapers – those serving every small community in Northern Ireland – continue to be under-used. British media coverage has been very inconsistent: the interest of the popular press declined as the violence became repetitious, leaving the field to more serious newspapers. The *Observer* and *Times* have taken a close interest in the issue, and the *Sunday Times* has conducted useful, if occasionally flashy, investigations. The most consistent and reliable British coverage is currently supplied by the London *Independent*.

A still under-used, and very valuable, source of information are the underground and political newspapers which flourished especially in the early 1970s. These were produced by a wide variety of loyalist, republican, socialist and community organisations in an almost equally wide variety of formats. Some lasted only for a few issues; others have been published regularly for decades. A few transmogrified with bewildering rapidity, closing down to re-emerge under another name and format. Tracks through this complicated minefield were charted in a catalogue of Northern Ireland Newspapers 1737–1979 published by the Northern Ireland branch of the Library Association.[5] Consultation of the newspaper holdings in the Linen Hall and Central libraries is necessary for more recent changes.

The mutations which most Northern Irish political parties have undergone since 1969 are reflected most clearly in the information which they produce about themselves. Four of the five main Northern Ireland parties – the UUP, the DUP, the SDLP and the Alliance Party – no longer produce a regular newspaper, preferring in some cases to concentrate on electronic means of communication. A few peripheral publications are still printed: the Young Unionists produce *Ulster Review*, on an approximately quarterly basis; the *Protestant Telegraph* divides its text roughly evenly between the religious concerns of the Free Presbyterian Church and the DUP; *Alliance News* appears on a monthly basis. But the largest political newspaper is *An Phoblacht*, produced weekly by Sinn Féin and circulated widely outside Northern Ireland. All the parties produce other literature, especially during election campaigns. More to the point, it is now at least theoretically possible to contact most party offices by telephone, fax and through the Internet, a vast improvement since 1969.

It is not possible to consult all these newspapers and periodicals under a single roof. Belfast's Central Library has a good selection, and a small number of libraries also have partial collections of political newspapers. Nowhere in Northern Ireland is it possible to examine the back files of British popular newspapers, even in the Belfast offices of these newspapers; for this thankless task it is necessary to visit the British Library newspaper archives at Colindale in London. More recently, however, two important databases of newspaper cuttings relating to the Northern Ireland conflict have become available: the Northern Ireland Office (NIO) Press Cuttings, donated to the Linen Hall Library by the NIO, contains almost 1,700 files covering the period 1969–89; and the Community Relations Council has a database of cuttings on community relations/conflict issues covering the period 1992–5. Also available are microfilm copies of, among others, the *Irish Times, Belfast Newsletter, Guardian, Sunday Times, Observer* and *London Times*. Most important, the Linen Hall Library has produced *Northern Ireland Political Literature* on microfiche, which contains copies from the republican, loyalist and socialist presses, and community newspapers, for the years 1966–89. These include some of the most extreme political expressions to be found in any newspapers, and are a valuable research tool.

Some of the audio-visual materials circulating since the early 1970s are equally partisan. Propaganda films aimed at public opinion in Europe and North America have been produced both by the Provisional IRA and by the British government. Television and radio, however, constitute the great bulk of material. It is not easy to secure access to programmes wholly or primarily devoted to Northern Ireland, although earlier research suggests that the quantity is huge.[6] BBC news bulletins on national television, which include items on Northern Ireland, may be consulted in the British Film Archive in London, but programmes produced in Northern Ireland are not automatically available to researchers. Nevertheless, exceptions have been made in the past. Apart from these sources, the History Film and Sound Archive at the University of Ulster in Coleraine includes some valuable sound and visual records, and the Linen Hall Library has more than 320 videos.

Archives and collections of materials

Belinda Loftus has completed a most comprehensive description of archives relating to the Troubles, which will be published by the Linen Hall Library. It also considers a number of related archival problems, including storage, copyright, the holding of allegedly illegal material, user access and the impact of information technology, as well as the importance of collecting ephemeral material. Pamphlets, broadsheets, campaign buttons, posters, graffiti, songs and poetry – these are the ephemera of unrest. They share the qualities of being essential for anyone interested in political and social attitudes, and extraordinarily elusive. By their very nature ephemeral materials are intended to have an immediate impact, and have a short life. Retrospective collection is notoriously difficult, so there is a particular debt to those institutions which had sufficient prescience to build up contemporary collections.

By far the most important of these is the Linen Hall Library, which has been operating in some form since 1788. Its collection on the Irish Troubles dates back to 1966 and contains more than 7,500 books, pamphlets, manifestos, reports and political ephemera. Many of the historical items were themselves the ephemera of earlier periods of violence. It was natural, therefore, for the Linen Hall to begin a new Political Collection during the civil rights campaigns of the mid-1960s. It already contains the evidence presented to a number of public inquiries, including the Widgery Tribunal and the Opsahl Commission. The real strength naturally lies in its Northern Ireland ephemera, which includes 4,000 posters, although southern material is also well represented. The Linen Hall also keeps 1,700 periodicals, and more than 400 works of fiction with conflict-related themes.

The Central Library in Belfast started its ephemeral collection in 1977, relying on purchasing existing materials, and is particularly strong on papers relating to the civil rights campaigns of the 1960s. In the Irish Republic the largest archive is housed in Trinity College Dublin which, as a copyright deposit library, includes much of the relevant material printed in Britain. Its holdings of Dublin-produced ephemera are also good, although its collection of materials produced north of the border is less comprehensive. The National Library in Dublin also holds some relevant publications.

Computer-based information

The mid-1990s have witnessed a remarkable increase in conflict-related data available on the Internet. Since 1993 INCORE, located in Derry, has set up a Conflict Data Server on the Internet (http://www.incore.ulst.ac.uk). This service provides a growing number of country studies which include conflict-related data on each country, a guide to the Internet for social scientists and links to other services in conflict resolution and ethnicity on the Internet. Closely associated with the INCORE Conflict Data Server is the CAIN project, which is developing a data-based case study of the Northern Ireland conflict. It is aiming to provide direct access to a selection of materials for those engaged in research and teaching in conflict studies. CAIN is a collaboration between the University of Ulster, Queen's University,

Belfast and the Linen Hall library. The World Wide Web is also the principal delivery mechanism for CAIN (http://cain.ulst.ac.uk/).[7]

While the INCORE Conflict Data Server and the CAIN Project Data Server are likely to be the dominant Northern Ireland-based facility on the Internet, they are not the only available facilities for researchers interested in Northern Ireland. John Coakley's Guide to Irish Politics Resources on the Internet (http://www.ucd.ie/~politics/irpols.html) is an excellent intro-duction to a broad range of web sites – academic links, basic information and documents, official agencies, political organisa-tions, current affairs – relating to both parts of Ireland. The Law Faculty at Queen's University, Belfast, is compiling a computer-based collection of emergency legislation in a variety of countries. As mentioned, most of Northern Ireland's political parties now present their own materials on the Internet.

Subjects and issues

The registers of research mentioned earlier confirm the breadth of interest in the Irish conflict. Virtually no academic discipline has been unaffected. While the humanities and the social sci-ences dominate the interest of scholars, the compiler of the most recent research register, like his predecessors, found it impossible to disentangle purely conflict-related themes from broader interests and included among his categories 'agricul-ture' and 'health and welfare'.[8] This section acknowledges the inter-relationship between society in general and conflict issues, but aims to provide a brief introduction to some of those subjects and issues which have attracted greatest interest for researchers. Other popular themes which have been com-prehensively covered elsewhere, notably education,[9] are not considered here.

History

For the Irish, according to A.T.Q. Stewart, 'all history is applied history',[10] unconsciously underlining the importance of its study for social scientists. The marked increase in the number of general histories since the 1960s, however, has not made it any easier to prepare a selective bibliography for the general reader. The specialist, on the other hand, has a number of historiographies as convenient starting points, for example, Lee (1981) and Moody (1971). An annual bibliography called *Writings on Irish History*, previously printed in *Irish Historical Studies*, is available on microfiche by the Irish Committee of Historical Sciences.

Any advice for the general reader is inevitably more subjective. General histories by Lyons (1971), Foster (1988) and Lee (1989) have become standard references, and the Gill series on Irish history maintains a reliable standard. The picture is complicated by the growth of revisionist interpretations, usually challenging what the revisionists regard as a nationalist interpretation which dominated Irish historiography until the 1960s, and a counter-revisionist tendency in more recent years. The dispute came to a head in 1995–6 in publications associated with the 150th anniversary of the Irish famine. Brady (1994) has assembled a collection of the main articles, down through the years, which relate to the revisionism debate, and Boyce and O'Day (1996) edited a series of commissioned papers summarising the debate as it relates to different periods of history. On the more detailed history of Northern Ireland, a wide range of interpretations available are: Buckland (1979 and 1981), Stewart (1977), Harkness (1983) and Wichert (1991) who adopt traditional forms of historical analysis. Bardon (1992) is likely to remain the standard text for a generation.

Access to primary data is obviously more difficult for the historian. Depending on the subject under study, a visit to the Public Record Offices in Belfast or Dublin will almost certainly be necessary. Under the Public Record (Ireland) Act 1867, the holdings in many Irish repositories were centralised in Dublin, and annual reports were printed between 1869 and 1921. On 30 June 1922 the main record repository in the Four Courts building was destroyed by bomb and fire as the Irish civil war began. Fortunately indexes and catalogues were saved, and many records have subsequently been copied and are now available for consultation in Dublin.

The Public Record Office of Northern Ireland (PRONI) was set up in 1924, and attempted to replace some of the materials relating to Northern Ireland which had been destroyed in the fire. For many

years PRONI's most valuable holdings were the private collections which it obtained through purchase or donation. Since the
1970s, however, records of many of the old local authorities
have been deposited, and the Office has become responsible for
the records of the Northern Ireland government, which were
previously unavailable. Access to the latter is restricted to files
which are more than 30 years old, although some earlier government material is also withheld from public scrutiny. In some
cases this amounts to a serious obstruction to research. PRONI is
generally well regarded by researchers, and has excellent facilities
and staff in Belfast. Information about it is available on the
Internet (http://www.nics.gov.uk/pubsec/proni/prguide.htm).

Politics and religion

Flackes and Elliott (1988 and 1995) is the best starting point for
information about Northern Ireland's political parties and per-
sonalities. In recent years, however, the parties, especially Sinn
Féin, the PUP and the UDP – the republican and loyalist parties –
have become more open to direct approaches by researchers. It is
more difficult to chart a route through the secondary analyses.
Arthur and Jeffery (1996) is a good general introduction to politics in Northern Ireland; and Whyte (1990) is a critical analysis
of nationalist, unionist, Marxist and internal-conflict interpretations of the conflict, thus forming an excellent springboard for
further study. O'Malley (1983) deserves particular attention as it
is based on interviews with an interesting political cross-section.

   Among the many reviews of political options for resolving the
political paradox the most notable are: Rose (1976), with the
often quoted conclusion – 'the problem is that there is no solution'; Hadden and Boyle (1994), following the build-up to the
Downing Street Agreement with their proposed approach;
Townshend (1988) and Hadfield (1993), in which a range of
approaches are explored; and O'Leary and McGarry (1993), who
argue for a form of shared authority involving Northern Ireland,
Ireland and Britain.

   Clearly the churches also have an interest in the conflict
and, according to some analyses, a level of responsibility for it.

Violence in Ireland was written by a joint group on social questions, which was appointed by the Catholic hierarchy and the Irish Council of Churches in an attempt to find a cross-confessional approach to community violence. Apart from this, the Catholic Church has been responsible for very few publications, though some papers, especially on peace education, have been issued by the Irish Council of Churches. Gallagher and Worrall (1982) is still a reliable guide to publications by the main churches. Morrow (1991) is a substantial study of the relationship between the main churches and the conflict; McElroy (1991) deals with the Catholic Church and the Northern Ireland crisis.

Public policy

A strong case can be made that the immediate trigger for the Troubles was the failure of the Stormont regime to deliver fair allocation of public resources – housing, jobs and other public services. Since then public policy has been under constant scrutiny and, at least since the 1980s, the data upon which policy can be scrutinised have become more available. The scrutiny has been conducted by individuals, academic institutions and pressure groups. Hillyard (1983), for example, argues that the security policies and practices introduced in Northern Ireland were trial runs for their broader application in Britain. The CAJ is an important watchdog on Northern Ireland's legal administration and practices, and have been constantly critical of what they see as an over-readiness by government to resort to emergency laws and procedures. Dickson (1993) offers a measured review of these procedures.

The *Majority Minority Reviews*, produced by Gallagher (1989 and 1991) and Melaugh (1994) for the Centre for the Study of Conflict at the University of Ulster at Coleraine provide non-partisan reviews of the research evidence on education, employment and unemployment and housing. The Centre for Social Research at Queen's University, Belfast, has a particular interest in social attitudes, and is closely linked with the analyses emerging from the *Social Attitudes* Surveys, described in the next section.

The relationship between the Northern Ireland economy and the conflict is under-researched, apart from the Research Monograph and Occasional Papers of the Northern Ireland Economic Council, which include useful material on the economic consequences of the ceasefires. The need for non-partisan economic research is all the more regrettable because the most controversial and bitter disputes on public policy have been in the field of fair employment. The disputes about the reasons for higher unemployment rates for Catholics, particularly Catholic males, have occasionally taken on an ideological tinge. Gallagher (1991) provides an excellent review of the arguments and positions. Gudgin and Breen (1996) is also valuable because it includes comments by Murphy and Rowthorn, as well as a rejoinder to these comments by the authors. The production in 1996 of three reports on fair employment, dealing respectively with the law, policy aspects and public views and experiences, by the Standing Advisory Commission on Human Rights comprehensively covers the current law and practice; they were published under the general title *Employment Equality in Northern Ireland* (Magill and Rose; McLaughlin and Quirk; McVey and Hutson). Those wishing to follow the debate in greater detail should look to the various publications by Cormack, Gallagher and Osborne (1993), Compton (1995) and Smith and Chambers (1991).

Human rights

The concern among human rights academics and activists about Northern Ireland is easy to understand. Since its creation in 1921, the province has never really enjoyed a period when normal legal procedures were not in suspension. Extraordinary legislation had been authorised by the Special Powers Act since 1922, until it was replaced by new Emergency Provisions legislation in 1973. Hillyard (1983 and 1993) and others argue that emergency laws have become normalised in Northern Ireland, and are also abused in Britain.

Others have been campaigning for human rights reforms from within Northern Ireland. Foremost among these is the CAJ, which has monitored the administration of justice – including employment equality, emergency laws, human rights and the behaviour of the security forces – since 1971. The best guide to civil liberties in Northern Ireland was edited by Brice Dickson for the CAJ in 1990, and was updated in 1993. Abuses of civil liberties in Northern Ireland have also been documented in Jennings (1990).

A number of international organisations have reported unfavourably on the existence and operation of emergency laws and procedures in Northern Ireland. Internally the annual reports of the Standing Advisory Commission on Human Rights, a statutory body set up in 1973, chronicle concerns about police complaints procedures, the removal of the legal 'right to silence', the broadcasting ban on Sinn Féin and other alleged government curtailments of human rights. The interrogation approaches of the British army in the 1970s was the subject of severe criticism in reports and submissions by Amnesty International (1973 and 1977), the European Commission of Human Rights (1976) and the Association of Forensic Medical Officers (1977), which led to some of them being changed or dropped. The European Commission has also reported on the British government's use of plastic bullets (1984), on seven-day detention (1988) and on the Prevention of Terrorism Act (1988). The involvement of the European Court introduced an additional tier of justice beyond the House of Lords, and it has been used increasingly to challenge human rights practices in Northern Ireland. Its judgments are available from Strasbourg.

Public opinion: elections and surveys

Northern Ireland sends elected representatives to the European parliament, Westminster, local councils and, spasmodically, to a succession of assemblies within Northern Ireland. It is potentially a psephologist's paradise, and the analyses of election results until the early 1980s are detailed elsewhere.[11] The most comprehensive data on more recent elections are on the Internet, where Nicholas Whyte runs an excellent site on Northern Ireland election results since 1970 (http://www.unite.net/customers/alliance/elfull.html).

By contrast public opinion surveys, general and particular, have been conducted with increasing frequency by academics, newspapers and consultancy firms. Harris (1972), a classic anthropological study, although researched in the 1950s and published in 1972, provides insights into social intercourse in Northern Ireland which are simply not susceptible to quantitative surveys, the approach adopted in most studies. It is often difficult to secure access to the raw data from academic and private public opinion surveys, or even to their published results. In only a few cases have findings been published in sufficient detail to allow a proper assessment of methodology, or permit replication. Of these the most important is Rose's 1969 survey, which has also been the basis for follow-up research by Moxon-Browne and others.[12] A similarly unsatisfactory situation applies to the surveys and polls which have been conducted for the *Belfast Telegraph*, *Fortnight* and consultancy firms.

There is no central depository for such data in Northern Ireland. The ESRC archive at the University of Essex contains survey materials which relate to Northern Ireland, notably the regular *Northern Ireland Social Attitudes* data, which are freely available to researchers. Less systematic, but a fascinating insight into a wide range of popular views, was the Opsahl Report[13] which presented 554 written and taped submissions to a citizens' inquiry into the ways forward for Northern Ireland. For more orthodox surveys of public opinion one must turn to the official *Community Attitudes Survey*, a continuous survey of public attitudes and views on crime, law and order and policing published in the NISRA Occasional Paper series since 1992, and the *Social Attitudes Survey*, which has been analysed in books edited by Stringer and Robinson (1991, 1992 and 1993) and Breen, Devine and Robinson (1995) and Breen, Devine and Dowds (1996). However, the absence of a social attitudes archive for Northern Ireland, which would include both academic research data and the raw material from commercial surveys, continues to be an obstacle to research.

Quantifying the violence

The declaration of the 1994 IRA ceasefire, and its subsequent ending in 1996, has not diminished interest and analysis of patterns of violence. Indeed the level of violence since 1969 was undoubtedly the main reason for the subsequent avalanche of research and publications on Northern Ireland.

Most basic information on the violence itself comes from the RUC, Brewer and Magee (1991) providing a rare academic study of the culture of policing. The Chief Constable's Report, published annually since 1970, has an appendix on terrorist crimes, which records, among other statistics, the number of murders, explosions and security incidents. For a more detailed breakdown it is necessary to consult the security statistics which are issued each month by the RUC Press Office. Beyond these published data, the RUC Press Office occasionally provides additional facilities for what it describes as 'the serious academic researcher who is pursuing a reasonably "benign" thesis'.[14] The closeness of the 'information' and 'propaganda' roles implied in this quotation is inevitable during periods of violence, and is equally evident in the activities of the Army Information Office. Simon Hoggart from the *Guardian* was quick to point out the importance of this office as a source of information to the press: 'When the British press prints an account of an incident as if it were an established fact, and it is clear that the reporter himself is not on the spot, it is a 99 per cent certainty that it is the army's version that is being given.'[15]

No previous riots have lasted as long as the post-1969 violence, nor have been so carefully examined. The *Cameron Report* (1969) and the transcripts of the evidence taken by the Scarman Tribunal (1972) are available in the province's two university libraries. These reports, and the newspaper debates accompanying them, provide some basis for comparison with earlier riot reports, notably those into the 1857 and 1866 Belfast riots. The nineteenth-century reports include evidence on intimidation and enforced population movement, subjects which have been examined in closer detail during the more recent disturbances.[16] The effects of violence on Northern Ireland's social institutions – education, health and social welfare services, policing, housing and community action – was the subject of Darby and Williamson (1978), but follow-up research has been dispersed and irregular.

Paramilitary violence has never lacked interest among researchers. Bruce (1992) has greatly increased understanding of loyalist paramilitaries, who were unfashionable until the increase of loyalist violence in the early 1990s. The republicans, especially the IRA, have attracted much greater attention.[17] Townshend (1983) considered political violence within a broader historical tradition of violence in Ireland; the work has been underrated and deserves wider attention.

A major limitation in the official data is their lack of detail. Although the RUC statistics identify general categories of victims, for example, they do not discriminate between different groups of civilian casualties. The gap has been filled by academic commentators, notably Michael McKeown in the 1970s and Irish Information Partnership in the 1980s. An informative analysis of the patterns of violence, including breakdowns of both perpetrators and victims, was carried out by McGarry and O'Leary (1990). The most comprehensive analysis of Troubles-related deaths between 1969 and 1994 is that by Fay, Morrissey and Smyth (1997). The most meticulous detailing of individual deaths was published by Sutton (1994), with some hopes that it would be the definitive and final accounting. The renewal of the IRA campaign dashed that hope, but only time will determine if the analysis of Northern Ireland's violence will continue to exercise its previous grim interest.

Northern Ireland in a comparative setting

There has been an extensive, if fluctuating, interest in the Northern Ireland conflict from outside Ireland – educationalists interested in its segregated school system, churchmen in the apparently denominational basis of the conflict, students of violence and its effects, medical researchers examining the emergency procedures and surgical techniques in its hospitals. The earliest attempts to locate the Northern Ireland Troubles within a broader context of ethnic conflict were predominantly Marxist,[18] although Rose (1971) also examined parallels between Northern Ireland and southern USA.

More recently there has been a shift towards comparative analysis of ethnic conflicts and approaches to conflict resolution. Wright (1987) examined the Northern Ireland conflict from the perspectives of a number of other conflicts, notably Algeria. Darby, Dodge and Hepburn (1990) edited a collection of papers on political violence, including studies of France, Algeria and New Brunswick, looking at Northern Ireland from a comparative perspective. UNRISD has recently conducted two cross-national comparisons of positive and negative examples of conflict management,[19] and INCORE is currently researching peace processes in societies recently engaged in ethnic violence. The report, put together by Mary Albon for the Foundation for a Civil Society, on the 1995 conference on reconciliation and community, which included papers from South Africa, Latin America, the Middle East and Eastern Europe as well as Northern Ireland, is an interesting attempt to encourage cross-fertilisation between peace-makers in a number of ethnically divided societies. Northern Ireland features as a case-study in a number of books exploring the process and development of ethnic conflict.[20] The move towards comparative analysis is likely to continue, but may concentrate in the future on more specific details within the cycle of ethnic conflict and violence, including military studies of the control of terrorism.

Cultural studies

One of the most remarkable effects of the Troubles in Northern Ireland has been the cultural renaissance which accompanied it. This especially applies to literature, and to poetry in particular. Although the process predated the Troubles by a few years, local poets were caught between what Michael Longley described as charges of exploitation if they wrote about the Troubles and charges of evasion if they did not.[21] Frank Ormsby (1992) is an excellent anthology of what he describes as 'Troubles poetry', and includes work by Heaney, Hewitt, MacNeice, Mahon, Longley, Montague, Deane, Muldoon and dozens of others. This work follows an earlier anthology put together by Fiacc (1974). It is possible to follow the effect of the Troubles on the visual arts in Northern Ireland through Hewitt (1977) and Catto (1977), but the authoritative review of popular culture, especially popular music, has still to be written.

A number of magazines, notably *Fortnight* and the *Linen Hall Review*, publish and review developments in creative writing. The more recent interest in cultural pluralism and traditions is well reflected in the series of conference reports published by the Cultural Traditions Group.[22] The work of the Community Relations Council, of which the Cultural Traditions Group is now part, broadens the debate beyond the political; attention is drawn to its journal *Causeway* and to its publications, including Bryson and McCartney (1994), a rare consideration of the importance of symbols in a divided society. A more detailed study of the marches which annually raise tensions in Northern Ireland, and which test the limits of tolerance for the expression of cultural identity, is Jarman and Bryan (1996).

Conflict research centres in Ireland

Study of the Irish conflict has been greatly boosted by recent developments within Northern Ireland's two universities. The Centre for the Study of Conflict at the University of Ulster in Coleraine was formed in 1977, and became a formal part of the university's structure in 1980. Its activities include the publication of research papers, conferences and seminars. It also provides facilities for visiting researchers. The Urban Institute, also associated with the University of Ulster since 1995, has a particular interest in the problems of Belfast, which inevitably involves it with an orientation towards conflict.

The Centre for the Study of Conflict's increasing interest in comparative and collaborative research led in 1990 to the creation of the Ethnic Studies Network, which currently has more than 400 members, mainly scholars working on ethnic conflict in their own societies. This in turn, with the work of the Centre, formed the basis for the establishment of INCORE in 1993, now located close to the University of Ulster's Derry campus. INCORE is a joint project of the Tokyo-based United Nations University and the University of Ulster. Its special interests are the analysis, resolution and management of ethnic conflict, with particular attention to the concerns of the UN and the third world. INCORE's major functions are the conduct of research and the provision of training on ethnic conflict and conflict management. Its comparative approach locates the Northern Ireland conflict within the broader context of international ethnic conflict.

The Institute of Irish Studies at Queen's University, Belfast, has been in operation since 1970, and has a limited number of fellowships for visiting academics. Its interests include Irish literature, language, history and other branches of Irish studies, and the Federation for Ulster Local Studies is based there. Also located at Queen's, within the School of Social Sciences, is the Centre for Social Research. Its main research interests are social attitudes and social mobility in Northern Ireland, and it produced *Social Attitudes in Northern Ireland* annually until 1997. Few researchers who visit Northern Ireland fail to benefit from the Irish collection at the Linen Hall Library, to which reference has already been made.

The Irish Peace Institute Research Centre at the University of Limerick, instituted in 1994, is the only such centre in the Irish Republic. It works closely with the Centre for the Study of Conflict in Northern Ireland, and is also associated with the University of Ulster in presenting a Master's course in Peace and Conflict Studies. Its aim is to contribute to a lasting peace in Ireland. It has a particular, but not exclusive, interest in cross-border studies.

Centres outside Northern Ireland

British academic interest in Ireland has become more institutionalised since the formation of the British Association for Irish Studies. Most of the acknowledged centres of activity concerning the Northern Ireland conflict either have a local Irish community or have arisen from the work of individual researchers. The Institute of Irish Studies at Liverpool University, which publishes research reports and hosts conferences, has been influenced by both. The Irish Studies Centre at the University of North London has a particular interest in the Irish in Britain. The Department of Peace Studies at Bradford University has long had Irish connections, as has the Centre for the Study of Public Policy at the University of Strathclyde, while the recently formed Conference of Irish Historians Working in Britain meets biennially. The appointments of George Boyce (Swansea), Patrick Buckland (Liverpool), Marianne Elliott (Liverpool), Roy Foster (Oxford), Tony Hepburn (Sunderland), Brendan O'Leary (LSE) and Charles Townshend (Keele) to chairs on the basis of publications on Irish history or politics partly reflects the growing involvement of British universities in the study of Ireland. (All appointments current at the date of publication).

North American interest in Irish matters has a longer pedigree. The American Committee for Irish Studies (later the American Conference on Irish Studies) produces a regular newsheet for its members which contains book reviews, and has also published an important *Guide to Irish Studies in the United States* which has been irregularly updated. Its annual conference, which was held in Northern Ireland for the first time in 1995, jointly with the Canadian Association for Irish Studies, often includes papers on Northern Ireland, but really demonstrates that the predominant American interest in Ireland is literary or historical. *Eire-Ireland*, the quarterly publication of the Irish American Cultural Institute in New Jersey (formerly based in St Paul, Minnesota), also has a literary bias, but has published papers on Northern Ireland. A substantial and growing number of American colleges and universities, mainly on the east coast, have developed links with Irish universities, and some have built up collections of Irish materials. There is an interest in Ulster-Scots studies in the Carolinas, Stanford University in California holds a small collection of Irish materials and Notre Dame, Indiana, has had a long-standing interest in Ireland. However, there is no recognisable centre on the Northern Ireland conflict in North America, as there is on Basque issues in the University of Nevada.

Outside North America, most foreign research on Northern Ireland has come from Europe. The level of interest in Germany and the Netherlands was high in the early years of the Troubles, and three collections of documents were published in German between 1969 and 1976, and one in Dutch in 1984. In France, the Centre d'Etudes et de Recherches Irlandaises at the University of Lille is an important centre of study and, though its main focus is literary, there have been articles on the conflict in its journal *Etudes Irlandaises*. Other centres of interest are the universities of Rennes and Caen. The Centre d'Etudes Irlandaises, Paris, has become increasingly concerned with Northern Ireland, and publishes papers on this and related themes. Its director, Paul Brennan, has published a background book on the conflict geared to French students, as well as encouraging a substantial number of postgraduate studies in French universities. The Centre publishes the journal *L'Irlande, Politique et Sociale* from Paris, and deserves considerable credit for the revival of French academic interest in the Irish conflict during the 1990s. It was one of the prime movers in the establishment in 1995 of the European Federation of Centres of Irish Studies, whose institutional members come from Ireland, Britain, France, Germany and Portugal.

APPENDIX I

CHRONOLOGY

1914		Ulster Solemn League and Covenant to resist Home Rule signed.
1916		Easter rising in Dublin.
1919–21		Anglo-Irish war.
1921		Anglo-Irish treaty. First Norhtern Ireland (NI) parliament opens.
1922		Irish Free State established. Special Powers Act introduced in NI.
1932–8		Economic war between Britain and Irish Free State.
1937		New constitution for Irish Free State.
1939–45		IRA campaign in Britain.
1949		The Irish Free State becomes the Irish Republic Irish Republic leaves Commonwealth. The Ireland Act guarantees NI's position within the United Kingdom (UK).
1956		IRA campaign in NI starts.
1962		IRA campaign called off because of lack of support.
1965		Premiers of Northern and Southern governments (O'Neill and Lemass) meet at Stormont.
1966		Malvern Street murders by UVF.
1967		NICRA formed.
1968	August	Civil rights march to Dungannon.
	October	Civil rights march to Derry, despite government ban, followed by rioting.
	December	NICRA declares truce – no marches or demonstrations.
1969	January	PD march attacked by loyalists at Burntollet.
	12-14 August	Apprentice Boys' march in Derry attacked. Followed by rioting in Derry, Dungannon, Dungiven, Lurgan, Newry and Armagh. Four men and a boy killed in Belfast.
	August	Army called in to restore order.

	October	Hunt Report on police reform – RUC to be disarmed, 'B' Specials to be abolished and replaced by the UDR.
1970	January	IRA split – Provisional IRA formed.
	April	Alliance Party formed.
	July	British army imposes curfew on Lower Falls area of Belfast.
	August	SDLP formed.
	September	Provisional IRA bombing campaign started in Belfast.
1971	February	First British soldier killed by Provisional IRA.
	July	SDLP announce boycott of Stormont, following two deaths in Derry, and set up alternative assembly.
	August	Internment without trial introduced. Riots in many towns.
	October	DUP formed.
	December	Fifteen killed in loyalist bombing of McGurk's bar, Belfast.
1972		Worst year of troubles – 478 people killed.
	January	'Bloody Sunday' in Derry – 13 men killed by the army, followed by four days' rioting in Derry, Belfast and Dublin.
	February	Bombing of Parachute Regiment's headquarters at Aldershot by Official IRA – 6 civilians and 1 padre killed.
	March	NI government replaced by Direct Rule from Westminster.
	June	IRA ceasefire.
	July	'Bloody Friday' – 22 IRA bomb explosions in Belfast – nine dead and 130 injured. Operation 'Motorman' – Army moves into Andersonstown and the Bogside. Claudy car bomb – 8 killed.
	December	Provisional IRA confirms Christmas truce.
1973	March	London car bombs – 1 killed and 180 injured. Vanguard Unionist Progressive Party (VUPP) formed with UDA support.
	April	Northern Ireland (Emergency Provisions) Act passed.
	July	Northern Ireland Constitution Act abolishes Stormont Parliament.
	November	UVF 43-day ceasefire begins.
	December	Sunningdale Agreement to establish Council of Ireland.

1974	January	Northern Ireland Power Sharing Executive takes office supported by SDLP, Alliance and part of Unionist Party.
	May	General Strike called by UWC. Four car bombs in Monaghan and Dublin – 28 killed and 100 injured. Power Sharing Executive falls: Direct Rule restored.
	November	IRA bomb in Birmingham. 21 killed.
1975	February	Provisional IRA ceasefire. Feud between official IRA and Irish Republican Socialist Party. UVF/UDA feud.
1976		Special Category status withdrawn from new prisoners.
	August	Peace People founded.
	December	Fair Employment Act.
1977	May	Second loyalist strike called by DUP.
1978	February	IRA bomb at La Mon restaurant kills 12.
1979	March	Airey Neave, Conservative NI spokesman, killed by Irish National Liberation Army (INLA).
	August	Eighteen soldiers killed by IRA at Warren point. Lord Mountbatten killed by IRA in Sligo.
1980	October– December	First hunger strikes in Maze prison.
1981	March	Second hunger strikes.
	April	Bobby Sands elected MP.
	May	Bobby Sands dies.
	October	Hunger strike called off.
1982	July	Northern Ireland Assembly set up. Two bombs in London – 8 killed and 52 injured.
	November	Northern Ireland Assembly opens. SDLP boycott it.
	December	Seventeen people, including 11 soldiers, killed by bomb at Droppin Well pub in Co. Londonderry.
1983	May	New Ireland Forum begins meetings in Dublin.
	September	Mass breakout from Maze Prison.
	December	IRA bomb at Harrods in London kills 5.
1984	October	IRA bomb at Conservative Party conference in Brighton.
1985	February	Nine RUC members killed in mortar attack in Newry.
	November	Anglo-Irish Agreement signed between British and Irish governments.
1986	March	Unionist strike, or 'Day of Action'.

1987	April	Northern Ireland Assembly dissolved.
	May	Eight IRA men killed by SAS at Loughall, Co. Armagh.
	October	Cargo ship *Eksund* seized, carrying 150 tons of explosives for IRA from Libya.
	November	Eleven killed and 63 injured at Enniskillen Remembrance Day ceremony.
1988	*March*	Three IRA members shot dead by SAS in Gibraltar. Two army corporals killed by mob at West Belfast funeral.
	August	Eight soldiers killed by IRA bomb in Ballygawley, Co. Tyrone.
	October	Twelve paramilitary organisations banned from direct broadcasting.
1989	*September*	IRA bomb army barracks in Kent: 11 killed.
1991	*March*	Brooke talks announced.
1992		UDA banned.
1993	*March*	Two children killed by bomb in Warrington – Peace Initiative '93 set up.
	April	Talks start between John Hume (SDLP) and Gerry Adams (Sinn Féin).
	October	Shankill bomb. Greysteel killings.
	December	Downing Street Declaration.
1994	*January*	Dublin government lifts broadcasting ban on Sinn Féin.
	June	Loughinisland killings – six Catholics shot.
	August	IRA declares ceasefire.
	September	Adams is first Sinn Féin leader to meet Irish Prime Minister. John Major lifts broadcasting ban. Patrick Mayhew announces reopening of 10 cross-border crossings.
	October	Loyalist paramilitaries declare ceasefire. USA lifts ban on official contact with Sinn Féin.
	November	EU announces Delors package of £240m to support peace process.
	December	Sinn Féin and loyalist delegations enter pre-negotiation discussions with government in Stormont. Albert Reynolds' Fianna Fáil–Labour government in Irish Republic collapses. Replaced by Fine Gael–Labour coalition under John Bruton.
1995	*February*	Publication of *Frameworks for the Future*.
	May	Investment conference in Washington, DC.
	July	Confrontations during Orange marches.
	September	James Molyneaux resigns as leader of UUP.

		David Trimble elected as new leader.
	November	President Clinton visits Northern Ireland.
1996	*January*	Mitchell Report on Decommissioning published.
	February	Canary Wharf bomb in London: IRA calls off ceasefire. Joint Communiqué by British and Irish governments on ground rules for talks.
	March	'Proximity talks' start with political parties. Chairman and member of Police Authority (PA) sacked. PA report on policing published.
	June	Garda killed in Irish Republic by IRA during bank robbery. IRA bombs in Manchester and Germany. Elections to the Northern Ireland Forum. Multi-party talks start.
	July	Confrontations between Orangemen and residents at Drumcree. First post-ceasefire bomb in Northern Ireland destroys Enniskillen hotel.
	August	Protestant businesses boycotted in some towns.
	September	Apprentice Boys' march in Derry successfully negotiated.
	October	IRA bomb at Thiepval Barracks in Lisburn, followed by other attacks in Northern Ireland.
1997	*January*	IRA and loyalist attacks continue; Court House attacked in Belfast.
	May	Westminster elections: Sinn Féin wins two seats.
	June	Northern Ireland local government elections: Unionists lose control of Belfast City Council. Nationalist mayors in Belfast and Derry. Elections and new government, headed by Bertie Ahern of Fianna Fáil, in Irish Republic. Two RUC men killed by IRA in Lurgan.
	July	Violence around Orange march at Drumcree. Orange Order cancels or re-routes four potentially confrontational marches on 12 July. Sinn Féin leaders urge IRA ceasefire. IRA ceasefire announced.

APPENDIX II

SOURCES OF DISPUTE:
KEY POLITICAL AND CONSTITUTIONAL
DOCUMENTS

List of Contents

No single publication includes all the key documents necessary to trace the evolution of the Northern Ireland question. Patrick Buckland published a documentary collection on Irish Unionism 1885–1923 and Jack Magee's *Northern Ireland: Crisis and Conflict* has a chapter on the period 1969–73. Tony Hepburn's *The Conflict of Nationality in Modern Ireland,* which presents extracts from important documents and a commentary, is unfortunately out of print. The most recent documentary collection is *Irish Historical Documents since 1800,* edited by Alan O'Day and John Stevenson. The collection which follows concentrates primarily on extracts from official landmark documents, but includes other insights and commentaries.

The Ulster Solemn League and Covenant, Belfast, September 1912

In 1912 Ulster unionists began to prepare their resistance to Irish Home Rule. The passage of the Home Rule bill in the Commons, coupled with the abolition of the Lords' veto, meant that Home Rule would probably come into force by 1914. The Ulster Volunteers began to drill openly, guns were landed to arm them, and civil war between North and South seemed likely but for the outbreak of the First World War. The Solemn League and Covenant, signed by 471,414 men and women of Ulster birth, summed up the spirit of resistance to Home Rule.

Being convinced in our consciences that Home Rule would be disastrous to the material well-being of Ulster as well as of the whole of Ireland, subversive of our civil and religious freedom, destructive of our citizenship and perilous to the unity of the Empire, we, whose names are under-written, men of Ulster, loyal subjects of His Gracious Majesty King George V, humbly relying on the God whom our fathers in days of stress and trial confidently trusted, do hereby pledge ourselves in solemn Covenant throughout this our time of threatened calamity to stand by one another in defending for ourselves and our children our cherished position of equal citizenship in the United Kingdom, and using all means which may be found necessary to defeat the present conspiracy to set up a Home Rule Parliament in Ireland. And in the event of such a Parliament being forced upon us we further solemnly and mutually pledge ourselves to refuse to recognise its authority. In sure confidence that God will defend the right we hereto subscribe our names. And further, we individually declare that we have not already signed this Covenant. God save the King.

Source: Ulster Unionist Council Papers, Northern Ireland Public Records Office, D1327/3/21

Proclamation of the Irish Republic: Poblacht na hEireann, Dublin, 26 April 1916

The proclamation of the Irish Republic by the leaders of the 1916 rising in Dublin is a key document in Irish republican tradition and provides its absolute legitimation. The rising failed and most of the leaders were executed, but it sparked off the War of Independence, partition and Irish independence. The proclamation was cited as justification in every subsequent IRA campaign.

Poblacht na hEireann

The provisional government of the Irish Republic to the people of Ireland:

Irishmen and Irishwomen: In the name of God and of the dead generations from which she receives her old tradition of nationhood, Ireland, through us, summons her children to her flag and strikes for her freedom.

Having organised and trained her manhood through her secret revolutionary organisation, the Irish Republican Brotherhood, and through her open military organisations, the Irish Volunteers, and the Irish Citizen Army, having patiently perfected her discipline, having resolutely waited for the right moment to reveal itself, she now seizes that moment, and, supported by her exiled children in America and by gallant allies in Europe, but relying in the first on her own strength, she strikes in full confidence of victory.

We declare the right of the people of Ireland to the ownership of Ireland, and to the unfettered control of Irish destinies, to be sovereign and indefeasible. The long usurpation of that right by a foreign people and government has not extinguished the right, nor can it ever be extinguished except by the destruction of the Irish people. In every generation the Irish people have asserted their right to national freedom and sovereignty; six times during the past three hundred years they have asserted it in arms. Standing on that fundamental right and again asserting it in arms in the face of the world, we hereby proclaim the Irish republic as a sovereign independent state, and we pledge our lives and the lives of our comrades-in-arms to the cause of its freedom, of its welfare, and of its exaltation among the nations.

The Irish republic is entitled to, and hereby claims, the allegiance of every Irishman and Irishwoman. The republic guarantees religious and civil liberty, equal rights and equal opportunities to all its citizens, and declares its resolve to pursue the happiness and prosperity of the whole nation and of all its party, cherishing all the children of the nation equally, and oblivious of the differences carefully fostered by an alien government, which have divided a minority from the majority in the past.

Until our arms have brought the opportune moment for the establishment of a permanent national government, representative of the whole people of Ireland, and elected by the suffrages of all her men and women, the Provisional Government, hereby constituted, will administer the civil and military affairs of the republic in trust for the people. We place the cause of the Irish republic under the protection of the Most High God, whose blessing we invoke upon our arms, and we pray that no one who serves that cause will dishonour it by cowardice, inhumanity, or rapine. In this supreme hour the Irish nation must, by its valour and discipline, and by the readiness of its children to sacrifice themselves for the common good, prove itself worthy of the august destiny to which it is called.

Signed on behalf of the provisional government,

Thomas J. Clarke, Sean MacDiarmada, Thomas MacDonagh, P. H. Pearse, Eamonn Ceannt, James Connolly, Joseph Plunkett.

Source: *The Times*, 26 April 1916

The Government of Ireland Act 1920

The Government of Ireland Act laid the foundations of what later became known as the Stormont system in Northern Ireland, establishing the supremacy of Westminster (which was invoked when Direct Rule was introduced in 1972), and a devolved executive and legislature comprising a Senate and House of Commons with responsibilities for local affairs. Less well remembered is that similar structures were envisaged for Southern Ireland, and a Council of Ireland to deal with common interests. Neither came into force.

1.1 On and after the appointed day there shall be established for Southern Ireland a parliament to be called the parliament of Southern Ireland consisting of His Majesty, the Senate of Southern Ireland, and the House of Commons of Southern Ireland, and there shall be established for Northern Ireland a parliament to be called the parliament of Northern Ireland consisting of His Majesty, the Senate of Northern Ireland and the House of Commons of Northern Ireland ...

2 For the purpose of this act, Northern Ireland shall consist of the parliamentary counties of Antrim, Armagh, Down, Fermanagh, Londonderry and Tyrone, and the parliamentary boroughs of Belfast and Londonderry, and Southern Ireland shall consist of so much of Ireland as is not comprised within the said parliamentary counties and boroughs.

2.1 With a view to the eventual establishment of a parliament for the whole of Ireland, and to bringing about harmonisation between the parliaments and governments of Southern Ireland and Northern Ireland, and to the promotion of mutual intercourse and uniformity in relation to matters affecting the whole of Ireland, and to providing for the administration of services which the two parliaments mutually agree should be administered uniformly throughout the whole of Ireland, or which by virtue of this Act are to be so administered, there shall be constituted as soon as may be after the appointed day, a council to be called the Council of Ireland.

2.2 Subject as hereinafter provided, the Council of Ireland shall consist of a person nominated by the Lord Lieutenant acting in accordance with instructions from His Majesty who shall be president, and forty other persons, of whom seven shall be members of the Senate of Southern Ireland, thirteen shall be members of the House of Commons of Southern Ireland, seven shall be members of the Senate of Northern Ireland, and thirteen shall be members of the House of Commons of Northern Ireland ....

4.1 Subject to the provisions of this act, the Parliament of Southern Ireland and the Parliament of Northern Ireland shall respectively have power to make laws for peace, order and good government of Southern Ireland and Northern Ireland with the following limitations, namely, that they shall not have power to make laws except in respect of matters exclusively relating to the portion of Ireland within their jurisdiction, or some part thereof, and (without prejudice to that general limitation) that they shall not have power to make laws in respect of the following matters in particular: the crown, war and peace, foreign trade, the armed forces, etc., ...

5.1 In the exercise of their power to make laws under this act neither the Parliament of Southern Ireland nor the Parliament of Northern Ireland shall make a law so as either directly or indirectly to establish or endow any religion, or prohibit or restrict the free exercise thereof, or give a preference, privilege or advantage, or impose any disability or disadvantage, on account of religious belief ....

75 Notwithstanding the establishment of the Parliaments of Southern and Northern Ireland, or the Parliament of Ireland, or anything contained in this Act, the supreme authority of the Parliament of the United Kingdom shall remain unaffected and

undiminished over all persons, matters and things in Ireland and every part thereof.

Source: Government Stationery Office, London, HMSO, 1920

The Anglo-Irish Treaty, December 1921

Following a truce in July 1921 the war between the British and the IRA was ended by the signing of the Anglo-Irish Treaty in December. This followed negotiations between the British led by Lloyd George and the Irish by Arthur Griffith and Michael Collins. This accorded the 26-county Southern Ireland with full dominion status. Although the Articles of Agreement for the treaty received the approval of the Dáil, or Irish parliament, it led to a split and civil war.

1. Ireland shall have the same constitutional status in the community of nations known as the British Empire as the Dominion of Canada, the Commonwealth of Australia, the Dominion of New Zealand, and the Union of South Africa, with a parliament having powers to make laws for the peace and good government of Ireland and an executive responsible to that parliament, and shall be styled and known as the Irish Free State ....
11. Until the expiration of one month from the passing of the act of parliament for the ratification of this instrument, the powers of the parliament and the government of the Irish Free State shall not be exercisable as respects Northern Ireland, and the provisions of the Government of Ireland Act, 1920, shall, so far as they relate to Northern Ireland, remain of full force and effect, and no election shall be held for the return of members to serve in the parliament of the Irish Free State for constituencies in Northern Ireland, unless a resolution is passed by both houses of the parliament of Northern Ireland in favour of the holding of such elections before the end of the said month.

12. If before the expiration of the said month, an address is presented to his majesty by both houses of parliament of Northern Ireland to that effect, the powers of the parliament and government of the Irish Free State shall no longer extend to Northern Ireland, and the provisions of the Government of Ireland Act, 1920 (including those relating to the Council of Ireland), shall so far as they relate to Northern Ireland, continue to be of full force and effect, and this instrument shall have effect subject to the necessary modifications. Provided that if such an address is so presented a commission consisting of three persons, one to be appointed by the government of the Irish Free State, one to be appointed by the government of Northern Ireland, and one who shall be chairman to be appointed by the British government shall determine in accordance with the wishes of the inhabitants, so far as may be compatible with economic and geographic conditions, the boundaries between Northern Ireland and the rest of Ireland, and for the purposes of the Government of Ireland Act, 1920, and of this instrument, the boundary of Northern Ireland shall be such as may be determined by such commission...

Source: *Articles of Agreement for a Treaty between Great Britain and Ireland* [Cmd.1560], 1921

The Constitution of Ireland 1937

The 1937 Irish constitution marked the move towards a republic and challenged Northern unionists in two main ways: first, it laid claim to the entire island, including Northern Ireland; and second, it was heavily influenced by Catholic moral teaching and republican cultural aspirations. The Catholic Church was singled out as having a 'special position', and Catholic family doctrine incorporated by forbidding the dissolution of marriage (41.3) and discouraging working mothers (41.2). Irish became the first official language (8.1).

1. The Irish nation hereby affirms its inalienable, indefeasible, and sovereign right to choose its own form of Government, to determine its relations with other nations, and to develop its life, political, economic and cultural, in accordance with its own genius and traditions.
2. The national territory consists of the whole island of Ireland, its islands and the territorial seas.
3. Pending the re-integration of the national territory, and without prejudice to the right of the Parliament and Government established by this Constitution to exercise jurisdiction over the whole of that territory, the laws enacted by that Parliament shall have the like area and extent of application as the laws of Saorstat Eireann and the like extra-territorial effect ...
4. The name of the state is Eire, or in the English language, Ireland ...
44.1 The State acknowledges that the homage of public worship is due to Almighty God. It shall hold His Name in reverence, and shall respect and honour religion.
44.2 The State recognises the special position of the Holy Catholic Apostolic and Roman Church as the guardian of the Faith professed by the great majority of the citizens.
44.3 The State also recognises the Church of Ireland, the Presbyterian Church in Ireland, the Methodist Church in Ireland, the Religious Society of Friends in Ireland, as well as the Jewish Congregations and the other religious denominations existing in Ireland at the date of the coming into operation of this Constitution.

Source: Government Stationery Office, Dublin, HMSO, 1937

The years of change: statements by leading politicians, 1968–74

The years between the civil rights marches in 1968 and the fall of the Power Sharing Executive in 1974 were a watershed in the history of Northern Ireland, which saw loyalist murders, wide civil protest, growing resistance to it and the introduction of the British army in 1969. The Provisional IRA was formed in the following year and began its campaign of violence. Ultimately, after the Northern Ireland Government introduced internment in 1971 in a vain attempt to control the deteriorating situation, Stormont was abolished and replaced by Direct Rule from Westminster. 1974 saw the fall of Northern Ireland's only power-sharing experiment following the strike by the UWC. These extracts illustrate some of the attitudes and positions behind these events.

Newspaper interview with Lord Brookeborough (LB), ex-Premier of Northern Ireland, 30 October 1968

Q: *Have the persistent allegations of discrimination against Catholics in the North worried you?*
LB: Yes; one doesn't like the idea. But I would like to make this plain. The Nationalists always say there is discrimination against the Roman Catholics. Well, there is no discrimination against Roman Catholics qua Roman Catholics, because they worship in a different way. What there is, is a feeling of resentment that most, and let me emphasise the word most, that most Roman Catholics are anti-British and anti-Northern Ireland. This is nothing to do with religion at all. But there is this feeling of resentment that here is a man who is out to destroy Northern Ireland if he can possibly do it. That, I think, is it. They say 'Why aren't we given more higher positions?' But how can you give somebody who is your enemy a higher position in order to allow him to come and destroy you?
Q: *Are you not talking in terms of what might have been true in the 1920s?*
LB: No, I'm sure it still holds. I'm perfectly certain that if they got a chance they would push Northern Ireland into the Republic.
Q: *Is it not the democratic right of anyone in Northern Ireland to be a Nationalist and an anti-partitionist?*
LB: Yes, absolutely his democratic right.
Q: *And therefore to expect completely equal treatment from the state?*

LB: Well, it's very difficult to answer that, but surely nobody is going to put an enemy where he can destroy you?
Q: *Even if he is going to use constitutional methods to do it?*
LB: No. I wouldn't.

Source: *Irish Times*, 30 October 1968

Statement by Terence O'Neill, Premier of Northern Ireland, 5 January 1969

I want the people of Ulster to understand in plain terms the events which have taken place since January 1st. The march to Londonderry planned by the so-called People's Democracy was, from the outset, a foolhardy and irresponsible undertaking. At best, those who planned it were careless of the effects it would have; at worst, they embraced with enthusiasm the prospect of adverse publicity causing further damage to the interests of Northern Ireland as a whole....

Clearly Ulster has now had enough. We are all sick of marchers and counter-marchers. Unless these warring minorities rapidly return to their senses we will have to consider a further reinforcement of the regular police by greater use of the Special Constabulary for normal police duties....

I think we must also have an urgent look at the Public Order Act itself to see whether we ought to ask Parliament for further powers to control those elements which are seeking to hold the entire community to ransom.

Enough is enough. We have heard sufficient for now about civil rights; let us hear a little about civic responsibility. For it is a short step from the throwing of paving stones to the laying of tombstones and I for one can think of no cause in Ulster today which will he advanced by the death of a single Ulsterman.

Source: *Belfast Telegraph*, 6 January 1969

Newspaper interview with Terence O'Neill, 10 May 1969

It is frightfully hard to explain to Protestants that if you give Roman Catholics a good job and a good house, they will live like Protestants, because they will see neighbours with cars and television sets; they will refuse to have eighteen children. But if a Roman Catholic is jobless, and lives in the most ghastly hovel, he will rear eighteen children on National Assistance. If you treat Roman Catholics with due consideration and kindness, they will live like Protestants in spite of the authoritative nature of their Church...

Source: *Belfast Telegraph*, 10 May 1969

Speech by Jack Lynch, Irish Taoiseach, following violence in Derry, 13 August 1969

It is evident that the Stormont Government is no longer in control of the situation. Indeed the present situation is the inevitable outcome of the policies pursued for decades by successive Stormont Governments. It is clear, also, that the Irish Government can no longer stand by and see innocent people injured and perhaps worse.

Source: White, B., *John Hume: Statesman of the Troubles*, Belfast, 1984

Remarks by serving British Marines officer following Internment, August 1971

The British army, as the instrument of internment, has become the object of Catholic animosity. Since that day the street battles, countless explosions, migrations from mixed areas and cold-blooded killings have done little to reassure us that internment would, by the removal of the gunner, provide a return to a semblance of law and order, a basis for a political solution to Ulster's problems. Ironically, it appears to have produced the opposite effect... It has, in fact, increased terrorist activity, perhaps boosted IRA recruitment, polarised further the Catholic and Protestant communities and reduced the ranks of the much needed Catholic moderates. In a worsening situation it is difficult to imagine a solution.

Source: Hamill, D., *Pig in the middle: The Army in Northern Ireland*, London, Methuen, 1985

The Downing Street Declaration, August 1969

1 The United Kingdom Government reaffirm that nothing which has happened in recent weeks in Northern Ireland derogates from the clear pledges made by successive United Kingdom Governments that Northern Ireland should not cease to be a part of the United Kingdom without the consent of the people of Northern Ireland or from the provision in Section 1 of the Ireland Act, 1949, that in no event will Northern Ireland or any part thereof cease to be part of the United Kingdom without the consent of the Parliament of Northern Ireland. The border is not an issue...

3 The United Kingdom Government have ultimate responsibility for the protection of those who live in Northern Ireland when, as in the past week, a breakdown of law and order has occurred. In this spirit, the United Kingdom Government responded to the requests of the Northern Ireland Government for military assistance in Londonderry and Belfast in order to restore law and order. They emphasize again that troops will be withdrawn when law and order has been restored...

5 The United Kingdom Government have welcomed the decision of the Northern Ireland Government relating to local government franchise, the revision of local government areas, the allocation of houses, the creation of a Parliamentary Commissioner for Administration in Northern Ireland [Ombudsman] and machinery to consider citizens' grievances against other public authorities...

Source: *The Times*, 20 August 1969

Newspaper report on Bloody Sunday, January 1972

The tragic and inevitable Doomsday situation which had been universally forecast for Northern Ireland arrived in Londonderry yesterday afternoon when soldiers, firing into a large crowd of civil rights demonstrators, shot and killed 13 civilians.

Fifteen more people, including a woman, were wounded by gunfire and another woman was seriously injured after being knocked down by an armoured car. The army reported two military casualties and said that its soldiers had arrested between 50 and 60 people who had been allegedly involved in the illegal protest march.

After the shooting, which lasted for about 25 minutes in and around the Rossville Flats area of Bogside, the streets had all the appearence of the aftermath of Sharpeville. Where only moments before thousands of men and women had been milling around drifting slowly towards a protest meeting to be held at Free Derry Corner, there was a handful of bleeding bodies, some lying still, mothers still moving with pain, on the white concrete of the square.

The army's official explanation for the killing was that their troops had fired in response to a number of snipers who had opened up on them from below the flats. But those of us at the meeting heard only one shot before the soldiers opened up with their high-velocity rifles. And, while it is impossible to be absolutely sure, one came away with the firm impression, reinforced by dozens of eye witnesses, that the soldiers, men of the 1st Battalion the Parachute Regiment, flown in specifically from Belfast, may have fired needlessly into the huge crowd.

Source: Winchester, S., *Guardian*, 30 January 1972

Speech by William Whitelaw, Secretary of State for Northern Ireland, 13 June 1972

We don't intend to let part of the United Kingdom ... default from the rule of law at the behest of ruthless conspiracy. The disrespect for law rooted there tends to spread like a cancer to other places. I will take the sternest measures to stop the spread of that cancer elsewhere ... Our troops and our money are an eloquent testimony of our concern...

Source: *New York Times*, 13 June 1972

Speech by Harold Wilson, Leader of Labour Party, denouncing UWC strike, 25 May 1974

In a deliberate and calculated attempt to use every undemocratic and unparliamentary means for the purpose of bringing down the whole constitution of Northern Ireland so as to set up there a sectarian and undemocratic state... British taxpayers have seen the taxes they have poured out, almost without regard to cost... Yet people who benefit from all this now viciously defy Westminster, purporting to act as though they were an elected government; people who spend their lives sponging on Westminster and British democracy and then systematically assault democratic methods. Who do these people think they are?

Source: Buckland, P., *A History of Northern Ireland*, Dublin, Gill and Macmillan, 1981, p.171

The Anglo-Irish Agreement, 15 November 1985

The Anglo-Irish Agreement, signed by Margaret Thatcher for the British government and by Garrett Fitzgerald for the government of the Irish Republic, marked a fundamental change in approaches to Northern Ireland. It was the first formal acceptance by the British government that the Irish government should have a voice on Northern Ireland through an Intergovernmental Conference, and by the Irish government that any change in the constitutional status of Northern Ireland required the support of a majority in Northern Ireland, and that the majority did not currently want such a change. It was bitterly opposed by the unionist community.

1 The Governments (of the United Kingdom and the Irish Republic)
(a) affirm that any change in the status of Northern Ireland would only come about with the consent of a majority of the people of Northern Ireland;

(b) recognise that the present wish of a majority of the people of Northern Ireland is for no change in the status of Northern Ireland; **(c)** declare that, if in the future a majority of the people of Northern Ireland clearly wish for and formally consent to the establishment of a united Ireland, they will introduce and support in the respective Parliaments legislation to give effect to that wish.

2(a) There is hereby established, within the framework of the Anglo-Irish Intergovernmental Council set up after the meeting between the two heads of Government on 6 November 1981, an Intergovernmental Conference (hereinafter referred to as 'the Conference'), concerned with Northern Ireland and with relations between the two parts of the island of Ireland, to deal, as set out in this Agreement, on a regular basis with

(i) political matters;

(ii) security and related matters;

(iii) legal matters, including the administration of justice;

(iv) the promotion of cross-border co-operation.

(b) The United Kingdom Government accept that the Irish Government will put forward views and proposals on matters relating to Northern Ireland within the field of activity of the Conference in so far as those matters are not the responsibility of a devolved administration in Northern Ireland. In the interest of promoting peace and stability, determined efforts shall be made through the Conference to resolve any differences. The Conference will be mainly concerned with Northern Ireland; but some of the matters under consideration will involve co-operative action in both parts of the island of Ireland, and possibly also in Great Britain. Some of the proposals considered in respect of Northern Ireland may also be found to have application by the Irish Government. There is no derogation from the sovereignty of either the United Kingdom Government or the Irish Government, and each retains responsibility for the decisions and administration of government within its own jurisdiction.

3 The Conference shall meet at Ministerial or official level, as required. The business of the Conference will thus receive attention at the highest level. Regular and frequent Ministerial meetings shall be held; and in particular special meetings shall be convened at the request of either side. Officials may meet in subordinate groups. Membership of the Conference and of sub-groups shall be small and flexible. When the Conference meets at Ministerial level the Secretary of State for Northern Ireland and an Irish Minister designated as the Permanent Irish Ministerial Representative shall be joint Chairmen. Within the framework of the Conference other British and Irish Ministers may hold or attend meetings as appropriate: when legal matters are under consideration the Attorneys General may attend. Ministers may be accompanied by their officials and their professional advisers: for example, when questions of security policy or security co-operation are being discussed, they may be accompanied by the Chief Constable of the Royal Ulster Constabulary and the Commissioner of the Garda Siochana; or when questions of economic or social policy or co-operation are being discussed, they may be accompanied by officials of the relevant Departments. A Secretariat shall be established by the two Governments to service the Conference on a continuing basis in the discharge of its functions as set out in this Agreement.

4(a) In relation to matters coming within its field of activity, the Conference shall be a framework within which the United Kingdom Government and the Irish Government work together

(i) for the accommodation of the rights and identities of the two traditions which exist in Northern Ireland; and

(ii) for peace, stability and prosperity throughout the island of Ireland by promoting reconciliation, respect for human rights, co-operation against terrorism and the development of economic, social and cultural co-operation.

(b) It is the declared policy of the United Kingdom Government that responsibility in respect of certain matters within the powers of the Secretary of State for Northern Ireland should be devolved within Northern Ireland on a basis which would secure widespread acceptance throughout the community. The Irish Government support that policy.

(c) Both Governments recognise that devolution can be achieved only with the co-operation of constitutional representatives within Northern Ireland of both traditions there. The Conference shall be a framework within which the Irish Government may put forward views and proposals on the modalities of bringing about devolution in Northern Ireland, in so far as they relate to the interests of the minority community.

5(a) The Conference shall concern itself with measures to recognise and accommodate the rights and identities of the two traditions in Northern Ireland, to protect human rights and to prevent discrimination. Matters to be considered in this area include measures to foster the cultural heritage of both traditions, changes in electoral arrangements, the use of flags and emblems, the avoidance of economic and social discrimination and the advantages and disadvantages of a Bill of Rights in some form in Northern Ireland.

(b) The discussion of these matters shall be mainly concerned with Northern Ireland, but the possible application of any measures pursuant to this Article by the Irish Government in their jurisdiction shall not be excluded.

(c) If it should prove impossible to achieve and sustain devolution on a basis which secures widespread acceptance in Northern Ireland, the Conference shall be a framework within which the Irish Government may, where the interests of the minority community are significantly or especially affected, put forward views on proposals for major legislation and on major policy issues, which are within the purview of the Northern Ireland Departments and which remain the responsibility of the Secretary of State for Northern Ireland ....

7(a) The Conference shall consider
(i) security policy;
(ii) relations between the security forces and the community;
(iii) prisons policy.

(b) The Conference shall consider the security situation at its regular meetings and thus provide an opportunity to address policy issues, serious incidents and forthcoming events.

(c) The two Governments agree that there is a need for a programme of special measures in Northern Ireland to improve relations between the security forces and the community, with the object in particular of making the security forces more readily accepted by the nationalist community. Such a programme shall be developed, for the Conference's consideration, and may include the establishment of local consultative machinery, training in community relations, crime prevention schemes involving the community, improvements in arrangements for handling complaints, and action to increase the proportion of members of the minority in the Royal Ulster Constabulary. Elements of the programme may be considered by the Irish Government suitable for application within their jurisdiction.

(d) The Conference may consider policy issues relating to prisons. Individual cases may be raised as appropriate, so that information can be provided or enquiries instituted.

8 The Conference shall deal with issues of concern to both countries relating to the enforcement of the criminal law. In particular it shall consider whether there are areas of the criminal law applying in the North and in the South respectively which might with benefit be harmonised. The two Governments agree on the importance of public confidence in the administration of justice. The Conference shall seek, with the help of advice from experts as appropriate, measures which would give substantial expression to this aim, considering inter alia the possibility of mixed courts in both jurisdictions for the trial of certain offences. The Conference shall also be concerned with policy aspects of extradition and extraterritorial jurisdiction as between North and South.

9(a) With a view to enhancing cross-border co-operation on security matters, the Conference shall set in hand a programme of work to be undertaken by the Chief Constable of the Royal Ulster Constabulary and the Commissioner of the Garda Siochana and, where appropriate, groups of officials in such areas as threat assessments, exchange of information, liaison structures, technical co-operation, training of personnel, and operational resources.

(b) The Conference shall have no operational responsibilities; responsibility for police operations shall remain with the heads of the respective police forces, the Chief Constable of the Royal Ulster Constabulary maintaining his links with the Secretary of State for Northern Ireland and the Commissioner of the Garda Siochana his links with the Minister for Justice.

10(a) The two Governments shall co-operate to promote the economic and social development of those areas of both parts of Ireland which have suffered most severely from the consequences of the instability of recent years, and shall consider the possibility

of securing international support for this work.
(b) If it should prove impossible to achieve and sustain devolution on a basis which secures widespread acceptance in Northern Ireland, the Conference shall be a framework for the promotion of co-operation between the two parts of Ireland concerning cross-border aspects of economic, social and cultural matters in relation to which the Secretary of State for Northern Ireland continues to exercise authority.
(c) If responsibility is devolved in respect of certain matters in the economic, social or cultural areas currently within the responsibility of the Secretary of State for Northern Ireland, machinery will need to be established by the responsible authorities in the North and South for practical co-operation in respect of cross-border aspects of these issues ...

Source: Government Stationery Office, London, HMSO, 1985

The Downing Street Declaration, 15 December 1993

The Downing Street Declaration, signed by John Major, the UK Prime Minister, and Albert Reynolds, the Irish Taoiseach, was intended to pave the way to involving Sinn Féin in negotiations, and followed secret talks between Sinn Féin and British officials. It was followed by the IRA ceasefire in August 1994. Note how some clauses apply to both the Taoiseach and the Prime Minister, and others to one or the other.

4 The Prime Minister, on behalf of the British Government, reaffirms that they will uphold the democratic wish of a greater number of the people of Northern Ireland on the issue of whether they prefer to support the Union or a sovereign united Ireland. On this basis, he reiterates, on behalf of the British Government, that they have no selfish strategic or economic interest in Northern Ireland. Their primary interest is to see peace, stability and reconciliation established by agreement among all the people who inhabit the island, and they will work together with the Irish Government to achieve such an agreement, which will embrace the totality of relationships. The role of the British Government will be to encourage, facilitate and enable the achievement of such agreement over a period through a process of dialogue and cooperation based on full respect for the rights and identities of both traditions in Ireland. They accept that such agreement may, as of right, take the form of agreed structures for the island as a whole, including a united Ireland achieved by peaceful means on the following basis. The British Government agree that it is for the people of the island of Ireland alone, by agreement between the two parts respectively, to exercise their right of self-determination on the basis of consent, freely and concurrently given, North and South, to bring about a united Ireland, if that is their wish. They reaffirm as a binding obligation that they will, for their part, introduce the necessary legislation to give effect to this, or equally to any measure of agreement on future relationships in Ireland which the people living in Ireland may themselves freely so determine without external impediment ...

5 The Taoiseach, on behalf of the Irish Government, considers that the lessons of Irish history, and especially of Northern Ireland, show that stability and well-being will not be found under any political system which is refused allegiance or rejected on grounds of identity by a significant minority of those governed by it. For this reason, it would be wrong to attempt to impose a united Ireland, in the absence of the freely given consent of a majority of the people of Northern Ireland. He accepts, on behalf of the Irish Government, that the democratic right of self-determination by the people of Ireland as a whole must be achieved and exercised with and subject to the agreement and consent of a majority of the people of Northern Ireland and must, consistent with justice and equity, respect the democratic dignity and the civil rights and religious liberties of both communities, including:

- the right of free political thought;
- the right to freedom and expression of religion;
- the right to pursue democratically national and political aspirations;
- the right to seek constitutional change by peaceful and legitimate means;

- the right to live wherever one chooses without hindrance;
- the right to equal opportunity in all social and economic activity, regardless of class, creed, sex or colour.

These would be reflected in any future political and constitutional arrangements emerging from a new and more broadly based agreement.

6 The Taoiseach however recognises the genuine difficulties and barriers to building relationships of trust either within or beyond Northern Ireland, from which both traditions suffer... The Taoiseach will examine with his colleagues any elements in the democratic life and organisation of the Irish State that can be represented to the Irish Government in the course of political dialogue as a real and substantial threat to their way of life and ethos, or that can be represented as not being fully consistent with a modern democratic and pluralist society, and undertakes to examine any possible ways of removing such obstacles. Such an examination would of course have due regard to the desire to preserve those inherited values that are largely shared throughout the island or that belong to the cultural and historical roots of the people of this island in all their diversity. The Taoiseach hopes that over time a meeting of hearts and minds will develop, which will bring all the people of Ireland together, and will work towards that objective, but he pledges in the meantime that as a result of the efforts that will be made to build mutual confidence no Northern Unionist should ever have to fear in future that this ideal will be pursued either by threat or coercion.

7 ...The Taoiseach also acknowledges the presence in the Constitution of the Republic of elements which are deeply resented by Northern Unionists, but which, at the same time, reflect hopes and ideals which lie deep in the hearts of many Irish men and women North and South. But as we move towards a new era of understanding in which new relationships of trust may grow and bring peace to the island of Ireland, the Taoiseach believes that the time has come to consider together how best the hopes and identities of all can be expressed in more balanced ways, which no longer engender division and the lack of trust to which he has referred. He confirms that, in the event of an overall settlement, the Irish Government will, as part of a balanced constitu-

tional accommodation, put forward and support proposals for change in the Irish Constitution which would fully reflect the principle of consent in Northern Ireland ....

9 The British and Irish Governments will seek, along with the Northern Ireland constitutional parties through a process of political dialogue, to create institutions and structures which, while respecting the diversity of the people of Ireland, would enable them to work together in all areas of common interest. This will help over a period to build the trust necessary to end past divisions, leading to an agreed and peaceful future. Such structures would, of course, include institutional recognition of the special links that exist between the peoples of Britain and Ireland as part of the totality of relationships, while taking account of newly forged links with the rest of Europe.

10 The British and Irish Governments reiterate that the achievement of peace must involve a permanent end to the use of, or support for, paramilitary violence. They confirm that, in these circumstances, democratically mandated parties which establish a commitment to exclusively peaceful methods and which have shown that they abide by the democratic process, are free to participate fully in democratic politics and to join in dialogue in due course between the Governments and the political parties on the way ahead.

11 The Irish Government would make their own arrangements within their jurisdiction to enable democratic parties to consult together and share in dialogue about the political future. The Taoiseach's intention is that these arrangements could include the establishment, in consultation with other parties, of a Forum for Peace and Reconciliation to make recommendations on ways in which agreement and trust between both traditions in Ireland can be promoted and established.

Source: Government Stationery Office, London, HMSO, 1993

Frameworks for the Future: a summary, February 1995

The *Frameworks* document, agreed by the UK and Irish governments and published after the declaration of the IRA ceasefire, set out the broad directions which both governments envisaged for negotiations. The IRA cited failure to move sufficiently rapidly towards its implementation as the justification for ending the ceasefire in February 1996.

Part I A framework for accountable government in Northern Ireland

These proposals:
– outline the British Government's understanding of where agreement might be found amongst the political parties and the wider community on new democratic institutions within Northern Ireland;
– identify the characteristics that should underlie any such new institutions;
– propose and describe in greater detail:
  • a single unicameral Assembly of about 90 members elected for a fixed term;
  • legislative and executive responsibility over as wide range of subjects as in 1973;
  • elections to the Assembly by a form of proportional representation;
  • possibly a separate Panel, perhaps of three people elected within Northern Ireland, to complement the working of the Assembly;
– a system of Assembly Committees, constituted broadly in proportion to party strengths in the Assembly;
– a system of detailed checks and balances intended to sustain confidence in the institutions.

Part II A new framework for agreement

These proposals:
– reaffirm the guiding principles of self-determination, the consent of the governed, exclusively democratic and peaceful means, and full respect and protection for the rights and identities of both traditions;
– provide for an agreed new approach to traditional constitutional doctrines on both sides:

- the British Government will propose changes to its constitutional legislation, so as to incorporate a commitment to continuing willingness to accept the will of a majority of the people living in Northern Ireland, and a commitment to exercise their jurisdiction with rigorous impartiality on behalf of all the people of Northern Ireland, in a way which does not prejudice their freedom to determine Northern Ireland's constitutional status, whether in remaining a part of the United Kingdom or in forming part of a united Ireland;
- the Irish Government will introduce and support proposals for changes in the Irish Constitution, so that no territorial claim of right to jurisdiction over Northern Ireland contrary to the will of a majority of its people is asserted, and so that the Irish Government recognise the legitimacy of whatever choice is freely exercised by a majority of the people of Northern Ireland with regard to its constitutional status;

– commend direct dialogue with the relevant political parties in Northern Ireland in developing new internal structures;
– propose a North/South body, comprising elected representatives from, and accountable to, a Northern Ireland Assembly and the Irish Parliament, to deal with matters designated by the two Governments in the first instance in agreement with the parties;
– describe ways in which such a body could work with executive, harmonising or consultative functions, by way of authority delegated to its members by the Assembly;
– envisage that all decisions within the North/South body would be by agreement between the two sides;
– set out criteria for the designation of functions, and suggest a

range of functions that might be designated from the outset, for agreement with the parties;
– envisage the Northern Ireland Assembly and the Irish Parliament being able, by agreement, to designate further functions or to move functions already designated between the three categories;
– envisage that the body will have an important role, in consultation with the two Governments, in developing an agreed approach for the whole island in respect of the challenges and opportunities of the European Union;
– envisage a Parliamentary forum, with representatives from new Northern Ireland institutions and the Irish Parliament, to consider matters of mutual interest;
– envisage a new and more broadly based Agreement between the British and Irish Governments to develop and extend co-operation;
– envisage a standing Intergovernmental Conference which would consider matters of mutual interest, but not those transferred to new political institutions in Northern Ireland;
– envisage that representatives of agreed political institutions in Northern Ireland may be formally associated with the work of the Conference;
– provide for a complementary undertaking by both Governments to ensure protection for specified civil, political, social and cultural rights.

These proposals do not provide for joint authority by the British and Irish Governments over Northern Ireland. They do not predetermine any outcome to the Talks process. Agreement by the parties, and then by the people, is the key.

Source: Government Stationery Office, London, HMSO, 1994

The Mitchell Principles and the Joint Communiqué, January and February 1996

In January 1996 the Mitchell Committee, established to find an escape route from the impasse over decommissioning arms, announced its findings. These included a set of principles to which parties had to agree before admission to all-party talks. The selection by the British government of one marginal suggestion – that elections would be held for a Northern Ireland Forum – seems to have convinced the IRA that the British would obstruct progress towards talks. The IRA ceasefire ended with the Docklands bomb in London on February 1996. Within a week the two governments issued a joint communiqué announcing an agreed path to all-party negotiations. This included consultations with Northern Ireland parties about elections to an assembly in Northern Ireland on 10 June 1996, followed by 'all-party negotiations' and possibly a referendum. Sinn Féin's involvement in the talks would depend on the restoration of the IRA ceasefire and acceptance of the principles agreed by the Mitchell Commission.

The Mitchell Principles, January 1996

The International Body on Arms Decommissioning recommended that participants in all-party negotiations must agree:
– To democratic and exclusively peaceful means of resolving political issues
– To the total disarmament of all paramilitaries
– That such disarmament must be verifiable by an independent commission
– To renounce and oppose any effort to use force or the threat of force to influence the course of the outcome of all-party negotiations
– To abide by the letter of any agreement reached in all-party negotiations and to resort to democratic and exclusively peaceful methods in trying to alter any aspect of that outcome with which they may disagree
– To urge that 'punishment' killings and beatings stop and to take effective steps to prevent such actions.

Source: *Irish Times*, 25 January 1996

Anglo-Irish Communiqué, February 1996

2...The Prime Minister and the Taoiseach noted with profound regret the statement announcing the ending of the IRA ceasefire and called for its immediate and unequivocal restoration.

3 They unreservedly condemned the murderous IRA attack in London's Docklands and subsequent acts of terrorism for which there can never be any justification. They expressed sympathy for the victims and their common resolve to bring the perpetrators to justice, to do everything possible to protect the public from further such atrocities, and to cooperate intensively at all levels to these ends ...

5 The Prime Minister and the Taoiseach agreed that the IRA's abandonment of its announced cessation was a fundamental breach of the declared basis on which both governments had engaged Sinn Féin in political dialogue. Accordingly, both governments are agreed that the resumption of ministerial dialogue with Sinn Féin and their participation in negotiations, requires the restoration of the ceasefire of August 1994.

6...Having undertaken the intensive consultations and the elective process as set out below, all-party negotiations will be convened on Monday June 10th, 1996.

7... The Prime Minister reaffirmed the British government's view that, having taken account of the differing positions of the parties and the view of the International Body, an elective process would offer a viable direct and speedy route to all-party negotiations...

8 The Prime Minister and the Taoiseach agreed that details of an elective process were for the parties in Northern Ireland, together with the British government, to determine. The Prime Minister confirmed that the necessary legislation for a broadly acceptable elective process would be processed as rapidly as possible ...

10 The Prime Minister and the Taoiseach agreed that the two governments would conduct intensive multilateral consultations with the relevant Northern Ireland parties in whatever configuration was acceptable to those concerned, beginning on Monday March 4th, and ending on Wednesday March 13th.

The purpose of the consultations will be to:

(a) reach widespread agreement on proposals for a broadly acceptable elective process leading directly and without preconditions to all-party negotiations on June 10th 1996;
(b) reach widespread agreement on the basis, participation, structure, format and agenda of substantive all-party negotiations; and
(c) consider whether there might be advantage in holding a referendum in Northern Ireland with a parallel referendum held by the Irish Government in its own jurisdiction on the same day as in Northern Ireland. The purpose of such a referendum would be to mandate support for a process to create lasting stability, based on the repudiation of violence for any political purpose.
11 ....The Taoiseach and the Prime Minister agreed that the two Governments will review the outcome of these consultations immediately after their conclusion on March 13. Following that, the British Government will bring forward legislation on the elective process, based on a judgment on what seems most broadly acceptable, and decisions will be announced, as appropriate, on the issues referred to earlier.

In the absence of the cessation of violence for which both governments look, the two governments affirmed their determination to continue to work in partnership with those parties which are exclusively committed to peaceful methods to secure a comprehensive negotiated settlement.

The Taoiseach and the Prime Minister expressed their hope that all parties with an electoral mandate would be able to participate in all-party negotiations.

They recognise that confidence building measures will be necessary. As one such measure, all participants would need to make clear at the beginning of the discussions their total and absolute commitment to the principles of democracy and non-violence set out in the report of the International Body.

They would also need to address, at that stage, its proposals on decommissioning.

Confidence building would also require that the parties have reassurance that a meaningful and inclusive process of negotiations is genuinely being offered to address the legitimate concerns of their traditions and the need for new political arrangements with which all can identify.

The two governments called upon Sinn Féin and the IRA to make Sinn Féin's participation in the process of such negotiations possible.

Source: Northern Ireland Information Service, February 1996

NOTES

Chapter 1
Ethnic conflict: plus ça change...?

1 Wallensteen, P. and Sollenburg, M., *States in Armed Conflict,* Department of Peace and Conflict Research, Uppsala, University of Uppsala, 1995.
2 *New York Times,* 14 May 1992.
3 Kidron, M. and Segal, R., *The New State of the World Atlas,* London, Pluto, 1984.
4 The estimate was made by the Commonwealth Secretary-General, Emeka Anyaoku, following a presentation entitled 'Space in which hope can grow' at the Initiative on Conflict Resolution and Ethnicity (INCORE) in 1996.
5 This extract is from Jonathan Swift's *On Poetry,* written in 1730.
6 Darby, J., *What's Wrong with Conflict?,* Occasional Paper 3, Coleraine, Centre for the Study of Conflict, 1991.
7 Shibutani, T. and Kwan, K.L., 'Changes in life conditions conducive to interracial conflict' in G. Marx (ed.), *Racial Conflict,* Boston, Little, Brown, 1971, p.135.
8 Coleman, J., 'The dynamics of conflict' in G. Marx (ed.), *Racial Conflict,* Boston, Little, Brown, 1971, p.256.
9 See Minority Rights Group (MRG) Reports and book series, including McDowell, D., *The Kurds: A Nation Denied,* London, Minority Rights Publications, 1992; Poulton, H., *The Balkans: Minorities and States in Conflict,* London, Minority Rights Publications, 1993 (2nd edn.); and Walker, C.J., *Armenia and Karabagh: The Struggle for Unity,* London, Minority Rights Publications, 1991.
10 Gurr, T.R., 'Third world minorities at risk' in S.J. Brown and K.M. Schraub (eds), *Resolving Third World Conflict,* Washington, USIP, 1992. As further illustration, Walker Connor estimated that, in the early 1970s, only about 10 per cent of states could claim to be nation states in the sense that the state's boundaries coincided with those of the nation, and that the state's population shared a single ethnic culture (Connor, W., 'Nation building and nation destroying' in *Ethnonationalism,* New Jersey, Princeton University Press, 1994).
11 Institute of Geographers, Moscow, 1991.
12 De Silva, K.M. and May, R.J. (eds), *Internationalisation of Ethnic Conflict,* London, Pinter, 1991.

13 Simpson, G. and Yinger, J., *Racial and Cultural Minorities*, New York, Harper & Row, 1965.
14 A good introduction to Track Two diplomacy is McDonald, J. and Bendahmane, D. (eds), *Conflict Resolution: Track Two Diplomacy*, Washington, Foreign Service Institute, 1987, esp. J. Montville's chapter, 'Track Two diplomacy'.
15 Horowitz, D., *Ethnic Groups in Conflict*, California, University of California Press, 1985.
16 See Montville, J. 'Track Two diplomacy' in McDonald and Bendahmane (eds.), *Conflict Resolution: Track Two Diplomacy.*
17 Boutros-Ghali, B., *An Agenda for Peace*, New York, United Nations, 1992.
18 Ibid., p.9.
19 Article 2 of the Universal Declaration of Human Rights.
20 Boutros-Ghali, *An Agenda for Peace*, p.10.

Chapter 2
Historical inheritances

1 The recent treatment of history is described in Chapter 8. At this point, the following books are recommended: Beckett, J.C., *The Making of Modern Ireland*, London, Faber & Faber, 1966; Foster, R.F., *Modern Ireland: 1600–1972*, Harmondsworth, Penguin, 1988; Lee, J., *Ireland 1921–1985: Politics and Society*, Cambridge, CUP, 1989; Lyons, F.S.L., *Ireland Since the Famine*, London, Weidenfeld & Nicholson, 1971; and, for Northern Ireland, Bardon, J., *A History of Ulster*, Belfast, Blackstaff, 1992.
2 The term 'Ulster' is popularly used in Ireland to describe two different areas. One is the nine counties of the traditional province: Antrim, Down, Armagh, (London)derry, Tyrone, Fermanagh, Donegal, Monaghan and Cavan. The other is the administrative and political unit which since 1921 has formed the state of Northern Ireland; it comprises the first six counties detailed above. In this book the term 'Northern Ireland' will be preferred, as the best in a long list of contested alternatives, when describing the latter area.
3 Lennon, C., *The Incomplete Conquest*, Dublin, Gill & Macmillan, 1995.
4 Beckett, *The Making of Modern Ireland*, p.222.
5 Boyd, A., *A Holy War in Belfast*, Tralee, Anvil, 1969, p.2.
6 Beckett, J.C. and Glasscock, R., *Belfast: The Origin and Growth of an Industrial City*, London, BBC, 1967, p.47.
7 Barrow, J., *Tour Round Ireland*, London, John Murray, 1836, p.36.
8 See Boyd, *A Holy War in Belfast.*
9 Lyons, F.S.L., *Ireland Since the Famine*, p.682.
10 Quoted in Shearman, H., *Northern Ireland 1921–1971*, Belfast, HMSO, 1971, p.16.
11 *Cameron Report*, 1969. See also, for example, Whyte, J., *Interpreting Northern Ireland*, Oxford, Blackwell, 1990.
12 O'Dowd, L., Rolston, B. and Tomlinson, B., *Northern Ireland Between*

Civil Rights and Civil War, London, CSE Books, 1980, p.66. For a more recent analysis of patterns of employment in the 1960s, see Eversley, D., *Religion and Employment in Northern Ireland,* London, Sage, 1989.
13 IRA press statement announcing the end of their 1956 campaign, 1962.
14 O'Neill, T., *Ulster at the Crossroads,* London, Faber & Faber, 1969, p.23.
15 Sheehy, M., *Divided We Stand,* London, Faber & Faber, 1955, p.66.
16 Wilson, A., *Northern Ireland and the Ulster Conflict,* Belfast, Blackstaff, 1995, p.16.

Chapter 3
The people of Northern Ireland

1 The cartoon by Martyn Turner appeared in *Fortnight,* which was published in Belfast, June 1976.
2 A useful guide to current population trends and likely future developments is a publication by the Northern Ireland Economic Council, *Demographic Trends in Northern Ireland,* Occasional Paper no. 2, Belfast, NIEC, 1995.
3 I am grateful to Tony Gallagher for data he has calculated from the 1991 census, indicating that Catholics form about 53 per cent of the under-14 population. Further details available from Registrar-General, *The Northern Ireland Census 1991: Religious Report,* HMSO, Belfast, 1993.
4 Compton, P., *Demographic Review: Northern Ireland 1995,* Belfast, Northern Ireland Economic Development Office, 1995.
5 Cairns, E., 'Is Northern Ireland a conservative society?' in P. Stringer and G. Robinson (eds), *Social Attitudes in Northern Ireland,* Belfast, Blackstaff, 1991, p.142.
6 Beckett, J.C. and Glasscock, R., *Belfast: The Origin and Growth of an Industrial City,* London, BBC, 1967, p.188.
7 Stewart, A.T.Q., *The Narrow Ground,* London, Faber & Faber, 1977.
8 Cormack, R. J., Gallagher, A. M. and Osborne, R. D., *Fair Shares? Religion and the 1991 Population Census,* Belfast, Fair Employment Commission, 1994, p.55. See also the Labour Force Surveys published and annually by the Northern Ireland Statistics and Research Agency, Belfast.
9 Cormack, R., Gallagher, A.M. and Osborne, R., *Fair Enough? Religion and the 1991 Population Census,* Belfast, Fair Employment Commission, 1993, p.17. See also the Labour Force Surveys published annually by the Northern Ireland Statistics and Research Agency, Belfast.
10 Moloney, E., 'Criticism for RUC in British report', *Sunday Tribune,* Dublin, 1 May 1994. It is still difficult to find accurate statistics on Catholic membership of the RUC.
11 Geary, R. and Morrison, J., 'The perception of crime', in P. Stringer

and G. Robinson (eds), *Social Attitudes in Northern Ireland*, Belfast, Blackstaff, 1992, p.78.

12 Clarke, L., 'Apartheid takes root after 25 years of segregation', *Sunday Times*, London, 14 August 1994.

13 Sugden, J. and Bairner, A., *Sport, Sectarianism and Society in a Divided Ireland*, Leicester, Leicester University Press, 1993, p.1.

14 McGiven, N.P., dissertation cited in Sugden and Bairner, op. cit.

Chapter 4
The Northern Ireland problem

1 Bruce, S., *God Save Ulster*, Oxford, OUP, 1986, p. 236. Bruce's book is the most persuasive of those arguing that the conflict has a religious basis. Also see Hickey, J., *Religion and the Northern Ireland Problem*, Dublin, Gill & Macmillan, 1984.

2 The most thorough and recent review of how the conflict has been interpreted by academics and others is Whyte, J., *Interpreting Northern Ireland*, Oxford, Blackwell, 1990. See also Darby, J., *Conflict in Northern Ireland*, Dublin, Gill & Macmillan, 1976, pp.250–4.

3 Whyte devotes a chapter to reviewing Marxist interpretations of Northern Ireland, and the subject has also been reviewed by Darby *op. cit.* and O'Leary, B., 'Explaining Northern Ireland: A brief study guide,'*Politics*, vol. 5, no. 1, 1985. See also Bew P., Gibbon, P. and Patterson, H., *Northern Ireland 1921–94*, London, Serif, 1995.

4 In Moody, T. W. and Martin, F., *The Course of Irish History*, Cork, Mercier, 1967.

5 These statistics are amalgamated by the author from the following official sources: *Continuous Household Survey*, Belfast, HMSO, 1988–1992; Department of Education, Northern Ireland, *School Leavers' Survey*, Belfast, HMSO, 1990, and *Annual School Census*, Belfast, HMSO, 1991; OPCS, General Registrar's Office for Scotland and the Department of Finance in Northern Ireland, *The Labour Force Survey*, London, HMSO, 1982; Policy Planning and Research Unit (PPRU), *Disability Study*, Belfast, PPRU, 1992; Policy Research Institute (PRI), *Spatial and Social Variations in the Distribution of Health Indicators in Northern Ireland*, Belfast, PRI, 1990; Department of Education Northern Ireland (DENI) , Statistical Bulletin, Belfast, DENI, 1996.

6 For a comprehensive review of employment patterns, see Gallagher, A.M., *Majority Minority Review no. 2: Employment, Unemployment and Religion in Northern Ireland*, Coleraine, Centre for the Study of Conflict, 1991.

7 *Continuous Household Survey* (CHS), Belfast, HMSO, 1988–92.

8 Boyd, A., *A Holy War in Belfast*, Tralee, Anvil, 1969.

9 The controls on Northern Ireland's violence are described in Darby, J. (ed.), *Northern Ireland: The Background to the Conflict*, Belfast, Appletree,

1983. A useful account of IRA violence is O'Brien, B., *The Long War: the IRA and Sinn Féin*, Dublin, O'Brien Press, 1993. The most up-to-date analysis of deaths during the Troubles is Sutton, M., *An Index of Deaths from the Conflict in Ireland 1969–93*, Belfast, Beyond the Pale, 1994.

10 Murray, D., *Worlds Apart: Segregated Schools in Northern Ireland*, Belfast, Appletree, 1985, is a rare detailed study of two schools. For a broader guide to the literature on education see Dunn, S., *Education and the Conflict in Northern Ireland: A Guide to the Literature*, Coleraine, Centre for the Study of Conflict, 1986.

11 Gallagher, A.M. and Dunn, S., 'Community relations in Northern Ireland: attitudes to contact and integration,' in P. Stringer, and G. Robinson (eds), *Social Attitudes in Northern Ireland*, Belfast, Blackstaff, 1991.

Chapter 5
Northern Ireland 1969–94: the years of violence

1 Cormack, R. J., Osborne, R.D., Gallagher, A.M., Fisher, N. and Poland, M., 'Higher Education participation of Northern Irish students', *Higher Education Quarterly*, vol. 48, no. 3, pp.207–26.

2 Guelke, A. (ed.), *Northern Ireland: The International Perspective*, Dublin, Gill & Macmillan, 1992, p.3.

3 Adrian Guelke has written an interesting overview of Northern Ireland from an international perspective, which examines the influence of Britain, the Irish Republic, the United States and Europe: ibid. Wilson, A., *Irish America and the Ulster Conflict*, Belfast, Blackstaff, 1995, concentrates on the United States, and brings the story up to the IRA ceasefire in 1994.

4 Guelke, *Northern Ireland*, p.195.

5 *Belfast Telegraph*, 30 January 1990.

6 The Cameron Report, *Disturbances in Northern Ireland*, HMSO, 1969, p.56.

7 Smith, D. and Chambers, G., *Inequality in Northern Ireland*, Oxford, Clarendon, 1991, p.370. See also Melaugh, M., 'Housing' in P. Stringer and G. Robinson (eds), *Social Attitudes in Northern Ireland*, Belfast, Blackstaff, 1991, p.125.

8 Gallagher, A.M., *Majority Minority Review no. 2: Employment, Unemployment and Religion in Northern Ireland*, Coleraine, Centre for the Study of Conflict, 1991.

9 McKittrick, D., 'Ulster job discrimination is still rife', *Independent*, 22 August 1994.

10 Fair Employment Agency, *Report of an Investigation by the Fair Employment Agency of Northern Ireland into the Non-Industrial Northern Ireland Civil Service*, Belfast, FEA, 1983.

11 Press release, Northern Ireland Office, Belfast, 21 July 1994.

12 Gallagher, A.M., *Majority Minority Review no. 2*, pp.55–61.

13 Darby, J., 'Race and religion: Some observations on desegregation in America and Northern Ireland', *Integrateducation* (Amherst, MA) XVIII, 5, 1981.
14 Ibid.
15 Department of Education Northern Ireland, Statistical Bulletin, SB2/96, DENI, Belfast, 1996.
16 Gallagher, A.M., *Majority Minority Review no. 1: Education and Religion in Northern Ireland*, Coleraine, Centre for the Study of Conflict, 1989, pp.37–8.
17 Hillyard, P., 'Law and order' in J. Darby, *Northern Ireland: The Background to the Conflict*, Belfast and Syracuse, New York, Appletree, 1983, p.58.
18 Ibid., p.60.
19 Gallagher, A.M., 'Civil liberties and the state' in P. Stringer and G. Robinson (eds), *Social Attitudes in Northern Ireland*, Belfast, Blackstaff, 1991.
20 White, B., 'The state of the Police', *Belfast Telegraph*, 21 September 1973.
21 Gallagher, A.M., 'Justice and the law in Northern Ireland', in R. Jowell, L. Brook and B. Taylor (eds), *British Social Attitudes: The 8th Report*, Aldershot, Dartmouth, 1991, p.68.
22 Darby, J. and Dunn, S., 'Segregated schools and the research evidence', in R. Cormack, R. Miller and R. Osborne (eds.), *Education and Policy in Northern Ireland*, Belfast, Policy Research Institute, 1987.
23 Smith, A. and Robinson, A., *Education for Mutual Understanding: Perceptions and Policy*, Coleraine, Centre for the Study of Conflict, 1992.
24 See Bryson, L. and McCartney, C., *Clashing Symbols*, Belfast, Institute of Irish Studies and Community Relations Council, 1994, for an interesting review of the importance of symbols in a divided society.

Chapter 6
Northern Ireland 1994–7: beyond the ceasefires

1 'IRA is cause, not symptom', *Sunday Tribune*, 24 August 1994.
2 *Frameworks for the Future*, Belfast, HMSO, 1995.
3 *Belfast Telegraph*, 5 January 1996.
4 *Irish Times*, 8 January 1996.
5 Poll reported in *Belfast Telegraph*, 16 January 1996.
6 *Sunday Business Post* (Dublin), 10 December 1995.
7 Report of the International Body on Arms Decommissioning (the Mitchell Committee), London, 1996.
8 I am grateful to Roger McGinty for information gathered on the various attempts to find a way out of the decommissioning issue. All the dates refer to references in the *Irish Times*.
9 *Irish Times*, 22 June 1996.
10 See report in the *Observer* (London), 16 June 1996.

11 McKittrick, D., 'The bombs that blew away Ulster', *Independent*, 26 December 1996.
12 *Guardian*, 25 February 1995.
13 *Irish Times*, 14 September 1996.
14 McKittrick, D., 'The week John Major went Nationalist', *Independent*, 23 February 1995.
15 See, for example, a speech by Bishop Mahaffey reported in *Irish Independent*, 27 March 1995.
16 *Belfast Telegraph*, 30 March 1996.
17 Police Authority for Northern Ireland, *Everyone's Police: Partnership for Change*, Belfast, PANI, 1996, App. 6.
18 Ibid.
19 *Irish Times*, 27 March 1996.
20 *Belfast Telegraph*, 16 January 1997.
21 *Irish Times*, 5 March 1996.
22 *Irish Times*, 30 April 1996, and *Business Telegraph* (supplement to the *Belfast Telegraph*), 3 September 1996.
23 *Belfast Telegraph*, 2 July, 1996.
24 *Daily Telegraph* (London), 21 July 1996.
25 *Irish Times*, 11 January 1997.
26 Hadden, T., Irwin, C. and Boal, F., *Separation or Sharing, The People's Choice*, Belfast, Fortnight Educational Trust, 1996.
27 *Belfast Telegraph*, 19 July 1996.
28 O'Connor, F., 'Confusion, and betrayal plague IRA', *Belfast Telegraph*, 20 December 1996.
29 See Cairns, E., *Caught in Crossfire*, Belfast, Appletree, 1987.

Chapter 7
Minority rights: an audit

1 Rose, R., *Governing without Consensus*, London, Faber & Faber, 1971, p.139.
2 Gallagher, A.M., 'Equality, contact and pluralism: attitudes to community relations', in R. Breen, P. Devine and G. Robinson (eds), *Social Attitudes in Northern Ireland*, Belfast, Appletree, 1995, p.25.
3 Smith, D. and Chalmers, G., *Inequality in Northern Ireland*, Oxford, Clarendon, 1991, p.370.
4 Ibid., p.378. In 1996 the Standing Advisory Commission on Human Rights published a useful three-volume review on employment equality in Northern Ireland (Magill, D. and Rose, S., *Fair Employment Law in Northern Ireland: Debates and Issues*, Belfast, Standing Advisory Commission on Human Rights (SACHR),1996; McLaughlin, E. and Quirk, P., *Policy Aspects of Employment Equality in Northern Ireland*, Belfast, SACHR, 1996; and McVey, J. and Hutson, N., *Public Views and Experiences of Fair Employment and Equality Issues in Northern Ireland*, Belfast, SACHR, 1996).

5   Hadden, T. and Hillyard, P., *Justice in Northern Ireland*, London, Cobden Trust, 1973.
6   Cairns, E., 'Is Northern Ireland a conservative society?' in P. Stringer and G. Robinson (eds), *Social Attitudes in Northern Ireland*, Belfast, Blackstaff, 1991, pp.143–4.
7   The figures on the incidence of mixed marriages are confused and often contradictory. The most recent review of the data is contained in Morgan, V., Smith, M., Robinson, G. and Fraser, G., *Mixed Marriages in Northern Ireland*, Coleraine, Centre for the Study of Conflict Studies, 1996.
8   Watson, D., 'Fund Irish schools, say Protestants', *Belfast Telegraph*, 28 December 1994.
9   Poll published in the *Irish Times*, 3 December 1993.
10 Gallagher, A.M., 'Community relations' in R. Breen, P. Devine, and G. Robinson, (eds), *Social Attitudes in Northern Ireland*, Belfast, Appletree, 1995, p.19.
11 Compton, P., 'An evaluation of the changing religious composition of the population of Northern Ireland', *Economic and Social Review*, vol. 16, 1995, pp.201–24. The earlier relationship between birth and emigration rates is discussed in Darby, J., *Conflict in Northern Ireland*, Dublin, Gill & Macmillan, 1976, pp.39–43.
12 Clarke, L., 'Apartheid takes root after 25 years of segregation', *Sunday Times*, 14 August 1994.
13 An excellent discussion of the Catholic community is O'Connor, F., *In Search of a State: Catholics in Northern Ireland*, Belfast, Blackstaff, 1993. No equivalent review has been written on the Protestant community, but a good introduction is Boal, F.W., Campbell, J.A. and Livingstone, D.N., 'The Protestant mosaic: a majority of minorities' in P.J. Roche, and B. Barton, (eds), *The Northern Ireland Question: Myth and Reality*, Alder-shot, Avebury, 1991, pp.99–129.
14 *Irish Times*, 13 July 1996.
15 Clarke, 'Apartheid takes root'.
16 Gallagher, A.M, 'Community relations', p.16. See also Breen, R., Devine, P., and Dowds, L., *Social Attitudes in Northern Ireland*, Belfast, Appletree, 1996.

Chapter 8
Northern Ireland: broader lessons?

1   Horowitz, D., *Ethnic Groups in Conflict*, California, University of California Press, 1985.
2   Simmel published very little, but his views are outlined and discussed in Coser, L., *The Functions of Social Conflict*, London, Routledge & Kegan Paul, 1956.
3   From a speech given by the UN Secretary General, Boutros Boutros-Ghali,

at the United Nations University, Tokyo, January 1993.
4   See Harff, B. and Gurr, T.R., 'Toward empirical theory of genocides and
    politicides: identification and measurement of cases since 1945',
    'International Studies Quarterly, vol. 32, 1988, pp.35–67, and Singer, D.J.
    and Small, M. (eds), *Resort to Arms: International and Civil Wars,
    1816–1980,* California, Sage, 1982.
5   Childers, E. and Urquhart, B., *Renewing the United Nations System,*
    Uppsala, Dag Hammarskjold Foundation, 1994, p.17.

Chapter 9
Finding out more about Northern Ireland

1   The three registers, while concentrating on research relating to the
    Troubles, in reality define 'conflict-related' generously. They are:
    Darby, J., *Register of Research into the Irish Conflict,* Belfast, Northern
    Ireland Community Relations Commission, 1972; Darby, J., Dodge, N.
    and Hepburn, A.C., *Register of Research into the Irish Conflict,* Coleraine,
    Centre for the Study of Conflict, 1981; and Ó'Maoláin, C., *Register of
    Research on Northern Ireland,* Coleraine, Centre for the Study of Conflict,
    1993.
2   The series is produced by Longman in collaboration with the British
    Library.
3   Martyn Turner's cartoons, some of which are featured in this book,
    have been published in collections since the 1970s. Particularly
    recommended are *Illuminations,* Kilkenny, Boethius, 1986 (a cartoonist's
    reflections on Irish history) and *Pack up your Troubles,* Belfast,
    Blackstaff, 1995 (a selection of Turner's cartoons over the 25 years of
    Northern Ireland's violence). The most recent collection is *The NOble
    Art of Politics,* Belfast, Blackstaff, 1996.
4   There is an index of the first 300 issues: Rolston, B., *Fortnight:
    the Index, Nos 1–300,* Belfast, Fortnight, 1993.
5   Adams, J.R.R., no date. Also useful is Howard, P., 'The paper war', three
    articles published in *Fortnight* in January and February 1974.
6   A report published in *Belfast Bulletin* in 1979, found that, on television
    alone, and not counting news broadcasts, 162 programmes 'wholly or
    primarily' devoted to Northern Ireland were shown between 1968 and
    1978.
7   The INCORE Data Server and CAIN are located with INCORE at
    Aberfoyle House in Derry.
8   Ó'Maoláin, *Register of Research* on Northern Ireland, pp.ix–xii.
9   See Dunn, S., Ó'Maoláin, C. and McClean, S., 'Sources of information:
    books, research and data' in S. Dunn (ed.), *Facets of the Conflict in
    Northern Ireland,* New York, St. Martin's Press, 1995, pp.258–9.
10 Stewart, A.T.Q., *The Narrow Ground,* London, Faber & Faber, 1977, p.16.
11 See Darby, J. (ed.), *Northern Ireland: The Background to the Conflict,*

Belfast and Syracuse, Appletree, New York, 1983, pp.235–6.

12 Richard Rose's 1969 research instrument is described in detail in Rose, R., *Governing Without Consensus*, London, Faber & Faber, 1971; Moxon-Browne, E., *Nation, Class and Creed in Northern Ireland*, Aldershot, Gower, 1983, follows a similar model.

13 Pollak, A. (ed.), *A Citizen's Enquiry: The Opsahl Report on Northern Ireland*, Dublin, Lilliput, 1993 is an excellent combination of oral hearings and written submissions.

14 Hoggart, S., 'The Army PR men in Northern Ireland', *New Society*, 11 October 1973.

15 Ibid.

16 Darby, J. and Morris, G., *Intimidation in Housing*, Belfast, Northern Ireland Community Relations Commission, 1974.

17 The IRA has been the subject of a number of books. One of the most notable early examples, which has been updated, is Bowyer Bell, J., *The Irish Troubles: A Generation of Violence*, Dublin, Gill & Macmillan, 1993. More recent reliable references are Bishop, P. and Mallie, E., *The Provisional IRA*, London, Heinemann, 1987, and O'Brien, B., *The Long War: The IRA and Sinn Féin*, Dublin, O'Brien, 1993. Holland, J. and McDonald, H., *The INLA: The Inside Story*, Dublin, Torc, 1994, is a substantial study of the INLA.

18 See Darby, J., *Conflict in Northern Ireland*, Dublin, Gill & Macmillan, 1976, especially the section on comparative analyses of conflict (pp.177–9), and Whyte, J., *Interpreting Northern Ireland*, Oxford, Blackwell, 1990, especially the chapter on Marxist interpretations (pp.175–93).

19 UNRISD, Geneva, 1992.

20 Two good examples are Montville, J.V. (ed.), *Conflict and Peacemaking in Multiethnic Societies*, Boston, MA., Lexington, 1991, and Marger, M., *Race and Ethnic Relations: American and Global Perspectives*, California, Wadsworth, 1985.

21 Quoted in Ormsby, F. (ed.), *A Rage for Order: Poetry of the Northern Ireland Troubles*, Belfast, Blackstaff, 1992.

22 The Northern Ireland Cultural Traditions Group, which operates as part of the Community Relations Council, was established to encourage more plural approaches to cultural diversity, and its work is described in publications edited by Crozier, M. (ed.), *Varieties of Irishness*, Belfast, Institute of Irish Studies, 1989 and 1990; and Crozier, M. and Sanders, N. (eds), *A Cultural Traditions Directory*, Belfast, Institute of Irish Studies, 1992. The Cultures of Ireland Group was formed in the Irish Republic in 1991 to encourage similar approaches south of the border.

BIBLIOGRAPHY

Adams, P., *Northern Ireland Newspapers*, Belfast, Library Association, Northern Ireland Branch, 1980.

Albon, M. (rapporteur), *Reconciliation and Community: The Future of Peace in Northern Ireland*, New York, Foundation for a Civil Society, 1996.

American Conference on Irish Studies, *Irish Studies in the United States*, periodic

Anderson, Benedict, *Imagined Communities*, London, Verso, 1993 (updated 1996)

Anyaoku, E., *Space in which Hope can Grow*, Derry, INCORE, 1996.

Arthur, P. and Jeffery, K., *Northern Ireland since 1968*, Oxford, OUP, 1996.

Bardon, J., *A History of Ulster*, Belfast, Blackstaff, 1992

Barrow, J., *Tour Round Ireland*, London, John Murray, 1836.

Beckett, J.C., *The Making of Modern Ireland*, London, Faber & Faber, 1966.

Beckett, J.C. and Glasscock, R., *Belfast: The Origin and Growth of an Industrial City*, London, BBC, 1967.

Bew, P. and Gillespie, G., *Northern Ireland: A Chronology of the Troubles*, Dublin, Gill & Macmillan, 1993.

Bew, P., Gibbon, P. and Patterson, H., *Northern Ireland, 1921–94*, London, Serif, 1995.

Bishop, P. and Mallie, E., *The Provisional IRA*, London, Heinemann, 1987.

Boal, F.W., Campbell, J.A. and Livingstone, D.N., 'The Protestant mosaic: a majority of minorities' in P.J. Roche and B. Barton (eds), *The Northern Ireland Question: Myth and Reality*, Aldershot, Avebury, 1991.

Boutros-Ghali, B., *An Agenda for Peace*, New York, UN, 1992.

Bowyer Bell, J., *The Irish Troubles: A Generation of Violence*, Dublin, Gill & Macmillan,1993.

Boyce, G. and O'Day, A. (eds), *The Making of Modern Irish History: Revisionism and the Revisionist Controversy*, London, Routledge & Kegan Paul, 1996.

Boyd, A., *Holy War in Belfast*, Tralee, Anvil, 1969.

Boyle, K. and Hadden, T., *Northern Ireland: The Choice*, London, Penguin, 1994.

Brady, C. (ed.), *Interpreting Irish History*, Dublin, Irish Academic Press, 1994.

Breen, R., Devine, P. and Dowds, L., *Social Attitudes in Northern Ireland*, Belfast, Appletree, 1996.

Breen, R., Devine, P. and Robinson, G. (eds), *Social Attitudes in Northern Ireland*, Belfast, Appletree, 1995.

227

Brennan, P., *The Conflict in Northern Ireland*, Paris, Longman, 1991.
Brennan, P. and Deutsch, R., *L'Irlande du Nord: Chronologie 1968–1991*, Paris, Presses de la Sorbonne, 1993.
Brewer, J.D. and Magee, K., *Inside the RUC*, Oxford, Clarendon, 1991.
Bruce, S., *God Save Ulster*, Oxford, OUP, 1986.
Bruce, S., *The Red Hand: Protestant Paramilitaries in Northern Ireland*, Oxford, OUP, 1992.
Bryson, L. and McCartney, C., *Clashing Symbols*, Belfast, Institute of Irish Studies and Community Relations Council, 1994.
Buckland, P., *Irish Unionism 1885–1923*, Belfast, HMSO, 1973.
Buckland, P., *The Factory of Grievances: Devolved Government in Northern Ireland 1921–39*, Dublin, Gill & Macmillan,1979.
Buckland, P., *A History of Northern Ireland*, Dublin, Gill & Macmillan, 1981.
Cairns, E., *Caught in Crossfire*, Belfast, Appletree, 1987.
Cairns, E., 'Is Northern Ireland a conservative society?' in P. Stringer and G. Robinson (eds), *Social Attitudes in Northern Ireland*, Belfast, Blackstaff, 1991, pp.143–4.
Cameron Report, *Disturbances in Northern Ireland*, Belfast, HMSO, 1969.
Catto, M., *Art in Ulster II, 1957–1977*, Belfast, Blackstaff, 1977.
Childers, E. and Urquhart, B., *Renewing the United Nations System*, Uppsala, Dag Hammarskjold Foundation, 1994.
Clancy, P., et al., *Ireland: A Sociological Profile*, Dublin, Institute of Public Administration, 1988.
Coleman, J., 'The dynamics of conflict', in G. Marx (ed.), *Racial Conflict*, Boston, Little, Brown 1971, p.256.
Compton, P., 'An evaluation of the changing religious composition of the population of Northern Ireland', *Economic and Social Review*, vol. 16, 1995, pp.201–24.
Compton, P., *Demographic Review: Northern Ireland 1995*, Belfast, Northern Ireland Economic Development Office, 1995.
Connor, W., 'Nation building and nation destroying' in *Ethnonationalism*, New Jersey, Princeton University Press, 1994.
Continuous Household Survey (CHS), Belfast, HMSO, 1988–1992.
Cormack, R., Fisher, N., Gallagher, A.M., Osborne, R.D., and Poland, M., 'Higher education participation of Northern Irish Students', *Higher Education Quarterly*, vol. 48, no. 3, p.26–38.
Cormack, R., Gallagher, A.M. and Osborne, R., *Fair Enough? Religion and the 1991 Population Census*, Belfast, Fair Employment Commission, 1993.
Coser, L., *The Functions of Social Conflict*, London, Routledge & Kegan Paul, 1956.
Crozier, M. (ed.), *Varieties of Irishness*, Belfast, Institute of Irish Studies, 1989.
Crozier, M. (ed.), *Varieties of Britishness*, Belfast, Institute of Irish Studies, 1990.
Crozier, M. and Sanders, N. (eds), *A Cultural Traditions Directory*, Belfast, Institute of Irish Studies, 1992.
Current Research in Britain Series, British Library with Longman, London

Bibliography

Curtis, L., *Ireland: The Propaganda War*, London, Pluto,1984.

Darby, J., *Register of Research into the Irish Conflict*, Belfast, Northern Ireland Community Relations Commission, 1972.

Darby, J., *Conflict in Northern Ireland*, Dublin, Gill & Macmillan, 1976.

Darby, J., *Intimidation and the Controls on Conflict in Northern Ireland*, Belfast, Appletree, 1986.

Darby, J., *Dressed to Kill: Cartoonists and the Northern Ireland Conflict*, Belfast, Appletree, 1983.

Darby, J. (ed.), *Northern Ireland: The Background to the Conflict*, Belfast and Syracuse, New York, Appletree, 1983.

Darby, J., *What's Wrong with Conflict?*, Occasional Paper 3, Coleraine, Centre for the Study of Conflict, 1991.

Darby, J., Dodge, N. and Hepburn, A.C., *Register of Research into the Irish Conflict*, Coleraine, Centre for the Study of Conflict, 1981.

Darby, J., Dodge, N. and Hepburn, A.C., *Political Violence: Ireland in a Comparative Setting*, Belfast, Appletree,1990.

Darby, J. and Dunn, S., 'Segregated schools and the research evidence', in R. Cormack, R. Osborne and R. Miller (eds) *Education and Social Policy in Northern Ireland*, Belfast, Policy Research Institute, 1987.

Darby, J. and Morris, G., *Intimidation in Housing*, Belfast, Northern Ireland Community Relations Commission, 1974.

Darby, J. and Williamson, A. (eds), *Violence and the Social Services in Northern Ireland*, London, Heinemann, 1978.

De Silva, K.M. and May, R.J. (eds), *Internationalistion of Ethnic Conflict*, London, Pinter, 1991.

Dickson, B., *Civil Liberties in Northern Ireland*, Belfast, Committee on the Administration of Justice,1993.

Doherty, J.E. and Hickey, D.J., *A Chronology of Irish History since 1500*, Dublin, Gill & Macmillan, 1989.

Dunn, S., *Education and the Conflict in Northern Ireland: A Guide to the Literature*, Coleraine, Centre for the Study of Conflict, 1986.

Dunn, S. (ed.), *Facets of the Conflict in Northern Ireland*, New York, St. Martin's Press, 1995.

Dunn, S., O'Maolain, C. and McClean, S., 'Sources of information: books, research and data' in S. Dunn (ed.), *Facets of the Conflict in Northern Ireland*, New York, St. Martin's Press, 1995, pp.258–9.

Economic and Social Research Unit, *Register of Current Social Science Research in Ireland*, ESRC, Dublin, occasional.

Elliott, S., *Northern Ireland Parliamentary Election Results, 1921–72*, Chichester, Political Reference Publications,1973.

Eversley, D., *Religion and Employment in Northern Ireland*, London, Sage, 1987.

Fair Employment Agency, *Report of an Investigation by the Fair Employment Agency of Northern Ireland into the Non-Industrial Northern Ireland Civil Service*, Belfast, FEA, 1983.

Fay, M.T., Morrisey, M. and Smyth, M., *Mapping Troubles-related Deaths in*

Northern Ireland, (London)derry, INCORE, 1997

Fiacc, P. (ed.), *The Wearing of the Black*, Belfast, Blackstaff, 1974.

Flackes, W.D. and Elliott, S., *Northern Ireland: A Political Directory*, Belfast, Blackstaff, 1988, 1994, 1995.

Foster, R.F., *Modern Ireland: 1600–1972*, Harmondsworth, Penguin,1988.

Frameworks for the Future, Belfast, HMSO, 1995.

Gallagher, A.M., *Majority Minority Review, no. 1: Education and Religion in Northern Ireland*, Coleraine, Centre for the Study of Conflict, 1989.

Gallagher, A.M., *Majority Minority Review, no. 2: Employment, Unemployment and Religion in Northern Ireland*, Coleraine, Centre for the Study of Conflict,1991.

Gallagher, A.M., Osborne, R.D. and Cormack R. J., *Fair Shares? Religion and the 1991 Population Census*, Belfast, Fair Employment Commission, 1994.

Gallagher, E. and Worrall, F., *Christians in Ulster, 1968–80*, Oxford, OUP, 1982.

Geary, R. and Morrison, J., 'The perception of crime' in P. Stringer and G. Robinson (eds), *Social Attitudes in Northern Ireland*, Belfast, Blackstaff, 1992, pp.67–70.

Gudgin, G. and Breen, R., *Evaluation of the Ratio of Unemployment Rates as an Indication of Fair Employment*, Belfast, CCRU, 1996

Guelke, A. (ed.), *Northern Ireland: The International Perspective*, Dublin, Gill & Macmillan,1992.

Gurr, T.R., 'Third world minorities at risk' in S.J. Brown and K.M. Schraub, (eds), *Resolving Third World Conflict*, Washington, USIP, 1992.

Hadfield, B. (ed.), *Northern Ireland: Politics and the Constitution*, Buckingham, Open University, 1993.

Hadden, T. and Boyle, K., *The Anglo-Irish Agreement: Commentary, Text and Official Review*, London, Sweet & Maxwell, 1994.

Hadden, T. and Hillyard, P., *Justice in Northern Ireland*, London, Cobden Trust, 1973.

Hadden, T., Irmin, C. and Boal, F., *Separation or Sharing: the People's Choice*, Belfast, Fortnight Educational Trust, 1996.

Hamill, D., *Pig in the Middle: The Army in Northern Ireland*, London, Methuen,1985.

Harff, B. and Gurr, T.R., 'Toward empirical theory of genocides and politicides: identification and measurement of cases since 1945', *International Studies Quarterly*, vol. 32, 1988, pp.35-67.

Harkness, D., *Northern Ireland since 1920*, Dublin, Gill & Macmillan, 1983.

Harris, R., *Prejudice and Tolerance in Ulster*, Manchester, Manchester University Press,1972.

Hayes, M., *A Police Ombudsman for Northern Ireland?*, Belfast, HMSO, 1997.

Hepburn, A.C., *The Conflict of Nationality in Modern Ireland*, London, Edward Arnold, 1980.

Hewitt, J., *Art in Ulster I, 1557–1957*, Belfast, Blackstaff, 1977.

Hickey, J., *Religion and the Northern Ireland Problem*, Dublin, Gill & Macmillan, 1984.

Hillyard, P., 'Law and order' in J. Darby (ed.), *Northern Ireland: The Background to the Conflict*, Belfast and Syracuse, New York, Appletree, 1983.

Hillyard, P., *Suspect Community: People's Experiences of the Prevention of Terrorism Act in Britain*, London, Pluto, 1993.

Hoggart, S., 'The army PR men in Northern Ireland', *New Society*, 11 October 1973.

Holland, J. and McDonald, H., *The INLA: The Inside Story*, Dublin, Torc Press, 1994.

Horowitz, D., *Ethnic Groups in Conflict*, California, University of California Press, 1985.

Hunt Committee, *Report of the Advisory Committee on Police in Northern Ireland*, Cmd. 535, Belfast, HMSO, 1969.

Jackson, H. and McHardy, A., *Two Irelands: the Problem of the Double Minority*, London, Minority Rights Group, 1984 (reprint with Update, 1995).

Jarman, N. and Bryan, D., *Parade and Protest*, Coleraine, Centre for the Study of Conflict, 1996.

Jennings, A. (ed.), *Justice under Fire: The Abuse of Civil Liberties in Northern Ireland*, London, Pluto, 1990.

Kidron, M. and Segal, R., *The New State of the World Atlas*, London, Pluto, 1984.

Lee, J., *Irish Historiography 1970–1979*, Cork, Cork University Press, 1981.

Lee, J., *Ireland 1921–1985: Politics and Society*, Cambridge, CUP, 1989.

Lennon, C., *The Incomplete Conquest*, Dublin, Gill & Macmillan, 1995.

Linen Hall Library, *Northern Ireland Political Literature on Microfiche*, Belfast, Linen Hall Library, 1992.

Lydon, J. and MacCurtain, M., *The Gill History of Ireland*, Dublin, Gill & Macmillan, 12 books published between the mid 1970s and 1980s.

Lyons, F.S.L., *Ireland Since the Famine*, London, Weidenfeld & Nicolson, 1971.

McDonald, J. and Bendahmane, D. (eds), *Conflict Resolution: Track Two Diplomacy*, Washington, Foreign Service Institute, 1987.

McDowell, D., *The Kurds: A Nation Denied*, London, Minority Rights Publications, 1992.

McElroy, G., *The Catholic Church and the Northern Ireland Crisis*, Dublin, Gill & Macmillan, 1991.

McGarry, J. and O'Leary, B. (eds), *The Future of Northern Ireland*, Oxford, Clarendon, 1990.

McGiven, N.P., 'An examination of Association Football support as a way of determining national identity in Northern Ireland', BA Dissertation, cited in J. Sugden and A. Bairner, *Sport, Sectarianism and Society in a Divided Ireland*, Leicester University Press, Leicester, 1993.

McLaughlin, E. and Quirk, P., *Policy Aspects of Employment Equality in Northern Ireland*, Belfast, SACHR, 1996.

McVey, J. and Hutson, N., *Public Views and Experiences of Fair Employment and Equality Issues in Northern Ireland*, Belfast, SACHR, 1996.

Magee, J., *Northern Ireland: Crisis and Conflict*, London, Routledge & Kegan Paul,   1975.

Magill, D. and Rose, S., *Fair Employment Law in Northern Ireland: Debates and Issues*, Belfast, SACHR,1996.

Mansbach, R., *Northern Ireland, Half a Century of Partition*, New York, Facts on File,1973.

Marger, M., *Race and Ethnic Relations: American and Global Perspectives*, California, Wadsworth, 1985.

Melaugh, M., *Majority Minority Review, no. 3. Housing and Religion in Northern Ireland*, Coleraine, Centre for the Study of Conflict, 1994.

Montville, J.V. (ed.), *Conflict and Peacemaking in Multiethnic Societies*, Boston, MA, Lexington, 1991.

Moody, T.W. (ed.), *Irish Historiography, 1936–70*, Dublin, Irish Committee for Irish Studies, 1971.

Moody, T.W. and Martin F., *The Course of Irish History*, Cork, Mercier, 1967.

Morgan,V., Smith, M., Robinson, G. and Fraser, G., *Mixed Marriages in Northern Ireland*, Coleraine, Centre for the Study of Conflict, 1996.

Morrow, D., *The Churches and Inter-Community Relations*, Coleraine, Centre for the Study of Conflict, 1991.

Moxon-Browne, E., *Nation, Class and Creed in Northern Ireland*, Aldershot, Gower, 1983.

Murray, D., *Worlds Apart: Segregated Schools in Northern Ireland*, Belfast, Appletree, 1985.

North Report, *Review of Parades and Marches in Northern Ireland*, Belfast, HMSO, 1997.

Northern Ireland Economic Council, *Demographic Trends in Northern Ireland*, Occasional Paper no. 2, Belfast, NIEC, 1995.

O'Brien, B., *The Long War: The IRA and Sinn Féin*, Dublin, O'Brien, 1993.

O'Connor, F., *In Search of a State: Catholics in Northern Ireland*, Belfast, Blackstaff, 1993.

O'Day, A. and Stevenson, J., *Irish Historical Documents since 1800*, Dublin, Gill & Macmillan,1992.

O'Dowd, L., Rolston, B. and Tomlinson, B., *Northern Ireland Between Civil Rights and Civil War*, London, CSE, 1980

O'Leary, B., 'Explaining Northern Ireland: a brief study guide', *Politics*, vol. 5, no. 1, 1985.

O'Leary, B. and McGarry, J., *The Politics of Antagonism: Understanding Northern Ireland*, London, Athlone, 1992.

O'Leary, B., and McGarry, J., *Northern Ireland: Sharing Authority*, London, Institute for Public Policy Research, 1993.

O'Malley, P., *The Uncivil Wars: Ireland Today*, Belfast, Blackstaff, 1983.

O'Malley, P., *Northern Ireland: Questions of Nuance*, Belfast, Blackstaff, 1990.

O'Maolain, C., *Register of Research on Northern Ireland*, Coleraine, Centre for the Study of Conflict, 1993.

O'Neill, T., *Ulster at the Crossroads*, London, Faber & Faber, 1969.

Ormsby, F. (ed.), *A Rage for Order: Poetry of the Northern Ireland Troubles*, Belfast, Blackstaff, 1992.

Osborne, R., Cormack, R. and Miller, R., *Education and Policy in Northern Ireland*, Belfast, Policy Research Institute, 1987.

Patterson, H., *Class Conflict and Sectarianism*, Belfast, Blackstaff, 1980.

Police Authority for Northern Ireland, *Everyone's Police: Partnership for Change*, Belfast, PANI, 1996, App. 6.

Pollak, A. (ed.), *A Citizen's Enquiry: The Opsahl Report on Northern Ireland*, Dublin, Lilliput, 1993.

Poulton, H., *The Balkans: Minorities and States in Conflict*, London, Minority Rights Publications, 1993 (2nd edn).

Registrar-General, *The Northern Ireland Census 1991: Religious Report*, Belfast, HMSO, 1993.

Roche, P.J. and Barton, B. (eds), *The Northern Ireland Question: Myth and Reality*, Aldershot, Avebury, 1991.

Rolston, B. (ed.), *The Media and Northern Ireland: Covering the Troubles*, London, Macmillan, 1991.

Rolston, B., *Fortnight: The Index, Nos 1–300*, Belfast, Fortnight Publications, 1993.

Rolston, B., et al. (eds), *A Social Science Bibliography of Northern Ireland, 1945–83*, Belfast, Queen's University, 1983.

Rose, R., *Governing without Consensus*, London, Faber & Faber, 1971.

Rose, R., *Northern Ireland: A Time for Choice*, London, Macmillan, 1976.

Scarman Tribunal, *Report of Tribunal of Inquiry into Violence and Civil Disturbances in Northern Ireland*, 1969, Cmd. 566, Belfast, HMSO, 1972.

Shearman, H., *Northern Ireland 1921–1971*, Belfast, HMSO, 1971.

Sheehy, M., *Divided We Stand*, London, Faber & Faber, 1955.

Shibutani, T. and Kwan, K.L., 'Changes in life conditions conducive to interracial conflict' in G. Marx (ed.), *Racial Conflict*, Boston, Little, Brown, 1971.

Simpson, G. and Yinger, J., *Racial and Cultural Minorities*, New York, Harper & Row, 1965.

Singer, J.D. and Small, M. (eds), *Resort to Arms: International and Civil Wars, 1816–1980*, California, Sage, 1982.

Smith, A. and Robinson, A., *Education for Mutual Understanding: Perceptions and Policy*, Coleraine, Centre for the Study of Conflict, 1992.

Smith, D.J. and Chambers, G., *Inequality in Northern Ireland*, Oxford, Clarendon, 1991.

Stewart, A.T.Q., *The Narrow Ground*, London, Faber & Faber, 1977.

Stringer, P. and Robinson, G. (eds), *Social Attitudes in Northern Ireland*, Belfast, Blackstaff, 1991, 1992, 1993.

Sugden, J. and Bairner, A., *Sport, Sectarianism and Society in a Divided Ireland*, Leicester University Press, Leicester, 1993.

Sutton, M., *An Index of Deaths from the Conflict in Ireland 1969–93,* Belfast, Beyond the Pale, 1994.

Townshend, C., *Political Violence in Ireland: Government and Resistance since 1848,* Oxford, Clarendon, 1983.

Townshend, C. (ed.), *Consensus in Ireland: Approaches and Recessions,* Oxford, Clarendon, 1988.

Turner, M., *Illuminations,* Kilkenny, Boethius, 1986.

Turner, M., *Pack Up Your Troubles: 25 Years of Northern Ireland Cartoons,* Belfast, Blackstaff, 1995.

Turner, M., *The NOble Art of Politics,* Belfast, Blackstaff, 1996.

Walker, C.J., *Armenia and Karabagh: The Struggle for Unity,* London, Minority Rights Publications, 1992.

Wichert, S., *Northern Ireland since 1945,* London, Longman,1991.

Whyte, J., *Interpreting Northern Ireland,* Oxford, Blackwell, 1990.

Wilson, A., *Irish America and the Ulster Conflict,* Belfast, Blackstaff, 1995.

Wright, F., *Northern Ireland: A Comparative Analysis,* Dublin, Gill & Macmillan, 1987.

INDEX